THE BEST OF

bamboo ridge

THE HAWAII WRITERS' QUARTERLY

Edited by
Eric Chock & Darrell H.Y. Lum

Bamboo Ridge Press
1986

Library of Congress Catalog Card Number: 83-73232
ISBN 0-910043-07-8
Copyright 1986 Bamboo Ridge Press

Some of the work in this book has previously appeared in
Bamboo Ridge, The Hawaii Writers' Quarterly, no. 1–29,
copyright 1978–1986. The table of contents cites the issue
and year of copyright for each previously published
selection.

Published by Bamboo Ridge Press and the Hawaii Ethnic
Resources Center: Talk Story, Inc.
Editorial advisory committee: Richard Hamasaki, Marie
Hara, Cheryl Harstad, James Harstad, Sheldon Hershinow,
Craig Howes, Dennis Kawaharada, Ruth Lucas, Wing Tek
Lum, Caroline Nakamura, Franklin Odo.
Cover: Gary Nomura
Line drawings: Darrell H.Y. Lum

Bamboo Ridge Press is a non-profit, tax exempt
organization formed to foster the appreciation,
understanding, and creation of literary, visual, audio-visual
and performing arts by and about Hawaii's people.
The publication of this book was supported in part by
grants from the State Foundation on Culture & the Arts
(SFCA) and the National Endowment for the Arts (NEA), a
Federal agency. The SFCA is funded by appropriations from
the Hawaii State Legislature and by grants from the NEA.
The grants were administered by the Hawaii Ethnic
Resources Center: Talk Story, Inc.

Bamboo Ridge Press
P.O. Box 61781
Honolulu, Hawaii 96839-1781

10 9 8 7 6 5   95 96 97 98

Contents _____

Prose

Local Literature and Lunch _____

There's an island surf shop called Local Motion where you can buy T-shirts that say "Locals Only." Anyone can shop there, even tourists. And locals and tourists alike buy "Locals Only" shirts because they're brightly colored, full of geometric New Wave designs, and they say "Hawaii" right there in front.

There's also a lunch that's quick and cheap that you can buy at drive-in restaurants and coffee shops called a "loco-moco." It's a bed of rice topped by a hamburger patty topped by an over-easy fried egg and smothered in brown gravy. Real locals then add salt, pepper, shoyu, and ketchup before digging in! And there's always saimin, a noodles-in-soup dish that you'll never find in Japan or China. It's a distinctly local invention along with the plate lunch. Watch where the truck drivers and businessmen and surfers always end up. It's usually at a lunch wagon (one of those delivery vans outfitted with a propane warming table and a flip-up side that reveals a serving counter), serving up a nutritional nightmare on a paper plate along the beaches, the waterfront, at construction sites, even right outside City Hall. A plate lunch of curry stew poured over two scoops of rice alongside a scoop of macaroni salad and a bit of kim chee (Korean style chili-pepper spiced cabbage) will run you about three dollars.

Then you can drive home to a nice little house in the suburbs: a modest twenty-year old, single wall, three bedroom, two bath place with a carport going for $150,000 or so . . . on leased land. This is all part of living in these islands. No wonder a number of Hawaii writers choose to describe themselves as local writers of "local literature" (as opposed to "Asian American" literature, largely a mainland term, or "Hawaiian" literature, which the locals know means native Hawaiian literature).

Things *are* different here. And, not surprisingly, the literature reflects it. Of course, there are the nature themes which according to some visiting writers appear too much and too often in local literature. But why shouldn't we write about nature when we know that the EDB (ethylene dimethyl-bromide, more simply, ant poison) sprayed on the pineapples shows up in the drinking water years after they stop using the insecticide? This isn't standing-in-awe-of or ain't-it-beautiful

3

nature writing that we're talking about. It's chemicals in the milk and the water, it's not washing the car or watering the lawn when there's a water shortage; it's volcanic ash in the air from an eruption two islands away or the sky grey with ash from burning sugar cane. It's the sting of wind-flung sand at the beach and going out even if it's raining because it'll probably stop by the time you get there. It's smashing a two-inch cockroach in your bathroom or listening to a gecko call all night from your ceiling. And you learn after the first time rolling around in the surf not knowing which way is up, "Never Turn Your Back To The Ocean."

Or at the first hint of a shipping strike, you find yourself in line at the supermarket behind all those mama-sans buying up the rice and Spam and vienna sausages. They have memories of shipping strikes that lasted months. They have memories of being a striker themselves or knowing someone who went hungry during a strike. And for many islanders, it doesn't take a lot of digging to find one's roots in the soil of Hawaii's sugar plantations: grandparents or great-grandparents who immigrated to the islands as contract laborers.

No wonder, then, the local literature which *Bamboo Ridge, The Hawaii Writers' Quarterly* has published over the years, has echoed this island life. Forget the "Golden Man" or the "melting pot" myths. The literature of local writers has a distinct sensitivity to ethnicity, the environment (in particular that valuable commodity, the land), a sense of personal lineage and family history, and the use of the sound, the languages, and the vocabulary of island people.

* * * * *

It was sometime around five years ago that the idea of having a "Best of" issue came up. People laughed when I first suggested it. At the time there were only twelve issues to consider. Laziness and procrastination in completing the task of reading through the stack of back issues kept delaying the project. Naturally, with the addition of each new issue, the job just kept getting bigger and bigger. Even with the help of an editorial advisory committee, it took us three years to finally get this out. The literature, like the lunches, are diverse, tasty, and speak of who we are and where we've come from.

4

We end this collection with the only piece of writing that was not previously published in *Bamboo Ridge*. Steve Sumida's article, "Waiting for the Big Fish: Recent Research in the Asian American Literature of Hawaii," summarizes the history of local literature and offers some thoughts about why it has largely been ignored and even denied to exist. Sumida's article and his forthcoming book are the first serious look at local literature by a scholar. Sumida along with Arnold Hiura and Marie Hara were the founders of the Hawaii Ethnic Resources Center: Talk Story, Inc., which for many years served as our own tax-exempt status. They put on the first ethnic American writers conference in Hawaii, "Talk Story: Words bind, words set free" in 1978 and published *Talk Story: An Anthology of Hawaii's Local Writers* in the same year. The conference and the book and the founding of Bamboo Ridge Press in 1978 were instrumental in helping define local literature. We recognize their contribution to *Bamboo Ridge* and to Hawaii's literary community. This is our past.

Getting this collection down to these 300 or so pages was a difficult task. This was supposed to only be lunch, but like all good local hosts, when you serve up lunch you should always have enough. Enjoy.

Darrell Lum

On Local Literature

In October 1980, the Writers of Hawaii Conference convened at the Hawaii State Capitol Auditorium for six nights to an audience of 200 people each night. It was sponsored by the Hawaii Literary Arts Council and Talk Story, Inc. with support from the Hawaii Committee for the Humanities and the State Foundation on Culture and the Arts. The following is an edited version of the opening night introduction, most of which is still relevant today. It is excerpted from Writers of Hawaii : A Focus On Our Literary Heritage, *edited by Eric Chock and Jody Manabe (Bamboo Ridge Press, 1981).*

I

Welcome everybody, to "Writers of Hawaii: A Focus On Our Literary Heritage." I am Eric Chock, president of the Hawaii Literary Arts Council. It was almost a year ago when the director of the State Foundation on Culture and the Arts, Mr. Preis, congratulated me on winning the HLAC presidency. And only half-jokingly he asked me, "Was this an election, or was it a revolution?" Must be my long hair, I guess. Some people are still afraid that the hippies are gonna take over.

Well, for Mr. Preis and everyone else, a late answer: I believe that this is part of not a revolutionary process, but an evolutionary process. And I hope that this is a process that will eventually lead to local literature being taught in the schools in Hawaii. Sounds a little strange, I know, to some people—local literature—Hawaii stories, written by Hawaii people, and taught to Hawaii's children in the schools. Sounds almost redundant.

But I hope that it will happen someday, in the schools, even at the college level. Because it will lead to more pride among Hawaii's people, and an awareness of Hawaii's directions, past and present. And also it will provide more opportunities for people, like me, who grew up here and want to be writers and who need clear models for exactly what that is—a Hawaii writer.

This process, this goal for the Hawaii Literary Arts Council, is as Mr. Preis once said, "To bring before the people of

Hawaii the great importance of literature." And this process is what we're continuing tonight.

But literature, and especially Modern Hawaiian Literature, what is that? And why is it so important? Literature is an activity that happens in a society, a culture, a group, any group. It is a shared sense of belonging and identity, expressed in words. Like any other kind of art, it is a way to understand life, to appreciate living and therefore to participate in life to the fullest of your potential. It should make you feel inspired about your life.

And how can it do that? Well, theoretically, literature helps you intensify your sense of individual identity in such a way that you feel like a so-called "universal being." What that means is that, in literature, the range of human experiences specific to your group is demonstrated to be characteristic of all people. Human traits are shown to occur naturally in all humans.

While the theory sounds simple, it's not so easily achieved. You would expect that in Hawaii, the world's most celebrated melting pot of cultures, we would have developed a literature which emphasizes and focuses on the humanity in people of all races. You would expect that with Hawaii's cultural blending, a literature would naturally emerge which expressed the infinite variety of ways in which people can share their lives, develop common goals, and achieve a sense of community pride. A literature which, in effect, expressed a sense of the word "aloha."

But what do we in Hawaii have as "our literature"? In Hawaii, which as John Dominis Holt said, "gave the world the word 'aloha,'" it is ironic that the most commonly held notion of our literature is that it is non-existent.

It is no secret that language has always been a crucial factor in Hawaii's history. It's no secret that the so-called "blending of cultures" often manifested itself in a clash of languages, sometimes in a competition for sovereignty. It's no secret that our own government, through its various organs, has attempted to suppress varying forms of languages in favor of one common language. And that ain't pidgin they talking about.

And though it may be a practical necessity—and I believe it is—it is again ironic that this chosen form of a common language is seemingly unable—seemingly unable—to produce a literature expressing a common Hawaiian life. And what indicators do we have of a lack of common literature?

If we did have a clearly defined common literature, a Hawaii literary tradition, wouldn't Hawaii's educational systems teach it and use it for educational purposes? They don't. And we wonder why they have problems teaching our kids to read and write. The answer is the problem, obviously. If there is no such thing as a Hawaii writer, how can you teach a Hawaii kid to write?

Should we also ask, why is it that there is so little emphasis in Hawaii's public educational systems placed on Hawaii's history? That is, of our sense of common background, our sense of common experiences—that sense of community again? Or should we take that a step higher and ask, why is it that in Hawaii's colleges and universities, in English departments and colleges of education, there is practically no mention, much less the study, of literature in Hawaii? In fact, there is denial that Hawaii literature of value exists.

And if you want statistics, take the Hawaii State Foundation on Culture and the Arts Report for fiscal year 1979. It reports that $1.7 million was spent on the arts: painting, dance, music, theater, literature. Why is it that out of over 1.7 million dollars, just over 2% of that sum is for literature? Just over 2%.

In all these factors, the main underlying point is that we in Hawaii are expected to believe that we are subordinate to the mainland. At best, we are expected to believe that we are really no different here and can even be *like* the mainland if we try hard enough. We are asked to reject the feeling that Hawaii is special. And when we become numbed and lose the feeling, it then becomes possible to accept mainland history and mainland culture as our own.

We are asked to accept mainland literature as the norm. In the process, our own literature loses its cohesiveness, our writings are categorized according to the framework of mainland, mainstream literary history, if at all. And without having had the chance to establish its own integrity and unique qualities, the literature of Hawaii is dissipated.

But there are those of us who believe *Hawaii no ka oi.* We know there exists a body of writings which we identify as the Modern Hawaiian Literary Tradition. We admit that it's a confusing conglomeration of writers representing a variety of cultures and viewpoints. We admit that much research must be done, much scholarship completed, before a working understanding of the literature becomes common knowledge here. But that's what scholars and universities are for, aren't they?

We know the literature exists. The art of writing has always occurred in Hawaii. And this conference is an attempt to make this tradition more visible, to clarify the different voices which contribute to the overall picture of the Hawaii we love.

Eric Chock

We saw three different store-ladies.
One couldn't stand us, almost daring us to buy.
I thought I saw a gold blade tucked
in her hair
and her nails looked red.
The second was nice. Like our mother—
how reasonable! "Yes, the slippers are expensive,
but they are cork . . ." We ended up
agreeing and praising the green slippers
with the pale butterflies.
The third was let's-get-down-to-business.
Horo horo!
"Yeah you can change the belt—you don't need the belt—
take the side seam out—
bargain yeah?"
Two girls on River Street
with a yukata in their hands.

Sheri Mae Akamine

In my body
there are caves
leading to different places.
I see blood and nothing but blood and dark.
Sometimes I see bones.
And veins and meat.
I am scared to be in the dark
so I think of my dog Pierre who died of heartbroken.
He's a poodle and is not supposed to be alone.
I let him go and he walked out of the gate.
Usually he runs.
I cried and cried
and I cannot forget about him.
My best dog I ever had for a long time.
Now I only have my cat Timothy
who is still a kitten that would want to mate.
And that's why I feel so lonely inside
of my great big body.
Nobody to love and care for.
Nothing but dark and death.
Sometimes I miss my father who left me
in Kindergarten. I visit him in summer.
He has his own family.
Now I am nothing to him.
But a body of dark and blood.
I live with my mother
who cares for me.
What else can anybody expect.

Anonymous 5th grader

Clear Eyes

Clear Eyes, Clear Eyes
When I slammed the cardoor
on my dad's thumb
he didn't cry, he kept
clear eyes, and when he
made a fist and hit the
top of the car and made
a dent in it
he had clear eyes
clear eyes

Tamatha F., Solomon Elementary

I am the eyeball looking at you
But when you look at me I turn around
But oh, when we look at each other
My eyeballs turn from brown to blue like yours
And when you look me straight in the eye
You see the sparkle like the diamonds.
My eyes are the key to you.

_ Kaipo, Royal Elementary_

Termites _____

On summer nights they swarm.
They seem to come out of the ground,
out of trees, they fill the air.
They wander down the streets,
wings glittering under streetlights.
They've kept these wings
all their lives
folded on their backs,
but in these insect starbursts
they fly toward whatever shines
in streetlights, headlights,
reflections in windows, or eyes.

We turn off the lights inside.
We watch as toads
gather at the porch light
and lick themselves silly.
Lizards haunt the windows,
stalking the winged or wingless bodies.
Sometimes they remain stationary,
content to eat what rushes past
the half-inch reach of their roll-up tongues.
If the creatures get in
we have candles flaming,
or white bowls of hot water
grandma leaves under a lamp
in a darkened room.
Looking out from the window,
it seems as though they're all bent
on living in our home.

Every summer they swarm.
Thousands.
Like drunken tourists
lost on New Year's Eve.
But in twenty minutes
their eyes are glazed with the glare of light,
their craziness for it so rapidly reversed,
and once again they crawl

for tunnels, baseboards,
any dark opening they can find.
On summer nights, thousands of wings
form feathery wreaths around each house.
Some of these have made it.
But out in front under the streetlight
mother shoots water like a gunner,
picking off stragglers
with the garden hose.

The Mango Tree

"One old Chinese man told me," he said, *"that he like for trim his tree so the thing is hollow like one umbrella, and the mangoes all stay hanging underneath. Then you can see where all the mangoes stay, and you know if ripe. If the branches stay growing all over the place, then no can see the mango, and the thing get ripe, and fall on the ground."*

And us guys, we no eat mango that fall down. Going get soft spots. And always get plenty, so can be choosy. But sometimes, by the end of mango season when hardly get already, and sometimes the wind blow em down, my mother, sometimes she put the fall down kind in the house with the others.

I was thinking about that as I was climbing up the tree. The wind was coming down from the pali, and I gotta lean into the wind every time she blow hard. My feet get the tingles cause sometimes the thing slip when I try for grip the bark with my toes. How long I never go up the tree! I stay scared the branch going broke cause too small for hold me, and when the wind blow, just like being on one see-saw. And when I start sawing that branch he told me for cut, the thing start for jerk, and hard for hold on with my feet. Plus I holding on to one branch above my head with one hand, and the fingers getting all cramp. My legs getting stiff and every few strokes my sawing arm all tired already, so when the wind blow strong again, I rest. I ride the branch just like one wave. One time when I wen look down I saw him with one big smile on his face. Can tell he trying not for laugh.

He getting old but he spend plenty time in that tree. Sometimes he climb up for cut one branch and he stay up for one hour, just looking around, figuring out the shape of the tree, what branches for cut and what not for cut. And from up there can see the whole valley. Can see the trees and the blue mountains. I used to have nightmares that the thing was going erupt and flood us out with lava, and I used to run around looking for my girlfriend so she could go with our family in our '50 Dodge when we run away to the ocean. But I never find her and I got lost. Only could see smoke, and people screaming, and the lava coming down.

The nightmare everytime end the same. I stay trapped on one trail in the mountains, right on one cliff. Me and some

19

guys. The trail was narrow so we walking single file. Some people carrying stuff, and my mother in front of me, she carrying some things wrapped in one cloth. One time she slip, and I grab for her, and she starting for fall and I scream "Oh no!" and then I wake up. And I look out my window at the mango tree and the blue mountains up the valley. The first time I wen dream this dream I was nine.

Since that time I wen dream plenty guys falling off the trail. And plenty times I wen grab for my mother's hand when she start for fall. But I never fall. I still stay lost on the cliff with the other guys. I still alive.

And my father still sitting in the mango tree just like one lookout, watching for me and my mother to come walking out of the mountain. Or maybe he stay listening to the pali wind for the sound one lady make if she falls. Or maybe he just sitting in his mango tree umbrella, rocking like one baby in the breeze, getting ripe where we can see him. And he's making sure no more extra branches getting in the way.

Eric Chock

Poem for George Helm
Aloha Week 1980 _____

I was in love with the word "aloha"
Even though I heard it over and over
I let the syllables ring in my ears
and I believed the king with outstretched hand
was welcoming everyone who wanted to live here
And I ignored the spear in his left hand
believing instead my fellow humans
and their love for these islands in the world
which allow us to rest from the currents
and moods of that vast ocean from which we all came
But George Helm's body is back in that ocean
I want to believe in the greatness of his spirit
that he still feels the meaning of that word
which is getting so hard to say

I thought there was hope for the word "aloha"
I believed when they said there are ways
in this modern technological world Oahu alone
could hold a million people
And we would become the Great Crossroads of the Pacific
if we used our native aloha spirit
our friendly wahines and our ancient hulas
They showed us our enormous potential
and we learned to love it
like a man who loves some thing in gold or silver
But these islands are made of lava and trees and sand
A man learns to swim with the ocean
and when he's tired he begins to search
for what he loves, for what will sustain him
George Helm is lost at sea
The bombing practice continues on Kahoolawe
I want to believe in what he was seeking
I want to believe that he is still swimming
toward that aina for which he feels
that word which is so hard to say

I want to believe in the word
But Brother George doesn't say it

He doesn't sing it in his smooth falsetto
in the melodies of aloha aina
There is no chance of seeing him walk up to the stage
pick up his guitar and smile the word at you across the room
The tourists, they twist their malihini tongues
The tour guides mouth it with smog-filled lungs
Politicians keep taking it out, dusting off the carcass
of a once-proud 3 syllable guaranteed vote-getter
You find its ghosts on dump trucks, magazines
airplanes, rent-a-cars
anywhere they want the dollar
They can sell you anything with aloha and a smile
even pineapples that came here from
(you guessed it) America!
They'll sell you too, servants of the USA
And if you don't believe they have the nerve
think of the ocean
They put up signs as close as they dare
And when his spirit comes back to land
the first thing he'll see is a big sign with that word
painted on, carved in, flashing with electricity
That word, so hard to say

I was going to believe that word
I was going to believe all those corporations
that seemed to spring up like mushrooms after a light rain
I was going to believe when they divided up
the home-land of a living people
and called it real estate   or 50th state
or   Aloha State
I was going to believe we would still be able
to go up to the mountains, out to the country beaches
to the ocean where waves wash the islands
the islands which remind us we've all traveled a long way to
      get here
We all wanted a garden of our own in the world
We believed we'd all have peace
(and a piece of the aloha and of the state if we worked for it)
We're all pursuing the same dream!
So many of us are trying to get to the mountains, the beaches
So many trying to swim in the waves
legs kicking, arms paddling like the arms

of George Helm stroking towards a familiar beach
which he respected and belonged to by birth
for which he felt something no word can express
except for that word which is hard to say
unless we all live it!

I want to live the word "aloha"
But the body of George Helm is lost at sea
the practice continues on Kahoolawe
the buildings follow the roads
the roads carry thousands of cars filled with people
following their dreams of Hawaii or Paradise
to Waikiki where girls sell their hips
singers sell their voices
the island which has been sold is lit up all night
while the king with outstretched hand
has forgotten how to use his spear
George Helm is dead
and that word is not forgotten
It rings in my ears every day
I want us to live the word "aloha"
but it's so hard just to say

Eric Chock

23

Tutu on the Curb _____

Tutu standing on the corner,
she look so nice!
Her hair all pin up in one bun,
one huge red hibiscus hanging out
over her right ear,
her blue Hawaiian print muu muu
blowing in the wind
as one bus driver blows one huge cloud
of smoke around her,
no wonder her hair so grey!
She squint and wiggle her nose
at the heat
and the thick stink fumes
the bus driver just futted all over her.
You can see her shrivel up
and shrink a little bit more.
Pretty soon, she going disappear
from the curb
forever.

_____ *Eric Chock*

Pa-ke

you speak of shadows
and I dream of journeys—

an old ship, iron and rusted
plates. Chinese workers for sugar
plantations. I move among
broken sandals and jade-
colored bile. once a week,
they wash the hold. the water
slides across the deck, over yellow
bodies. it clings to the rusted hull.

from the vats
of cooking rice, the steam
rises in the twilight. we gather
near the warmth with our wooden
bowls. the brown rice
is over-cooked. burnt rice
scraped for those at the end
of the line. someone says every man
who can walk off the ship in Hawai'i
is worth five
dollars. there are no more
men, only hollow trees. hunger,
a sparrow, flutters
among the branching bones, taking each
grain of rice. it sings and its voice
enchants the twilight
into a shadowed sigh.

Ling Wan has died. I helped
throw him into the sea. his
feet were cold and stiff. his
toenails were black. I wear his
sandals. I keep his last
words. they are,
"do not let me die."

the island, a broken piece
of jade, rises with the dawn.

and the deck is full of wandering
eyes. behind me is
Fan Wei, whose sickness covers
him with sweat, as though
he had been
laboring instead of eating
rats. gone is the pain
in my legs, where the skin
is raw from scratching at sores
as I slept. now we smile
into each other's faces. soon,
soon . . .

I push my way off the ship.
I do not limp but walk
onto the dock. a man passes
and taps me on the shoulder
with a stick. I am
number nine. I throw my bowl
into the sea. too soon
I have need for another.

the night on this island
also sighs. I have journeyed far,
thinking that I had left
nothing behind.

Herbert Chun

Songs from the Ancient and Modern

Marker at Kukuiolono Garden, Kalaheo, Kauai:
Chief Ola hid his feather cloak under this stone
to avoid capture and loss of the engagement.

I

The island is a flower closing.
I tend my husband after each battle.
He faces his brother near the Mana swamp.
Blood weaves among the rushes.
I lift a gourd of water to his lips.
But already he walks the cliffs at night.
I pierce my right eye with a stick.
The blackness is a door opening
to where the dead enter.
All through my body is the ache of the sea.
In the hollow place, I watch for him
riding the long wave in.

II

I rescue his red and yellow cloak
from beneath its stone.
Do not look
for the little birds
who no longer hide in the forest.
Tonight, in the dark,
the feathers will be
the flesh of my shoulders.

III

Why does she wear a skirt
thick as the cliffs as Polihale?
She teaches my son
to put words on paper.
He learns the language
of sticks breaking.

The tapa beaters thump
village gossip.
Fishermen sing to the shark.
I hear the flutter
of 'iwi birds
captured for feathers
and Grandfather's songs
between pages.

IV

I ride my bicycle past the mill,
through a burst of dust and molasses smoke.
In a foreign place
it is easier to feel nothing
than to be captured.
Down Elepaio Street, jars of water
border the yards. This
a ritual to keep out the dogs.
What is it about loss
that feels like a wound you want to keep open?
At the post office, men talk-story
in pidgin. I nod and assume
the blind smile of faith.
No trees shade the road
past the Buddhists' graveyard.
Still the heat
carries the scent of Plumeria.
And me pedaling backwards
to friends in cities,
across a sky as flat as the sea.

Jan Day Fehrman

Inheritance _____

my grandmother died
    before I had a face
she reclaims me now with silence
    and a brown photograph:
      her kimono, hair, face,
        the instep of her turned-in foot

I have no stock in this place
the woman in the picture is
      the sole estate of my inheritance
her immigrant's name and face,
    her incomplete passage

blood
there are no islands in its red surge
where the ground wires should be
    is only a space the color of sleep
if you look long enough into my left eye
   you will see my grandmother there
sitting with tabied feet
      and hands of silence
sitting in constant passage

_____ *Wanda Fujimoto*

Some years ago,
    my grandmother preferred the hides of alligators
    to tuck her feet or money in—
    wore green or brown swamptones to match.
    Those alligators ranged
    the streets and stores and church
    of her small Iowa town
    and a sudden waiting wit
    would snap her cronies
    right in two.
By the time she got her snakeskin cane—
    moved to her son's
    West Virginia home,
    she used her eyes, more than her tongue
    to sting a thought your way.
One day,
    as she was poling down the driveway
    toward the mail
    she passed a copperhead
    snake enough to ditch itself
    in her wake.
At ninety-four
    scaled skin held her together still.
    Basking mosttimes,
    she'd crack an eye,
    rasp a word or two
    and leave you laugh
    or thrashing
    in her grip.

Caroline Garrett

T'ang Fishermen

I will recognize you
by the way you appear
            robed in mist
sitting on a boat
            beneath a bamboo shelter
a teapot steams in front of you
            the wooden deck
and the sleeves of your gown damp
     your hair fastened into a knot
you are no longer
                    as you are now
driving in a blue truck
            to a green house on a hill
we are pulling the boat up
     on the shore beneath dripping leaves
our voices flow to each other
            like water over rocks
parting and coming together again
     all the way   from one
        cloud covered peak

Dana Naone Hall

Letter to Paris

Old letters accumulate like dust on my desk.
Yours arrive decorated with stamps
from another country.
Across the valley the dogs are at it again,
passing their messages along Palolo Avenue,
following the musical ice cream truck.
The ants keep crawling out of their holes,
anti-Semitic Frenchmen paint swastikas
on the Jewish confectioner's shop
on your street,
and the years keep slipping by.
Ten, twenty, thirty . . .
the years fall behind us
like crumbs in some dark forest.
You write of our lives
half over, lost, stewing in some witch's iron pot.
I want to deny it,
but the unwritten poems remain silent and dark,
and less is accomplished than imagined.
We blame the daily business of living
that's consuming our adult lives,
termites eating away at our dreams—
the cooking, the cleaning, the laundry
that never fails to overflow the hamper,
the chores that wait like beasts with feral eyes.
I remember a mutual friend's plaintive refrain:
"There must be more to this life!"
and I believe there is.
You have a daughter with dark hair and a gypsy name
and I just know that she must be beautiful.

_____ *Gail Harada*

Water Born _____

Moomomi Beach, narrow and hooked like a horseshoe
From centuries of wear, is reefless. Seas pound it
And strong currents often cut through
Carving pockets and cleaning stations out
Of the lava. I brought you there to dive,
To spear ulua, fish with an approach like a spaceship.
We moved easy, consumed,
Flippers never breaking the surface,
Drawn into an unnoticed current, and carried
Out to deep, purpling water.
Alerted by the color I turned to you
But you knew, your mottled eyes filled the window
Of your mask like a single bruise.
We pumped hard for shore
Burning our lungs up, making no headway,
I turned again, you'd fallen far behind,
All timing gone from your stroke.
I felt death by drowning
And went to hold you, taste the last water in your hair,
To slip under with you, and await the coming sharks,
Their fins dipped, bodies arched,
The beautiful pewter of their tails,
To accept death and be finally brave for us,
Bellow like an old hero
Into a deafening white mouth.
It lasted less than seconds
And I remembered about a current,
Go with it, ride till it slows and lets you off.
Panic lifted, order rose out of my chest
Like smoke, we breathed and were limp.
We hadn't gone far, a steady swim brought us in
East of the beach. Through it all you'd held on
To your 3-prong and stringer of poked fish.
We rested on a pile of warm stones
One of many that speckles Moomomi
And marks the ancient fallen.
You asked about them, their weapons and deaths,
Putting our scrape into perspective.
Picking up the spear and fish

We headed back,
Renewed, heroic, or as close as we'd ever get.

_____ *Norman Hindley*

Ass Why Hard _____

We sit out on the concrete slab
of our backyard patio, catching
the sun sifting through apricot
and lemon trees, both of us
studying: him, stacks of books
high as the egg crates we piled
in back of the old Hongo store;
me, my sports page and guide
to the races. He's getting ready
for the long pull up Bachelor
Arts Mountain. I'm trying to relax.

He's shrinking from what he was
in high school—a balloon of
a left guard or linebacker—
I can't remember which because
he was always on the bench
or else the *kamikaze* squad
on kickoffs, punts, and returns.

It's a scholar of a damn poet
he wants to be now, and
I guess they've got to be
skinny as I was at McKinley,
playing tailback and pounding
through the line, playing center
field and pounding the black
pocket of my Mel Ott's mitt.

If skinny's all it takes, then
I should have been the scholar.
We said "Go For Broke!" and busted,
"Suck Em Up!" and got screwed,
"Lucky Come Hawaii!" and lost it.

So I brought them all to California
on the G.I. Bill, studied amps
and wattage, cycles of Franklin's Juice,
flipped the lights on this house,
and my finger to the F.H.A.

For what? For my son to tan
himself under a canopy of smog
filtered light, over some books
that say Keats, Shakespeare, and Yeats?
That's what the mongoose say
chasing snakes through the Koolau.

Must be like my father-in-law
tells me, the Gospel According
to Kubota, "Ass why hard,
eh, Hongo? Ass why hard."

_____ *Garrett Kaoru Hongo*

C & H Sugar Strike
Kahuku, 1923 _____

You waken to food,
hot yellow tea on cold rice,
    a dash of *shoyu*,
    Louisiana Red,
a few tangles of *daikon*

    glistening like angel
hair in the *chazuke* bowl.
    You waken to a
    new wife, humming jazz
tunes over the kitchen sink,

    rinsing radishes
as she coaxes water out
    of the iron pump.
    You waken to the
old worries, shining like loose

    change in a churchplate,
tears of light beading under
    gaslamps while the hymns
    rummage through shallow
pockets, and the memories

    flicker into bloom
with the dawnlight bleeding through
    porchscreens into the
    kitchen where it falls
at your feet like scattered rice.

    A drift of incense
migrates from over the hills
    behind the village
    of quonset barracks,
rinses through the dirt sidestreets,

    reaches the table
and settles into your hands

where you read it like
a message—The burn
has started. The strike is killed.

Garrett Kaoru Hongo

To Buddy, on the Edge

Buddy calls the other day
tells me,
"got some good deals, brah,"
says the bay won't break again
till September,
and the south,
"got too much haoles."
He wants us to fly over,
pick up a few deals
and bring him Honolulu on the way home.
But I remember the last time,
the rented Cessna,
the eight pounds Buddy packed
in an old market box,
keeping the cockpit windows open while we smoked,
and the storm that nailed us
twenty minutes out of Lihue.
Oh, that was a mean mother,
and when we couldn't climb it,
you rammed into its heart at full throttle,
swallowed by that thick milk
and screaming rain,
air pockets big as craters.
But that Buddy,
laughing us right through it,
loving the edge
and living hard to stay there,
he wants to look for more storms.
"Fuckin' great ride," he says.

So I'm thinking
how that edge keeps lookin' better everytime,
and I want it all back again.
I call Buddy,
tell him we can get a plane this week.
"I sold it to some haole already,"
he says, "and the bay came up six feet yesterday.
Sorry brah."

Well Buddy. The next storm
comes in December,
and you know how summer
dulls the blade.

_____ *Dean H. Honma*

Fish Story

Yeah that time when we went Kapoho,
flew over that afternoon for catch ulua,
"plenny," you said had,
so we went pack the big poles, the lights
and cooler, the quart good whiskey from Christmas.
You tell some stories back then,
how much times you went lose big kine,
"nightime hard," you said, "but that's when they stay."
Okay, but me, my cousin tell Kapoho spooky,
he hear stories, guys see ghosts li'dat.
He tell the cliffs steep,
the water most times rough, that nightime
maybe better go someplace more safe.
But nah, not you, the fish more important,
that you no come this far for nothin'.
So what can I say?

By the time we reach Kapoho stay late,
almost dark,
wind picking up hard from the south.
You almost broke the rennacar going down that road,
fuckin' thing grinding over the lava,
but I figure you know where we stay.
We come to this place, one short field
where the flow came sideways,
and in the back had big ironwoods, the pine tree kine.
The edge of the field went drop straight down,
could tell was deep,
and the waves stay slappin' high up the cliff.
Brah, was hairy.
The kine you fall,
pau already.

After the lines out stay real dark cause
no more moon, no can see shit.
Only our fire, one small one,
just like the only light forever.
Come cold over there nightime, the wind
make noises from the ironwoods, the ocean

41

just like breathing.
Sometimes the bells on the poles stay ring,
the headlamps shine, but only the wind
or strong surge.

No more human kine sound cept us,
talking soft
and drinking whiskey.
I know you stay thinking,
and you know I stay thinking,
like us guys not supposed to be here,
like darker and more noisy
cause we stay.
But we no say nothin',
no even shine the light when just like get something
steppin' on the rocks.
And nothin' bite,
long time we wait, the tide drop,
the wind die and come quiet,
like only get us.
So we went to the car
and locked the doors,
left the fire behind, the poles still there
in the cracks.

Morningtime your reel stay stripped,
guarantee ulua.
The bell musta been clangin',
line singing from the spool.
Funny but, sometimes,
when you stay listen too hard,
no can hear nothin'.
Now, when you tell me you like go again,
I figure it ain't the fish so much.
You already catch plenny since then.
I think maybe you like take one from them
when stay dark and quiet,
bring back the fear we went leave behind.

Dean H. Honma

Ho. Just Cause I Speak Pidgin
No Mean I Dumb

Pidgin short.
Fast.
Match.

If I say
What are you going to do with that?
No say how
I feeling curious

What you going do with that?
Now you know.
I not just nīele.

I like know
but I ain't
no cop.

Pidgin safe.
Like Refuge, Pu'uhonua,
from the City.

Diane Kahanu

Order

The fields seemed chaotic to him—
butterflies flitting among the flowers,
bees zinging by like bullets,
dragonflies zipping at crazy angles,
grasshoppers with springy legs
leaping out of reach.

He captured them, one kind at a time,
and put them in his death chamber—
a mayonnaise jar with a paper towel
soaked with Black Flag inside.
He watched each go frenzied, then wind down
like a little toy running out of spring;
when it was still; he spread it out to dry.
Then he impaled the soft corpse,
the small tension in the pin
sending an imaginary pain through his chest.
He placed each new specimen
in line with the last:
neat rows like cars in a parking lot.

Dennis Kawaharada

rain quietude

In sleep made of sleep and remembrance, a few raindrops
sound in the dark. Like a chieftain, the wind moves through
    leaves,
and then the raindrops fall. But I am deceived by other
nights and desires; these are only small hands
shaken from the sky. No rainfall follows the path through
    the woods,
the night is clear of its sounds, and I can hear the ocean
    open
like a palm among small rocks.

I think of days when some ghost undulation
moved through stillborn
rain on the ocean.

I have seen that same movement of rain in the changing
    tones of sea
seen from a great height on clear days; and in clouds paled
    by wind
on the pali; and in a woman's distraction
when love has carried her to awkward hours
and the light in the room is strange; when she is exhausted,
wet, suspirant with desire, and things are still moving,
but moving less, and she wonders what of love will remain
when she has handed it down to herself through the years
and her hands have changed it, when even now it is
    strangely unapproachable
like something in perfect balance, and offhandedly, she says,
"I think it's going to rain."

Gary Kissick

Dear Reiko: 1968/1978 _____

I Kula

We buy books to keep our secrets:
mine, a leopard's skin,
yours, his wooden coffin.
Every page is lined
like your grandmother's field.
Quietly we begin to plant
among the rows of cabbages.
Soon they are covered with first growth,
aimless vines with no support.
Somewhere a leopard opens his eyes.

II Ofuro

Today I build the fire:
yellow newspaper,
too-green wood,
and everything is smoke!
Your auntie comforts me
with sweet potato dumplings.
There are new kittens
behind the bathhouse.
Soft as we are to each other.
We put them in our slippers
just inside the door;
they are that warm.
Tonight the bathwater
will smell of green fire,
and it will not matter.

III Graveyard

We carry water to your grandfather:
some of it spills
leaving withered footprints
that follow me
down the blank white steps.

We wash his stone carefully.
Solemn, we pull the weeds
that fill his bed.
We do not dig too deep.
We leave the roots.

IV Memorial

I am the proper kokeshi doll:
my wooden hands bend harmlessly
in my green lap,
a field of daisies
with dark pink centers.
The priest catches me—
"You don't understand a word, do you?"
I hide in the grass.
I cannot find you anywhere.

V Omiyage

Your grandmother takes us
to her garden for the last time:
we squat among flat, wet leaves,
afraid of worms and centipedes
and potatoes that will not let go.
But she finds them easily—
her fingers emerge,
brown as the earth
she has taken them from.
We run to where the loquats dangle,
already the size of a man's thumb.
We pluck them from the trees
and poke them into egg cartons
where each pale fruit glistens
in its own moist compartment,
waiting.

Reluctant to leave,
we race the length of the field,
the cabbages clumsy and mute around us—
our brothers' heads! No arms to hurt us!

So we kick them toward the dim lines
of the mountains.
And there I see
our grandmothers,
their backs bent,
carrying the sky.

Jody Manabe

Grandmother and the War _____

She memorized the Pledge of Allegiance,
The Star-Spangled Banner.
And everything "Japanese" was buried—
Her Buddha, the Rising Sun, her family's picture.
She made a garden on this mound and all
The days of war, she tended silence.
But late at night, she'd shake off
The dead leaves of her reticence and
Rising from the garden of her voices,
I'd hear her whisper,
"Grandchild, grandchild, we are Japanese,
Never forget that!"

_____ *Juliet S. Kono*

The Cane Cutters

It is early morning. The brave
Hawaiian moon sits in the saddle
Of morning, bucking its light.
A woman shivers as she trudges
Briskly, behind a man. She carries
The lunches and an old kerosene lantern
That trails fumes heavily into the gloom.
Surrounding them, piles of bagasse
Sit silently fat and rank. Unmindful,
The old-looking couple, stop to rest.
The man takes out two long knives.
They sparkle in the negligent light.
He fingers each honed edge and tenderly
Caresses the sharpness. Pleased,
He hands one to his wife. Together,
They work the tall burnt fields,
Long into the tiring hours. They sing,
And they dream to the pendulum
Swing of their machetes.

Juliet S. Kono

Yonsei

I hear the music
Ride the updraft
In this valley.
It is not yours.
You are thumbing
Your way to the North Shore:
Being dropped off
At Left Overs
Or Thompson Corner, first,
Then making your way down;
Shouldering a radio,
Smothering the speaker
Into your ear—
The one with the gold star
That glints and steals
Studs of moonlight
When your hair whips
Away from your face.
I can see the wide
Swagger of your body
As it moves.
Shadows of firm bones.
They hold your body
Across roads as each
Lean and tall muscle
Ripples you forward
In your dark, good health—
Each sinew curved,
Warm as sun.

You live so far away
From what connects you.
You have no recollection
Of old plantation towns,
Of rains that plummeted
Like the sheafs of cane,
The song of flumes,
The stink of rotting feet,
The indignities cast by hard labors.

Your blood runs free
From the redness of soil.
But you are mired
Into this locality.
A mixture of ideals
Basked in sun,
Wild surf and turbulent air.
And yet once a year
You come with me
In your dark brooding—
Like a craving—
To visit the ancestors'
Gravesites to pray.
You say nothing
About being held
To these traditions.
You pray, bow and
Burn incense. You travel
Backward in time
For a brief moment
And say dutiful words
Do the respectful gestures
And I know that
In my longest sleep
You would come
And I would not want.

Juliet S. Kono

Like Love

What you will remember are his hands,
his large hands that could encircle your arms
and how your fingers could not even meet
around his wrists. The coarse hairiness
of his arms against your face, your arms, your body,
and the roughness of his fingertips.
If you were lucky, you were on the grass,
not on hard concrete or dry dirt
where little stones would leave imprints
on your face, arms, and back.
    You would remember those little stones a long time
    pressing against your cheekbones, shoulder blades
    and tailbone.
And for a long time, the large hands of men,
    the hairy arms leading to large palms
    with fingers curling around
    steering wheels, cigarettes, water faucets,
    toothbrushes, spoons, and hammers
will make you remember.

Laurie Kuribayashi

Freeway Poem _____

He's right.
Freeway driving, like everything else
she's afraid of trying,
isn't as impossible as she'd thought.
He taught her, out of necessity
more than love, to synchronize
their travel with the other cars.

She learned not to think,
while winding around the curve
between Moanalua and Halawa,
about the parallel impact between
crashing at 50 mph on asphalt
and falling fifteen stories
to land spread-eagled on cement.
Images of Lee being gutted
by his stick shift on the H-1
and Clara's windshield guillotine
no longer come to mind
as she accelerates on the onramp
above Church of the Crossroads.

But he knows it's not enough
to face fear with rationality
and necessary action: he knows
freeway driving, like everything else
that frightens her, is filled
with uncertainty and so requires
a certain amount of faith,
in herself and others,
that she so rarely finds: as always
there are just too many variables
juxtaposing at too high a speed.

And she still can't tell, no matter
how she peers into that little mirror
screwed onto the car door,
how fast a car is coming at them;
she still feels that mystical anxiety

whenever the shadow of an overpass
passes through the car so fast
that it's almost non-existent;
and she still wishes she had that faith
to merge with the minimum of panic,
to believe that together
they could move safely forward,
parallel with the others.

Laurie Kuribayashi

Taking Her to the Open Market _____

Scales glisten;
pink whiskers jut out.
Some are the color
of mud, others
recall the embroidery
of coats placed
on babes one-month old.
Fat, round, small:
they lay on the crushed
ice, stall after stall.

"Look at the fresh fish!"
I exclaim, eager to impress
on her our respect
for the old
ways, and that I know
how to tell the firmness
a poached flesh will have
by the bulging
of its eyes, the blood
in the gills.

"They are dead,"
she replies. Taken aback,
I see
through her Hong Kong eyes
that fresh
means leaning over
a galvanized pan, eyeing
closely through the running
water at that
cluster of darting
shadows, seeking out the one
swimming most
vigorously: in demonstration
that it
has not yet
passed the point of no return.

"Sanitation,"
I mutter, "has killed off
more than germs."

Wing Tek Lum

I Caught Him Once _____

Gruff old fut
never showed it
even after Ma died
even near his own end
stomach mostly gone
except one time
I caught him
in his room
talking to his nurse
wistful
"I don't know how much longer . . ."
him just sitting there
face so pale
not moving
the nurse standing at his back
leaning over
expertly
to wipe the tears
as they welled up

_____ *Wing Tek Lum*

The Poet Imagines His Grandfather's Thoughts on the Day He Died _____

This is the first year
the Dragon Eyes tree has ever borne fruit:
let us see what this omen brings.
Atop one of its exposed roots
a small frog squats, not moving, not even blinking.
I remember when my children were young
and this whole front yard was a taro patch:
we would take them out at night with a lantern
blinding the frogs just long enough
to sneak a hook up under the belly.
In those days we grew taro
as far as the eye could see;
I even invented a new kind of trough
lined inside with a wire mesh
so we could peel the skins with ease.
The King bought our poi,
and gave me a pounder one day.
It is made of stone,
and looks like the clapper of a bell, smooth and heavy.
I keep it in my bedroom now—there—on the dresser.
The fish we call Big Eyes
lies on an oval plate beside it.
I have not been hungry today.
The full bowl of rice attracts a fly
buzzing in anticipation.
I hear the laughter of one of my grandchildren
from the next room: which one is it?
Maybe someday one of them will think of me
and see the rainbows that I have seen,
the opium den in Annam that frightened me so,
my mother's tears when I left home.

Dear ancestors, all this is still one in my mind.

_____ *Wing Tek Lum*

Riding the North Point Ferry

Wrinkles: like
valleys etched by glaciers
lumbering coarse
and deliberate, random
traces pointing to
that vast, dark sea. The skin
is an ochre
of old corn, with
splotches of
burnt embers from a summer
of mountain fires.
The brown
from a lifetime of tea or
tobacco or both
has stained her
uneven teeth. Ears and nose
are small, pudgy,
and on each
lobe a little knob of gold
tacked on.
She sits with one
leg raised, tucked
into her body, the heel
supported by
the seat, her arm
resting on her
knee—unlady-like to be
sure, though
in her black garments
a relaxed pose. I glance at
her eyes, mottled
now with a chicken fat-
yellow in the
pupils, gazing out at the harbor,
the neon lights beckoning
from the Kowloon
shore.

      Where
was I prepared for this
face? Not
from the land of
my birth, with our museums,
glass cases filled
with the porcelain of ancient
dynasties, restaurateurs (cheeks
of cupidity)
proffering hot
and sour delights, our bookstores
extolling Shangri-las in
paperback—all to deny
our scrutable
lives. We believe
that somewhere in the world our
exotica is real. Images
of all fairy tale
maidens: clear-eyed yet
coy, hair pure
as silk, skin like jade,
the small hands so clever and
refined—and when
held in my own, how
warm, yielding to the touch!
They are
fiction: like the wind-blown
waves across this
ferry's bow, an inconstant
surface of
reflection, glittering, oblivious
to the swollen
depths below.

        I know
that outward appearances are
no judge for
virtue within. And
even this old
woman, combing her loosed

hair at dawn,
must sometimes wonder
at that mirrored form, peering
from those eyes. Does
she recognize
that dark glow as
her own? We meet so many
dreams, so many tales
of woe. Which
ones are true? Which ones
our alibis? So hard to
choose.

       My grandparents
I recall sailed by
sea to settle in
that place we now call home.
I have crossed that
ocean too, flying this time
with the sun,
searching for a vision
for my own. The deck rocks gently.
By chance I find
myself beside this woman
on this crowded
boat: she is
for me reason enough to
have come here.

Chinese Hot Pot

My dream of America
is like *dá bìn lòuh*
with people of all persuasions and tastes
sitting down around a common pot
chopsticks and basket scoops here and there
some cooking squid and others beef
some tofu or watercress
all in one broth
like a stew that really isn't
as each one chooses what he wishes to eat
only that the pot and fire are shared
along with the good company
and the sweet soup
spooned out at the end of the meal.

Wing Tek Lum

Junior Got the Snakes _____

One Time
Junior got
the snakes
real bad, an
had only family
was drinking
in the cars
up Piihana,
and he was
some wild,
so brother
Bobby tell,
"Okay, Moke
take it out
on me, then,"
an bumbye
Junior stay
confused,
but still
he like fight
so Bobby
tell go
punch the stone,
an Junior go,
he blass em—
then his hand
stay·all
buss,
he sour,
swell head
mo worse
was,
but so much
the pain
he only hold
his hand
an walk
behind
the water tank,

an bumbye
I seen
he wen write
KILL YOU
on top.

_____ *Michael McPherson*

Poets Behind Barbed Wire _____

*The following is an excerpt from **Poets Behind Barbed Wire** (Bamboo Ridge Press, 1983), collected and edited by Dr. Jiro Nakano and his wife, Kay.*

Since early 1981, the Commission of Wartime Relocation and Internment of Civilians, created by Congress in 1980, has held a series of hearings where many Japanese Americans attested to the injustice, abuse and mistreatment of innocent people by the United States Government during World War II. Very few people, however, are aware that many of the Japanese internees recorded their life behind barbed wires through the Japanese poetic forms such as tanka and haiku. These short poems, being less cumbersome than long diaries, were ideal forms for these internees to express their pent-up emotions in view of the scarcity of writing paper.

_____ *Jiro Nakano, M.D. and Kay Nakano*

Arrest

Torawaruru
Toki wa kitarinu
Ame no yoi
Kokoro sadamete
Kutsu no oto kiku

The time has come
For my arrest
This dark rainy night.
I calm myself and listen
To the sound of the shoes.

Sojin Takei

At the Volcano Internment Camp _____

Shokudo ni
Kayou nomi fumu
Daichi nari
Ajiwau gotoku
Fumite ayumeri

As if to relish
Each step I take
On this great earth,
I walk—
To the mess hall.
The only walk allowed.

_____ *Muin Ozaki*

On the Ship to the Mainland _____

Nobishi tsume
Kamikirite futo
Ko no uso o
Shikarishi koto o
Omoidasareshi

Biting down my overgrown nails,
I suddenly remembered
That day
When I scolded my son
For biting his nails.

_____ *Muin Ozaki*

Fort Sill Internment Camp _____

Komi ageru
Ikidori ari
Hyakujyuichi to
Munehada i bango
Akaku kakareshi

A retching anguish rises
As the number "111"
Is painted
On my naked chest
In red.

Muin Ozaki

Haru Asaki
Kimi ga chibusa no
Fukurami ka
Tsukitateshi mochi no
Kiyoki tezawari

My hands lightly touch
The freshly pounded *mochi*
So like the swell
Of a maiden's breasts
This early spring day.

_____ *Sojin Takei*

Santa Fe Internment Camp _____

Ashi no ue ni
Ari noborikuru o
Jitto mitsume
Toki o sugoshite
Kuinu kono koro

Ants climbing up my foot—
I don't begrudge anymore
The time I spend
Just watching them.
Such is my life nowadays.

_____ *Sojin Takei*

Death at the Camp _____

Warera mina
Sarinishi ato no
Kono mushiro
Tare ka touran
Ikusa hate naba

When the war is over
And after we are gone
Who will visit
This lonely grave in the wild
Where my friend lies buried?

Keiho Soga

Homecoming

Akibae no
Yaseshi ga hitotsu
Tobimawaru
Nibuki yuhi no
Heya no akarumi

A thin autumn fly
Circling the room
Lit by a dim evening sunlight

Sojin Takei

Ikuman o
Kazofuru kuroki
Tori no mure
Kemuri o nashite
Doyomi tobitatsu

A flock of black birds
Ten thousand in number
Creates a commotion
As they fly up like smoke.

_____ *Sojin Takei*

Crack Seed _____

The bodhisattva
knew with a shock
that a certain glass jar
(mislabeled "crack seed")
contained human hearts.
Their owners had put them
(shriveled
and clinging
and soaking in brine)
out to bid.
Still darkly oozing,
the hearts vaguely remembered
their days of plum sweetness.
But mostly
they hugged the sharp shards
of the times
they'd been broken.

The bodhisattva
made a huge purchase.

Then she painstakingly picked
and showed the hard hearts
their still living
center.

_____ *Kathy Phillips*

Kuan Yin Mingles with the Ghosts, Now on Guided Tour, of the Slave Population Which Constructed the Great Wall of China ───────

—I kept my self-respect by loving every stone I carried.
—I kept my self-respect by hating every stone I carried.
—You mean anybody who really wants to cross it can cross it?
—It has aesthetic value.
—Yes, it's like wrapping eleven Florida islands in six million square feet of pink plastic.
—Some would argue that aesthetic values keep out barbarity.
—Here's my carving: up yours.
  I was blunt in those days.
  My individual bluntness has survived the centuries!
—The airplane makes the wall a joke.
—This wall makes the airplane a joke!
—The wall still baffles the goats.
—The wall still baffles the ghosts.
—I never said anything at the time, but at night I could see Kuan Yin sitting on the wall.
  Smiling. At ease.
—I never said anything at the time, but by day I could see Kuan Yin helping to lift stones.
—I kept working because I could hear Kuan Yin singing.
—I kept working because I could see Kuan Yin throwing stones down the mountainside.
  She was shouting the curses I couldn't shout.
—I gave birth under the wall.
  I prayed Kuan Yin to take the child before it grew bent picking stones.
—Did Kuan Yin take it?
—Yes

───────── *Kathy Phillips*

75

Kuan Yin Turns Her Photo Album to a Certain Point _____

When pressed, Kuan Yin explains
why she has not yet left the world.
She shuffles to files,
turns to a certain point,
has to force a long look.

It is a famous photo.
Thousands saw the girl
tearing burning clothes
from her napalmed body.
The thin naked girl.
The wide open mouth.
"Quan Am," she may have been screaming:
Kuan Yin in Vietnamese.

The girl would be twenty-five by now,
then forty-seven,
and then sixty,
if she survived:
the photo doesn't say.

"She may still be looking for me.
She may not be able to forget.
She may ask me,
why?"

"I have unfinished business,"
says Kuan Yin, packing her sparse bag with subtle salves.
"How is it that some are able to say,
'It is finished'?"

_____ *Kathy Phillips*

The Youngest Daughter _____

The sky has been dark
for many years.
My skin has become as damp
and pale as rice paper
and feels the way
mother's used to before the drying sun
parched it out there in the fields.

    Lately, when I touch myself,
my hands react as if
I had just touched something
hot enough to burn.
My skin, aspirin-colored,
tingles with migraine. Mother
has been massaging the left side of my face
especially in the evenings
when it flares up.

This morning
her breathing was graveled,
her voice gruff with affection
when I took her into the bath.
She was in a good humor,
making jokes about her great breasts,
floating in the milky water
like two walruses,
flaccid and whiskered around the nipples.
I scrubbed them with a sour taste
in my mouth, thinking:
six children and an old man
have sucked from these brown nipples.

I was almost tender
when I came to the blue bruises
that freckle her body,
places where she has been injecting insulin
for thirty years, ever since
I can remember. I soaped her slowly,
she sighed deeply, her eyes closed.

In the afternoons
when she has rested,
she prepares our ritual of tea and rice,
garnished with a shred of gingered fish,
a slice of pickled turnip,
a token for my white body.
We eat in the familiar silence.
She knows I am not to be trusted,
even now planning my escape.
As I toast to her health
with the tea she has poured,
a thousand cranes curtain the window,
fly up in a sudden breeze.

Cathy Song

Easter: Wahiawa, 1959 _____

1.
The rain stopped for one afternoon.
Father brought out
his movie camera and for a few
fragile hours,
we were all together
under a thin film
that separated the rain showers
from that part of the earth
like a hammock
held loosely by clothespins.

Grandmother took the opportunity
to hang the laundry
and mother and my aunts
filed out of the house
in pedal pushers and poodle cuts,
carrying the blue washed eggs.

Grandfather kept the children
penned in the porch,
clucking at us in his broken English
whenever we tried to peek
around him. There were bread crumbs
stuck to his blue-grey whiskers.

I looked from him to the sky,
a membrane of egg whites
straining under the weight
of the storm that threatened
to break.

We burst loose from Grandfather
when the mothers returned
from planting the eggs
around the soggy yard.
He followed us,
walking with stiff but sturdy legs,
curious at the excitement

shuddering through our small spines.
We dashed and disappeared
into bushes,
searching for the treasures;
the hard boiled eggs
which Grandmother had been simmering
in vinegar and blue color all morning.

2.
When Grandfather was a young boy
in Korea,
it was a long walk
to the river banks,
where, if he were lucky,
a quail egg or two
would gleam from the mud
like gigantic pearls.
He could never eat enough
of them.

It was another long walk
through the sugar cane fields
of Hawaii,
where he worked for eighteen years,
cutting the sweet stalks
with a machete. His right arm
grew disproportionately large
to the rest of his body.
He could hold three of us
grandchildren in that arm.

I want to think
that each stalk that fell
had brought him closer
to a clearing,
to that palpable distance.
From the porch
to the gardenia hedge
that day, he was enclosed
by his grandchildren,
scrambling around him
like beloved puppies

for whom he could at last buy
cratefuls of oranges,
basketfuls of sky blue eggs.

I found three that afternoon.
By evening, it was raining hard.
Grandfather and I
skipped supper. Instead,
we sat on the porch
and I ate what he peeled and cleaned
for me.
The delicate marine-colored shells
scattering across his lap
were something like what
the ocean gives
the beach after a rain.

Cathy Song

Tribe

for Andrea

I was born
on your fourth birthday,
song of the morning dove
spilling from the guava trees.

Grandparents came to look at me,
the number two girl
with dumpling cheeks and tofu skin.
They pinched and cuddled,
affectionately gruff, blowing garlic breath
across my unflinching face.
Lifting me into their brown speckled arms,
you stood guard, proud and protective
of this new fat sister, stern
like a little buddha

I rolled and rebounded,
gravity nestling its fist
in the center of my stubborn belly
whereas you were lithe
with the speed of a rabbit,
quick and cunning.
You hopped to errands,
fetching this and that.

We shared papaya boats
Mother emptied of tiny black seeds
that resembled caviar
and egg shells Father hollowed for whistles.
Our lungs expanded
as though they were balloon fish
fluttering out noiseless tunes.
We blew our songs to the gulch
that brought the eucalyptus smell of rain.

I don't remember
going there into the forest,
although you must have taken me

where the lilikoi vines
dripped sticky sap passionately,
their blossoms curling like bells or tongues.
I heard my first story from you.

Waving good-bye
at the edge of the grass,
you disappeared into the bushes
like a huntress, the only girl
in a gang of boys.
I knew bravery then
and what it meant to belong to a tribe
when you returned triumphant
just as the afternoon showers broke,
with all their marbles
bulging in the pockets
of your leopard spotted pedal pushers.
I heard your slippers slapping the mud
and running to meet you
at the screen door,
I saw you laugh, tossing up something
sunlit and flashing into the air:
you told me how Arnold had cried
to lose his precious tiger's eye.

Cathy Song

83

The White Porch

I wrap the blue towel
after washing,
around the damp
weight of hair, bulky
as a sleeping cat
and sit out on the porch.
Still dripping water,
it'll be dry by supper,
by the time the dust
settles off your shoes,
though it's only five
past noon. Think
of the luxury: how to use
the afternoon like the stretch
of lawn spread before me.
There's the laundry,
sun-warm clothes at twilight
and the mountain of beans
in my lap. Each one,
I'll break and snap
thoughtfully in half.

But there is this slow arousal.
The small buttons
of my cotton blouse
are pulling away from my body.
I feel the strain of threads,
the swollen magnolias
heavy as a flock of birds
in the tree. Already,
the orange sponge cake
is rising in the oven.
I know you'll say it makes
your mouth dry
and I'll watch you
drench your slice of it
in canned peaches
and lick the plate clean.

So much hair, my mother
used to say, grabbing
the thick braided rope
in her hands while we washed
the breakfast dishes, discussing
dresses and pastries.
My mind often elsewhere
as we did the morning chores together.
Sometimes, a few strands
would catch in her gold ring.
I worked hard then,
anticipating the blue hour
when I would let the rope down
at night; strips of sheets,
knotted and tied,
while she slept in tight blankets.
My hair, freshly washed
like a measure of wealth,
like a bridal veil.
Crouching in the grass,
you would wait for the signal,
for the movement of curtains
before releasing yourself
from the shadow of moths.
Cloth, hair and hands,
smuggling you in.

Cathy Song

On Being Local _____

All events and experiences are local, somewhere. And all human enhancements of events and experiences—all the arts—are regional in the sense that they derive from immediate relation to felt life.

It is this immediacy that distinguishes art. And paradoxically the more local the feeling in art, the more all people can share it; for that vivid encounter with the stuff of the world is our common ground.

Artists, knowing this mutual enrichment that extends everywhere, can act, and praise, and criticize, as insiders—the means of art is the life of all people. And that life grows and improves by being shared. Hence it is good to welcome any region you live in or come to or think of, for that is where life happens to be, right where you are.

_____ *William Stafford*

Forging a Passport _____

On the north side where wind and water
are turning even plastic into little
colored pieces of sand, a frigate bird
coasts over, its big W wings disappearing
down the trade wind, like anyone who waits
long enough and holds on, carried by a steadfast
local stance no matter how the wind blows.

With the passport like that you too could come in
over the guns, or hold that poise
before descent when a wave breaks.
You could be somebody else when the doves
ask, hold your wings partly folded
and float, saying, "I'm sorry, I'm sorry."

Out there where the water goes deep, something
profound and blue keeps the island, holds
a stillness none of us can overcome.
Can a passport say it's ok to be born?
The frigate bird strokes in from out there, telling
us in a million ways how to move,
how to stay still, how to live.

_____ *William Stafford*

The Kim Chee Test

for En Suk

It wasn't because
    I made your daughter happy,
    wore hair on all sides of my face,
    or voted for McGovern.

It was because on that day in 1972,
    in the only Korean restaurant in downtown LA,
    I passed what you called "the kim chee test."

My almost deft chopstick technique surprised you
    having no way of knowing
    that I had been practicing for weeks,
    trying to grasp
    even the greatest of difficulties—
    peas, peanuts, and jello.

"Is he eating it?" you shouted
    from the opposite end of that long, low table.
"Yea, I think he likes it!"
    one of your friends shouted back.

Kim chee:
    the best of it sears the tongue like a battle cry
    a warm scream of pride
    at being alive
    and Korean.
    It's hotter stuff
    than I was born to handle,
    but the taste is there.

That red-orange, peppery incandescence
    of won bok and daikon
    rose to me then as it has so often since,
    spikes of terrible light inexorably dawning.

I swallowed hard,
    struggling not to gasp
    or lurch too quickly

for the salving, golden remedy,
foaming icy at the brim.

Then I reflected:
this beer comes from where I come from:
the city of Cardinals, of mighty river meetings,
of the world's largest croquet wicket.

Congratulations to you,
my Korean father,
you chose the right brew,
you just passed the Michelob test.

_____ *Joseph Stanton*

Someday, But for Now _____

I take my place among you
I sit in the back of a classroom
and talk to the TV repairman
fixing the set in a living room somewhere
He picks up a piece of metal
and says, "this is how the system works"

I take my place among you
sit in the shade under a breadfruit tree
on a green metal bench
I talk to the farmer somewhere in the hills
growing lettuce
He has a handful of chicken shit
He tells me, "it's the salt of the earth"

I sit on the hood of a '68 Camaro
in a parking lot
it's raining
the manager wants to know where my raincoat is
I say, "it's alright, I don't mind getting wet"
He says, "get the coat"
I take my place among you and get the coat.

_____ *Gary Tachiyama*

Reviewing the Scene _____

I.
"Eleanor, don't do it!"
        he cried out.
Only her name was not Eleanor.
Her name was Elaine,
            and so,
she didn't listen.
She bounced three times
on the diving board
and made her swan dive
into the empty pool.

Or her name was Eleanor,
but she just flipped him the bird,
tested the board and made
that spectacular dive.

II.
In reviewing the scene,
each take had subtle differences.
Sometimes she bounced twice, not three times.
Sometimes it wouldn't be a board,
just the ragged edge of a cliff.
And sometimes even endings would change.

There would be the dive,
then a wide-angle pan
of a clear, empty pool.
Or maybe, the dive,
then a cut to footage where young boys
in blue Acme pool cleaning uniforms,
looking so much like service men,
tossed handfuls of chlorine
as they created a procession
past the pool and into red light.

Understandably, the scene
never ended overtly bloody.
It would take too much money.

It would leave us no sequel.
It would cost too many bodies.

III.
No clear choice could be made.
The panel of judges sitting on chairs
fronting one end of the pool
couldn't decide which image to project.
Even the highest performance score
averaged just below an 8.
        the high of an 8.9
        and the low of a 6.5
        were tossed out.
They all agreed, however,
at least a 9.5 was needed.

They also agreed that they wanted
the girl concrete and real—
"with the nakedness of motive
and action revealed, but not overtly so."

But they could not decide—
"Eleanor," the innocent,
the slut, the defiant,
the bruised and abused,
the cool and untouchable,
and even the loved.

All the labels given to women
and all their implications.

IV.
It was generally a crowd of men
sitting stiff and anxious
until the lights went out
and "Eleanor" was shaded,
then focused to form
on the screen.

And when the scene appeared,
it never occurred to them

to think why this jerk
was yelling, "Eleanor, don't do it!"
All they could relate to or feel toward him
was the urgency of his action
and the pathetic but well-intended
nature of his gesture.

No one would recognize him
for his performance.
It was like he worked at McDonald's.
He was not the star, she was.

They saw her and when she dived
they stuffed their faces with popcorn
and took long sips on their Cokes.
She was the hot number.
She exploded in their minds.

Then it was over.
The crowd of men scurried
or lumbered out into the streets.
"Damn, that's what you call a woman!"
                              one said,
"Damn good woman." But no one listened
or even cared why or how
this movie affected him.
It was none of their business
what gestures would come and go
like traffic lights
as he walked the streets
past "Eleanors" for sale.

_____ *Gary Tachiyama*

Tansu I

in old tansu drawers
the family crest disintegrates
on rust mottled kimonos.
what was once a wedding undergown
i will fashion into silken robes
for hostessing . . . seduction.

brilliant obi—
    threaded silver and fine gold—
binds me until
i cannot breathe
and feet too large for tabis
strut
      without grace
        before the mirror.

Raynette Takizawa

Faces on the Unpaved Road Past Mokulē'ia

Your long dark hair streams behind you
when you put on your tradewind mask.
You pick a path through fields of beach-rock
on the north shore of Ka'ena.
Between waves
you tap at the 'opihi navels
on the low bellies of black rocks.
The ocean spray dries in your eyes
and crusts on your eyelashes.
I pick off the limu stuck in the web of my throw-net.
I tie suji across rips torn by coral.
Your feet bleed from small cuts.
That's what you get
for walking on the beach-rock
without tabi.
I rub ice on the cuts.
It melts on your warm feet.

Wini Terada

The Last Turnings of the Season's Wheel

as the last turnings of the season's wheel
approach you
the mango tree at the east window is
fogged with thousands of brasspink blossoms
waiting to be left alive by gusts of tradewinds
and too much Manoa rain
left to grow into something beyond a flower

one last journey on the wooden ship is all you ask
though you are not spry and sturdy as at nineteen
craning your neck to see on approaching Honolulu Harbor
    the face
of the man in the photograph you held
and he also meeting you the first time
matching you to the image in his hand
those vivid adorations of youth do not bind you still
neither do the seizures of grief and confusion
that sent you on occasion to the mental hospital
raising nine children
for though Yoshio the firstborn died of influenza
and the third Seichi died also before his first year drowning
you still had to raise the memories of them
and those that might have been
over the years in wartimes
ironing shirts of canefield workers in your spare time
as you worked in the pineapple cannery
bringing home the cores for your children's snack
remembering after your husband died in his late forties
the touch of his shirts
and how he came home from carpentry
to the smell of bread in the brick oven outside
round loaves you baked Portuguese style
and the songs he taught you that he learned at parties
after you stayed up waiting
where he cooked for extra money
and carved beets into flowers
and white turnip into fishnets
and a papaya into a turtle with diamonds cut out over the
    back

96

inserting Lancer matchsticks for eyes
almost black the irises clouded vision
of his last hours as he lay the cancer
constricting purple and swollen his stomach

I can't stomach much of you these days
remembering what you were like before
and fearing what might have changed you
the mysterious cold that kept you up nights coughing
and wailing that demons were laughing at you
and coming to get you
though others suggested a psychiatrist
I believed you and too jittered for sleep one night
sat up in front of the TV blanking everything out
even as you came crawling down the hallway stealthily
like a cat craning your neck close to the carpet
as though sniffing out a scent
glancing furtive side to side
like a secret agent hiding behind the fan
and muttering to yourself you got to the kitchen
and grabbed the scissors and masking tape from the drawer

it seemed appropriate somehow to me
that you wrapped one by one in layers of old newspaper
the black and white photographs of your deceased
for though life could threaten them no longer
you feared for the lives of their images
the kimonos and gold threaded obi
were folded up and wrapped along with the dried up
     umbilical cords
of all nine children you saved
in tissue
indeed everything from the carved teakwood chest was
     salvaged
and dumped in a king size white pillowcase
which you slung over your creaky shoulder
like the last burden
till finally I got Mom up
who took it from you
and promised to hide it
at two a.m. on the porch
as you were readying for escape

she convinced you to go back to bed
as I watched bleary eyed from the dim hallway

you were admitted to Kuakini for testing
and given a strong diuretic
by the doctor I was leery of
because he was so offhand and old
but everyone said "she trusts him he speaks Okinawan"
and when Mr. and Mrs. Young from next door
visited you lying there you covered your face in your hands
    and cried
with some shame social or cultural
as you plummeted twenty five pounds down the scale

you never recovered that weight
or the smooth glow
that kept you in the garden
weeding or planting lettuce and comfrey
and the garden never recovered
from your absence
it still records the sighs
as you dropped to your knees in the soil
to let some earthworm squiggle back between the roots
and the faint sound of your white headkerchief flapping
in the valley breeze
as the mynahs stalked by
I saw only yesterday
the white crab flowers
on the jointed cactus claws
dropping down dusty green
the petals ever so susceptible to bruising
by any zephyr
and their faint scent as I walked the baby past
unmistakably sweet
from such an untended annual
in a rusted coffee can
one of your hundreds still lining the house

in my dream last night
I saw you no longer staring at your hands
as you do hour after hour silent in the chair
or at the table

complaining "nani kode mezurashii ne"
no matter what is set before you
I saw you at rest at last
in some larger hands or roots
cradling or branching through puddled water
around you
your back against the tree trunk
brown and flecked with lichen
and you were singing the nursery tune you taught me years
    ago
about the children seeing birds on the rooftops
on their way to school
and holding hands in a circle playing
then in the afternoon hearing the temple bells
in the mountains and heading home together

I remember the words timeless
like memory warps the heart
for what still lives that cannot be shared
as each leaves separate
what was known with others
like petals scattering on the waves
a life
circling its way out over blue water
the bird only glancing back once over the wing
at what was its home
as the season turns
opening the lotus
the wind rides over the body
its irresistible call
to some more comfortable environment
to rest
but I know you will not pause for long
you are too wise and pure
and will walk into some other clime
on a farther shore
greeting those
strangers to me
around you
with that same reserve calming
and graceful
and the work on your hands

will reflect not as scars of another time
colored by age or custom
but new clean and whole will enter
into your strength
as you fulfill some higher purpose
to its end
again

Debra Thomas

Where You Sleep

the moon nears our zenith
you lie asleep
the newborn hair spinning out from your scalp
like a spiral galaxy

I want to sleep where you sleep
is there music
or a speech
is a fairy dancing across green leaf stages
or are the stars rearranging themselves
into future clusters and systems

it is a gathered leaves and rain place
a hollow off the mainstream
a berth of clean silent air

Debra Thomas

etiquette

Eating a fish head is an art
which must be done
with refinement and
gusto.
Refinement because
as one dismantles the
brain, the eyes, the head
one must not offend the sensibilities of
others.
Gusto so that they maý be assured that the
head
is the most delectable of tastes
and it is.

Jean Yamasaki Toyama

Fever

They had burned my letters,
the ones from my brother,
and they had burned my wife's lacquer dresser,
and my daughter's porcelain dolls.
But that was the first time,
and it was I who smiled first at
the white-shadowed face of my son
against the curfew candlelight
that time.
My younger sons squealed at this
game in the dark,
at the swords in the attic unscathed,
at the thick black paper on the windows.

Only my wife turning
away from the yellow/white light
did not see the glory of the moment.
They had captured the saboteurs,
held behind army green walls
conspirators and patriots,
kamikaze zealots
and traitors,
but we were mute, and they passed us.

My father's books of poems,
my mother's koto,
the family scrolls
still wrapped in red silk
holding their breath in the floorboards beneath me
were silent in the dark.

They had passed us;
they, with their green/white eyes
and purgation missions
that smelled of kerosene.
They were burning the temples,
the schools,
some houses too.
But we had expected that,

and we let the vengeance take its course,
and let them take what they wanted,
who they wanted,
until they were quelled.
We were safe this first time.
Perhaps they had seen the plaques on the walls,
and the books and the surgical tools
in white cabinets,
and the metal-framed beds that were draped
in white sheets
and so passed us,
thinking perhaps,
that we, that I
with a Stanford degree
once donning the whites of their
surgical gowns
would deftly and surely
eviscerate
my seventeen summers in Nara.
Or perhaps they had simply known
this was the first time.

So I worked in my office,
in hospital wards,
in wailing half-empty
well-scrubbed houses of
wives without husbands,
mending and healing
the bodies of the jaundice-faced people.
Sometimes there were fevers,
and I'd go in the dark,
in my car, with black-covered headlights
that let only slits of yellow through
like cat's eyes.
I would go in the dark,
and knock at hidden doors
to find the sick blanched ones
with bodies on fire.
These were the ones who had been held,
the ones they had not passed,
and in their eyes, reflected
I saw the burnings of the shrines,

their pictures,
their tenuous links with homeland
forever charred.
So when they came that last time,
and shattered the floorboards
and the screams of my wife
that last time,
and scoured the attic
where my samurai swords
lay waiting, in white cloth,
that last time,
the faint upturnings
at the corners of my mouth
were not for glory
but comradeship.

They are burning my father's books of poems,
and the silk strings of my mother's koto
curl in the flames,
and the red wrapped scrolls
of my family dance
in yellow fire.

Jo Ann Uchida

Song at Hanalei

for Robert Cazimero

A gesture of the sea.
This wave does not recede
but unfurls until it's taken into sand.
The bay is a voice which gives itself,
wave after wave, and takes back nothing
yet every wave sinks to it again.

I heard your voice lifted from you
by a room of angles and spaces
and saw your eyes widen in surprise.
Is it silence or the constant untuned world
which demands so much of you?
Then you filled the room.

And if there were no walls

Could you breathe another wind into the world
or into the long light between stars?

While others hoard their breath,
thinking "my breath," as if it could be stolen,
I see you stand and trust its going
and its coming again.

There is something at the edge of your song
like the darkness which confines flame.
You travel to that edge, surrender into it
to be borne again on another breath.

_____ *Martha Webb*

The Anatomy of the Infinite _____

Woman. It is a word,
a question I have asked
of many men. I did not know
you had the answer, your mouth
with its tiny leap of tongue.
Your hips are the bend of water down-
streaming the place I was born,
and you taste of oranges
or cup-of-gold, which is a flower
like your own. Just when I think
you are all softness, you are bone;
and if I touch you my voice
moves softly from your throat, a surprise
of doves.

Since I no longer know
myself apart from you,
I will be content in our confusion.
As for that man whom we both love,
I know him better now for wanting you.
He has become the fire I could not feel
and like a vessel glowing in the kiln
I only harden to be broken, or be treasured.

Once again our bodies do not add
but multiply: we are not three, but nine,
or one, I cannot tell my numbers or my finites any more.

_____ *Martha Webb*

Las Horas de Verdad (The Hours of Truth)

Would the hours of truth discourage her
from breathing again from the dream?
After midnight when the streetlight
flooded her bed between the curtains' sway
she remembered his voice and ached between her shoulder
    blades.
She remembered the way he had shown her the constellations
without pointing
by shining his flashlight toward heaven.
Were these the hours of truth?

Not a single thought contained her.
Not her stallion limping in the wild lantana
his left fetlock burned by a rope
when he had bucked loose three nights ago
not the sweet green stain left on her hands
by the Hawaiian medicinal weed
she had squeezed through a cloth to heal him
not her sore thumb bruised
nor her shoulders wrenched
urging yesterday's gelding past the misted graveyard.

It was difficult visualizing his bed.
Did he lie alone in the smell his wife's perfume had left
in last week's sheets
or had she stayed
and were their long limbs tangled
their boney elbows and ribs renewing acquaintance?

Unfinished wine slept in a Japanese teacup beside her own
    bed.
The half she had drunk gave her mouth a sour taste.
The sound of the silent telephone unnerved her.
She turned east then west
her damp hair in twisted ropes slapped the pillow.
Are these the hours of truth, she repeated.

In evening light she rode a red dust ridge
upon the other horse

the shining red gelding as tame as a mud puddle.
Lyrics and arias pressed her mind
out of tune, words misplaced
but pressing
the way atoms must
when they expand and explode into another element.
Is it possible to learn
to go to the ones who come easily to us
and to like them?
These were the hours of truth.

Jill E. Widner

Trembling

The butterfly was caught
in an abandoned spider's web,
no one's nourishment.
She dismounted from her horse
and unglued its orange wings.
It followed her along the ravine for a while,
petroglyphs to the left
wasted overripe pineapple to the right.
Later when she had to pass the lone man in the brown jeep
with the rifle
parked on the side of the road
in the middle of the wilderness
she was sure it was the butterfly's heart
who kept her from harm.

Jill E. Widner

Anita Sky

I marinated her heart
oh Italian artichoke
I threw in her delicate entrails
parts I had touched in the dark of her moan
I threw in all the oils she had ever
soothed my bear-body with, basil, balm, musk, anise
I threw in the red of her floating pain
the black of her peasant eyes
I stirred in all my suffering
years in a factory, weeks on a train, a kid brother's death
I threw in the blue of her hair, small of her back
and for years after she left
I feasted on her body, I communed
with a landscape of sheep and cow and pasta
I lived on the juice of a woman
run off to her own infinite, Anita, Anita Sky

Rob Wilson

Strange Scent

Written 1978—Hawaii's Bicentennial

Hear the beating of the pahu
    distant and warning.
    Beware—a strange wave has washed upon the rocks
    even the crabs run from their homes.
In the night it passed over shining black water, gliding—not
    knowing where it came from
    or where it's going
    An omnipresence—there.
Me, I tried to sleep under starless sky
    but too dark
    too strange
    too still.
I feel I will never be the same again.

Tamara Laulani Wong-Morrison

The Luna Of The Landing _____

On a gusty afternoon, a lone mynah bird was startled out of a pine tree by the sound of footsteps rapidly approaching the edge of the cliff. He chattered angrily, then flew away as a youth with huge curious eyes stared up in his direction.

"Boy! Boy!" a voice called out hoarsely from the distance. The youth continued staring even after the bird had completely disappeared, until a wrinkled old man caught up to him.

"I tell you, no run away like that," the old man scolded. "You like fall down and get hurt?"

A gigantic smile spread over the boy's face. Then, without a word, he turned and immediately started down a winding trail which led across a sloped portion of the cliff wall. The old man started to voice a second warning but stopped because he knew that it would be of no avail. He hitched up an old knapsack, faded and frayed from years of constant use, and dropped out of sight after the youth.

The Hamakua coast on the island of Hawaii is a string of steep black lava cliffs dropping straight down into the sea. A man on shore can stand directly over the turbulent water and yet be hundreds of feet away from the surface, never being touched by the sea except for the salty mists which drift inland on days when the wind blows from the north.

Few are the coves which in past days allowed wary steamers to deliver supplies to the sugar cane plantations located at strategic spots along the coastline. Strong winches constructed at the top of the cliff wall stood ready to lift the cargo up to where mule trains waited. The job was long and difficult as well as hazardous because of the temperamental sea. Perhaps the ancient Hawaiian gods were alarmed at such intrusions upon their sacred burial grounds, for many hidden caves in the area contained the bones of kings and lords of old Hawaii. Whatever the reason for the turbulence, the ships had to approach the shore with extreme caution since there was no way of telling when the sea would belch forth a swell capable of hurling the ships against the rocks. Many men vanished under the raging sea to be lain in submerged crypts or carried away by predatory sharks.

But when those days passed, the coves were forgotten and tangled underbrush covered the mule trains leading to them. No one visited the landings except for fishermen who told stories about hearing the rusty winches being operated again on dark nights when the sea was in a less angry mood.

One of the coves was even more isolated than the rest because the sugar mill which it formerly served had been abandoned many years ago. A wide grove of mournful pine trees circled along the cliff rim high above the sea. It was through this grove of trees that the old man and the youth had just passed.

The old man shuffled cautiously down the trail, sometimes gaining leverage by grabbing hold of the tough-stemmed grass growing on either side. He was still strong and healthy, his figure showing few of the physical impediments which usually accompany old age. But though his legs showed no signs of weariness, the old man was aware that his once-sharp reflexes were no longer suitable for the steep trail. Over places where the youth would have scampered heedlessly across, the man conveyed himself with all four limbs.

A length of manila rope was coiled around the old man's waist, serving to hold up an ancient pair of pants. Several holes in the seat were covered with crude patches while others remained exposed to provide ventilation. It was difficult to say whether his shirt was tan colored or just covered with dust, but it had the long sleeves which are common among the plantation laborers who work with the thorny leaves of the sugar cane. An obsolete safety helmet balanced precariously on his head. A piece of sheet metal was soldered around the side for added protection from the sun so that the helmet resembled a shiny metal bonnet. The metal bonnet completely hid the old man's white hair but not the two huge ears which protruded from below it. The old man attributed his good health to his ears because of Japanese superstition which declared that large ears portended a long life.

At the bottom of the trail, the youth was waiting impatiently on an old concrete landing platform which was faded and covered with seaweed where it entered the water. In his stubby hands he grasped two bamboo fishing poles which he had retrieved from a crack in the cliff wall. As soon as the old man set foot on the landing, the boy ran to the water's edge where he laid the poles down and beckoned furiously with both of his hands. The old man smiled at the way the youth jumped up and down in gleeful anticipation while he attached hooks and lines to the poles.

When the old man had baited his hook, the boy dropped the line into the water and sat down on the edge of the landing. His face changed from one of anticipation to one of the most intense concentration. His huge eyes were focused deep into the water where he saw shadows gliding back and forth. When one of them approached the hook, he held his breath in expectation, his face frozen and his eyes piercing.

Suddenly, a small form moved where the water lapped against the slimy cement. The boy's attention was immediately directed to a black crab gathering seaweed with rapidly moving claws. How strange it looked with its eyes extended up into the air. The boy contorted his face into weird shapes, trying to extend his eyes into the air also. His face flushed and his eyes hurt but he could not get them to stand upright. A rage flashed through the boy. In anguish, he pulled at his hair and kicked his feet out wildly. He swung his pole viciously at the crab in bitter disappointment. With the crab's departure went the boy's rage. He turned his attention back to fishing and was soon hunched over with his former intense concentration, though he often paused to try to extend his eyes outward.

When the boy finally felt a twitch, he yanked the pole up hard enough for the fish to arch over him and land in back. With a triumphant cry, he jumped clumsily to his feet and fell on the fish as it squirmed furiously on the cement.

"Hooey," the old man chorused the boy's excitement. "As one nice size papio you catch, boy. Good eat, that one! We tell your mama cook 'um for you tonight."

The youth danced a happy victory jig over the landing, trailing the fish behind him. When he tired, the old man unhooked the remains of the fish and placed it in the knapsack. After his hook was again baited, the boy hunched over his pole with the same intense concentration. Each time the boy caught a fish, he danced for joy. But after a while, the sea grew restless and he lost all interest in fishing. He wandered away to chase crabs on the rocks off to one side of the landing.

Taking out a bag of tobacco from the knapsack, the old man slowly and carefully rolled himself a cigarette. After running his wet tongue over the cigarette, he raised his head to see where the boy was, then lighted up and settled back to fish. But his mind was not on fishing as he sat there blowing out blue clouds from under his silver bonnet. He looked out toward the horizon where the dark sky was creeping landward. Whitecapped swells were already arriving at the cove, speeding heralds of the approaching storm. The old man watched the waves hurl themselves at the peninsula which protruded from the opposite side of the landing from where the boy had gone. Each wave hissed angrily as it rushed upon the rocks, exploding into white foam at the impact. How often the two of them had sat and examined the same scene from the top of the cliff. Under the wailing pine trees they sat, each enjoying the sea in his own way. Sometimes the boy screamed encouragement to the pounding waves, rising to his feet in his excitement. At other times he sat in a trance, open-mouthedly staring.

The waves brought different emotions for the old man. They brought memories of the days when he had been the luna of the landing. At those times, he explained to the boy how to judge the wind and the sea in order to determine whether or not it was safe for a ship to enter the cove. He had spent many cold nights on the landing waiting for tardy steamers to come in. Many times he had given the order to start the winches and many times had given the muleteers their instructions on where to deliver the supplies. The luna was in charge of all operations at the landing and few were more important than he.

Looking up once again, the old man saw that the boy was zealously pursuing crabs, hurling rocks away to his right and left as he attempted to corner the elusive creatures. He and the boy belonged together. They understood each other as no one else did. Or perhaps it was just he who understood, the boy only instinctively attaching himself to the old man. One thing was certain though, this little cove was their private world and no one had the right to disturb their bond with each other and with their friend, the sea. No, not even the boy's parents should be allowed to interfere.

Deep within himself, the old man sensed (though he was unwilling to admit it) that he depended on the boy just as much as the boy depended on him. It would be so very lonely to have to visit the little cove by himself again. It never occurred to him to ask himself why he still came to the landing. If he had asked himself that question, he could not have given an answer. Or else he might have answered simply, "Me the luna of the landing."

No other explanation was needed. The old man's life had never been one of expanding horizons. When he first came to work at the landing, he had set only one goal for himself, to wear the shiny hat of the luna. After he became the luna, the little cove became his world. Everything had changed since then, but not the old man. He was still the luna. This was still his world though he was long retired and the landing was long outmoded. He was content with his memories, except that he could not speak to memories.

Long after the old man resolved himself to being the solitary sentinel of the cove, the boy had come. At first, he brought the boy only out of sympathy toward his parents. The youth was an intruder who feared the powers of the sea. But the boy's intense curiosity was too strong to keep him afraid for long and now the boy loved the cove almost as much as the old man.

More important, however, the cove itself had accepted the boy. It had befriended him and it had washed away the impurities. The youth was all right here, with a place where he belonged. Nowhere else would he find an environment which suited him more. If he was kept in a cage, the dynamo of emotion and energy inside the boy was sure to explode, while here at the old man's side, the cove could absorb all of the outbursts. None of the complications, the confusions, and the restrictions of society existed here to bewilder him. All the boy needed was freedom, freedom to explore the strange world that existed within his disproportional head. Both the man and the youth were useless to the world beyond the pine trees, and it was useless to them.

The shock of cold water splashing over his feet awakened the old man from his reverie. The tide was coming in as well as the storm. Glancing over his shoulder, he saw that the boy was nowhere in sight. After packing his knapsack and replacing the fishing poles in the crevice in the wall, the old man made his way over the moist rocks to the hidden spot where he knew he was most likely to find the boy. He walked until he came to the gaping mouth of an old lava tube which wormed its way into the cliff. Inside was the boy.

Lying very still on the floor, the youth was listening intensely to sounds coming out of a fissure. Apparently, the noises were produced by water rushing into a hollow chamber beneath the lava tube and somehow the fissure distorted the sound so that it resembled the clamor of distant voices. Whatever the voices were, they spoke intimate messages to the youth, for he never moved while he listened to them. They never spoke to the old man but it was obvious that the boy understood them so he was satisfied to sit and wait.

Having sat on the floor beside the boy, the old man said without looking at him, "Hey, boy. They sure making big noise today, hah? I think they talking about the big storm coming tonight."

The youth did not acknowledge the other's presence, which did not surprise the old man. He simply took out his tobacco and silently rolled himself another cigarette. His feet were folded under him and, with the boy close behind his back, he faced the entrance of the lava tube through which he watched the swells roll into the cove. The man and the youth sometimes spent hours here, the boy with his ear to the fissure and the man puffing on his hand-rolled cigarettes. For several minutes they continued as they were, man and boy together in comradeship, yet each engrossed in his own world. The old man knew that this was likely to be the last time he would ever share this silent bond with the boy. It marked the end of a phase of his life. As for the boy, perhaps occasionally a dim spark of remembrance would light in his mind, but for the most part, the old man and the voices would soon be forgotten.

Slowly, the old-timer turned toward his friend until he was staring directly at the prone figure, a great sadness shining in his eyes. He again spoke, more to himself than to the boy. "They telling you goodbye, boy. They know you not coming back no more. Your mama and papa sending you away to the city tomorrow." He had tried to convince them otherwise but they were sure of themselves and refused to be dissuaded. Each sentence was followed by a long pause, as though his words were intrusions within the silence. "You listen what they say and be good boy, okay?"

The youth still had his ear to the fissure, enthralled by the voices. "Get plenty nice things for see. You be real happy over there." He wished desperately that the boy could say, "No, I will not be happy." But the boy said nothing.

Tears trickled down the cracks on the old man's sunbaked cheeks. The fear and love poured out of his chest in one pleading sentence, "You no understand, boy?" The question was futile, merely a confirmation of fact. All self-control had left the old man. "How you can take care of yourself, boy? You almost one man but you no even talk yet. Nobody going to look out for you now."

Finally, the strange tone in the old man's voice caused the boy to look up at him. However, only curiosity appeared on the youth's face as he waited for his companion to give the usual sign that it was time to go. Two pairs of eyes met each other, one huge and waiting, the other moist and pitying. The old man looked deep into the other's eyes, trying to grab hold of just a little something inside the boy, but he could not see anything beyond the fog.

The eyes of the old man dropped first. He pushed himself to his feet and the youth quickly followed. From the landing, they watched the storm waves beating against the peninsula for the last time. One after another, as methodically as falling raindrops, the waves crashed onto the rocks. At regular intervals, an exceptionally large wave struck with such momentum that it hurled itself entirely over the piece of land.

After studying the sea for awhile, the old man looked thoughtfully at the boy's innocent face. No, it was not right for the boy to leave this place. It was unfair. He looked again at the peninsula as it was submerged by a giant wave, then he motioned toward it with his arm and said, "Come. We go catch some more crabs."

And together they set off.

Marshall M. Doi

121

Chapter I. Once In the First Times from *What You Like Know? An Oral Biography of Bonipasyo*

I was drenched with sweat, and so was *Tata,* Father. He had just taken off his squash hat and was wiping his salty lips with his short sleeves. I was already on my butt.

"Don't slouch on your ass, my son. You get lazy that way," he said.

And that's true, you know. When you sit and don't do anything with your hands, not moving, not talking to anyone, you can get lazy. And if you don't watch out, your thoughts can go all over the place, but never get you anywhere.

I squatted comfortably and opened the water pot to dip the coconut dipper for Tata to drink so I could drink. Ay, was I thirsty! But water is tastiest that way. After a few hours of continuous movement, working in the sunlight following your animal around and around, starting from the outside plowing, and circling inward, getting caught in the middle like the body of a butterfly between two wings, then taking the freedom to break through all those plow lines of life—ay, you're as hot as burning red embers. Sometimes you start in middle—that's the best way—from the inside, churning and plowing around and around, spiraling wider and wider. And if your calculation is balanced, you finish just right, leading onto the trail for home. When the Lord Sun clears the long shade of those bamboos, your skin burns and you are winded and dry inside. You can drink like a water buffalo. If you are weak, you can get dizzy. But no matter what, you look forward to that water in the pot, cooling in the shade where the dried leaves are so thick and moist with dew.

Tata gargled with the first sip then spat out the staleness and cleared his breath. "Hayhhh! Sweet is this water, ahemmm!"

He swallowed the next mouthful slowly. You always do that so you taste all the sweet wetness and don't choke. Tata handed me the water dipper, and I dripped a drop to appease the spirits of dead people and non-people, then took a long slow sip.

"Those sprouts will be good to cook over the *inabraw,* broth of your *Nana,* Mother, for our day meal my son," he said.

And I felt good and warm all the way around my ears. It would please everyone to taste it, and yes it's delicious. Ever tasted it?

"Yes, Tata," I agreed.

You answer parents like that. You address people by how you are related to each other. Not like nowadays here in Hawaii where kids just say, "Yes," as if talking without salt. That's tasteless and disrespectful in our custom, and if you ever spoke out of turn in those days, you got knuckles for lunch.

"Go on working hard, my son, that is the way of our life. It keeps boredom away which can confuse you to uselessness if you don't know how to handle it and see it through," he said in a breath of a lesson.

And like always, I answered obediently. That way I stayed silent and rested faster. Talking like this after work was the style of our Tata, his way of relaxing and thinking through the puzzles of his life-long curiosities.

"The soil is hard, and our animal is tired. But we have to harrow now so the soil won't dry deep," he said.

I was glad because it was really hot. I had gathered enough fresh feed for the day. That meant we didn't have to come back in the afternoon, and I could go riding with my friends to graze, maybe by the river.

"Tomorrow afternoon we'll plant . . ."

Suddenly, we heard women and children screaming, "Eiiiihhhh!" from our home to the east!

Tata took off like lightning, ripping his bolo knife in stride from the branch of the mother tree, and unsheathing it with his left hand, for Tata was left-handed, and our Apo was ambidextrous.

He charged down the pathway. I swallowed fast dropping the water dipper. Tying off the animal, I chased after him.

As he zigzagged, speeding through the corn rows, I entered the field pulling out my sickle from my right-hand pocket. Tata was hurdling the grass hedge when I came out of the corn rows.

Tata ran to the left of the house towards the north end by the grapefruit tree. I went to the south side behind the kitchen. The chickens were clucking danger and the dogs were barking for help at the corners of our front courtyard.

I was trembling when I peeked. Apo was flat on his back in the dirt with the big black boot of a *Kastila,* Spaniard, pushing on his stomach and a flashing silver saber pointed into his bare chest.

Apo had not let his head touch the dust. He held it up as if his heaving chest didn't even feel the sword point on his flesh. His eyes were fixed steady and strong, piercing with hate into the Spaniard above him.

Everything happened so fast. When Tata peeked and saw that, he screamed red, "Yaaahh!" with his bolo knife in front of him his eyes fiery with vengeance.

"Don't touch Tata!"

But a *mestizo,* half-breed, shot his musket into the dirt, shocking Tata in the legs, and he fell to his stomach.

When I saw that, I flew to my feet screaming—that's all I remembered. Like a lightning flash at night, the light went out in me. I had been smacked with a rifle butt.

Our Nana was cradling my head when my feelings came back. I was seeing fireflies twinkling against the blue sky, and hot blood was streaming down my nose into my mouth. That was the first time I ever really tasted so much human blood— my blood—and it tasted bittersweet.

Tata was held down by two Pilipinos at the whim of the Spaniards, you know, bossed around like their "boys." Two other stoolies were chasing chickens, catching our fattest mother hens and Apo's ace fighting cock.

Apo, seeing them *okininada,* cunt-of-mothers, take his cock, a winner killer of more than four battles, stared up at the towering Spaniard with the pointed helmet and leather chin-strap. Then with that fixed stare, he held the saber's edge and pushed it up off his chest. Jumping to his feet, kicking a left to the Spaniard's rib cage, he doubled the *yotniinana,* mother-fucker, croaking him in the dirt. But a mestizo butted him on the right temple! Apo went down, and his eyes did not move. For the rest of his life, Apo stared like that a lot—with sharp pointed eyes of concentrated love and hate.

"Do not be afraid for me," he shouted to us. "Look out for yourselves!" But all the men were held down.

Some of the men in our *barrio*, our village, came running when they heard the gunshot, but they had no guns, like our family. They could do nothing but look. Some women cried with the children, and a few others trembled prayers, but there were no godly miracles to help them. Our men were beaten this time, but inside, their guts were strengthened with humility.

They didn't say much in words, those robbers. They just commanded with fear and took what they wanted in greed; hit those of us who resisted, then left in a cloud of dust and a trail of horseshit.

The Spanish *tenyente*, lieutenant, led the way on a beautiful brown house, while the two *Don*, Mister, mestizos followed. Behind them were two pairs of Pilipino peons on foot carrying on their shoulders the four lengths of bamboo where the loot was hung. The procession of looters, the powerful rich and their stooges, was brought up in the rear by another Spanish officer riding full-dress on a prancing white female horse.

I cannot forget this memory, and perhaps it will never be erased in the mind among some of us Pilipinos who think. I can still see that Spanish bastard galloping through our tomatoes and eggplants. If I had a gun, for sure I would have shot him right through his neckbone. That would have been a sight to see—a robber of life bleeding in the dirt with his eyes pleading for mercy to live. Against the Spaniards, this was wishful thinking, of course, but every injustice must be resolved in a lifetime if there is to be peace and joy for here and now.

For a long time afterwards, our Apo was very quiet. He changed like night and day before our eyes. He kept to himself now—you know, not free with company. That was the big difference. His nature as a person had been very light hearted with a lot of get-up-and-go, fluidly full of fun. But now, during dinner, he would be locked very deep in silence. And he affected all of us in the house. We lost our appetites, too.

He was like that for many weeks until one evening he took over the kitchen with a spurt of life and told everyone to stay out. He prepared the whole dinner, chicken with papaya and fern sprouts, for he was a good cook. That evening he told Tata to roll out a cask of *basi,* sugar wine, and we all drank spirit with the dinner. He got a little happy and was his old self again, bubbling with life with no mention of any past. We were so glad, hoping he was cured.

The next morning, he was stone silent again, as if nothing really earth-shaking had changed from the day before. We knew his thoughts were heavy so we let him be, for you must respect the silence of a man because most of the time he is making peace with himself and the world around him.

Apo just went on with his daily chores, sometimes like a machine talking to no one. He fixed fences, twined *maguey* ropes, some hemp, and wove the lining inside of his squash hat. Our dinner table was like a casket before the crying starts, as if someone had died, and we were all like him because we were so close. When someone is heavy with thoughts, you must feel with that person to lighten his weight of burden.

Let me tell you how his sickness was. Suddenly, he would go crazy, falling, shaking like a fish out of water, and his mouth would lock and bubble like a mad dog. That's when *Ina Baket,* Grandmother, would tell everyone to get away, and she would pull his penis to bring back his life. That's a true practice I know, because people believed in that. I was with my cousin when he saved the life of a friend who fell down from a plum tree. My cousin just pulled his penis, and his breath just pulled back in.

Since then Apo would stare all the time, sometimes for half a day. Luckily, he always got sick close to home because he always told everyone he wanted only Ina to pull his life. I don't know if I could have saved him if I was there and he had another attack. Maybe. Who knows what we can do when death is facing us?

Only once did I see Ina pull Apo. It happened one afternoon while they were picking sweet potato leaves for the evening meal. They didn't see me coming after the animals. When I reached them, he was breathing deep and pale with cold, sticky sweat. After he came to, he walked around as if nothing had happened.

Clearly, Apo was dishonored. Dead air was all around him a lot. He was humiliated and degraded by the Spaniards and their collaborating peons. Dishonor shamed him speechless to us, his family, for allowing this kind of subservience to go on for so long. His parents had been subjected servants of the Spanish and their vices all the way back to the Grandparents-of-the-Foot and his Grandfather-of-the-Knee and their people of the same body.

Apo was a *Katipunero,* a revolutionary soldier in the war against the Spaniards. When the fighting broke out in the parts of Ilokos, most of the Spaniards fled our town of Laoag. Tata used to tell us children that after my eldest sister, Romana, the first child was born, there was no authority to hold them down in town anymore.

"Let's go live on our land," Apo had said, according to Tata, "Life is better there where you are not policed everyday, and you don't have to go far to find a living."

There weren't too many people then, and there was enough land for people to live on. These lands, which weren't far to the east of town, had been the land of our ancestors for a long, long time. While the Spaniards ruled, the land belonged to the church and to those who ruled and kissed the government. In their time, there were no papers to say who owned this, and who didn't own that. People just knew who owned what.

Those who lived in the barrios close to town were rounded up and made to live in town, and this made farming difficult because you had to stay out in the fields sometimes for weeks to tend the rice. It was the same when the harvest came. Tata would make a simple lean-to hut to live in for awhile when he was away from home.

The Spaniards could not fight much of a battle according to Tata. The war had started in the parts of the south of us close to Manila where the sugar plantations were. When the fighting began to spread like fear and fire to Pampanga, Katipunero runners came to Ilokos, but somehow the local Spaniards found out—you know if there is war you cannot hide it.

"They were fat cowards, really. They withdrew and escaped out of our grasps as if slipping on a slippery rock," said Tata. Maybe the victors of greediness must die cowardly.

The Spaniards escaped swiftly by boats from the town of Laoag because the river there in those days ran deep and wide and flowed swiftly to the sea. That river is adjacent to the grounds of the municipal building, the capitol, and the church. The Spaniards had guns to keep distance between themselves and the chasing Katipuneros.

In other towns farther from the river and the sea, like Pinili and Badoc, our Katipunero ambushed many of them. Tata used to laugh with his friends when they talked histories, drinking basi.

"We roasted the bodies over the fire sprinkled with holy water then fed them to the dogs and pigs!"

Most of the mestizos settled and became Pilipinos for the occasion of course, and managed to keep most of their land holdings.

Apo Lakay was old in years then, but he was as strong as a young man. He would still beat all of us pulling *cogon* grass for roofing when I was already a young man. People lived long and were strong in those days. Their bodies were not destroyed with over-work like us today who were abused in the cane-fields. The Lord Earth was fat and fertile. The soil was so fertile you didn't have to farm much. Plants were fruitful. People lived long and healthy because they ate only fresh foods— foods that still had life in it. Not like today. We eat chicken from the store that has been dead for who knows how long! Remember, you are what you eat, and if you eat out of boxes and cans, then what are you? And the vegetables at the super-market, why that *Japanee* has no shame to sell wilted every-thing! And the prices! There must be a hidden gun cocked behind every price to turn people into domestic dogs willing to pay whatever the price!

Ay, yes, Apo Lakay used to say that men would grow so old in years. They would stand around leaning on fences through all seasons gathering moss—some drinking basi, living so still they would stay in place for days, then work side-by-side with everyone when they were rested enough. They would not die! Ha-ha-ha-ha-ha! Yes, that's true. And it's very possible. They were still alive when I was growing up. Some of them had no more memories. They were everything that was happening and behind their beards that were down to their navels, they balanced in a peaceful quietness that was clearly strong. They were the last I saw who had killed time by naturally living so old. They were always worthy of everyone.

I don't believe that Apo Lakay killed anyone in the war against the Spanish, or ever in his lifetime. And yet he may have kept this a secret. If so, he became a stronger man and perhaps happier, too. But he died frustrated by a lifelong toil of patience.

There were some rich mestizos who were killed by other Katipuneros in our parts. This is to be expected when life has become a war just to make a living. The people who were high headed with education looked down on the have-nothings. You know those people—they are always formal because they don't know how to live easily in laughter. They have to tense shit all the time to make money, and when they see you eyeing them, they act as if you have offended them. Just like the *Haoles,* the white people, over here in Hawaii, they think they are so expensive and untouchable, you have to pay to look!

Apo said that he looted the *Pake,* Chinese, stores after the Spanish left. Practically all the stores were owned by Chinese.

You can bet that the prosperous ones were all owned by them. They were helpless because their protection from their Spanish bosses was gone. You see, the Chinese were the middlemen like here along with the Japanese and the Haoles in Hawaii.

Funny thing, I can remember now what Tata said, "I spat in the face of one of them."

And there isn't nothing more humiliating personally than being spat on. Well, maybe getting shitted on, of course, is worse. But taking spit in the face is part of the protection they bought with taxes, legally paid or not.

The year after I was born the Katipuneros became active again. The New *Katipunan* is what they were whispering and calling the organization. Most of them this time were the peers of our Tata, who were family men. The rich were getting filthy cocky again because they got back into government. The *Amerikanos* put back those who had been prick sucking for the Spaniards. Only now, Pilipinos were promoted to most of the positions the Spaniards held.

What the New Katipunan did, Tata said, was to take from the farms of the rich. Katipuneros did not destroy. They just took what they needed for their respective families, which was the gravy profit that would end up in the market in the next few days. They were just helping the rich harvest. If the Katipuneros were discovered during a harvest raid, they had no choice but drag the owners away, and you'd never see them again. There weren't too many killings mainly because every-one still knew each other, and from the beginning we were all related in blood. You could still reach the rich. There wasn't this army of police we have today to pickle your senses to make sure you are okay! Soldiers of the Amerikanos, Pilipinos like us who had no jobs and went into the army, came patrol-ling even at nights. They had rifles that made the Spanish guns seem like water pistols. After losing a friend and having one maimed for life and seeing families left without a father for the home, Tata and Apo decided then the times were too dangerous. The government could now pick you off one-by-one. So Tata and Apo went into hiding, by going to work in Ca-gayan. Apo told me I was about one year old at the time.

Virgilio Menor Felipe

Waiting For Henry

I like the feel of a cat's head, the fur close to the bone. I like the feel of a cat's skull, the shape of it. It is soothing to stroke a cat on the broad flat forehead, feeling the sculpted surfaces under the fur. The tips of a cat's ears are cool. My fingers run through the fur of cats.

I have one lover and one cat. I call my cat Henry after O. Henry and Henry James. My lover is named Jonathan Henry. After his grandfather. Sometimes I call him Henry because it is so much simpler than trying to say Jonathan. And sometimes I call him Jon.

Henry my cat rejects me all the time. Come to me, baby, come to me, lover, I say. He walks away, tail twitching high. I can see his lightly furred two-toned balls when he walks away. I think they are so precious. Cat balls are so cute. Henry knows I love him. That is why he can scratch me and make me bleed. That is why he rejects me so much. Cats are like that sometimes.

Jon my lover, the other Henry, is very patient all the time. Sometimes I wonder what he is thinking, he is always so terribly tactful. He is strong but not heavily muscled. Some would call him a "prize catch" (he is a promising medical student) but I would prefer not to look at him that way. Maybe I love Jonathan Henry. He never rejects me. Some people are like that.

During the afternoon, after work, I play with Henry my cat. I rub him and stroke his head. His beautiful head. I tickle his stomach and admire his cute cat balls. I carry him around the house checking the windows. I secure the latches of the screens in the kitchen and the bathroom. I do not want Henry to leave me. I do not want him to be hit by a car.

At night, Henry my lover comes. In the dark, we play out our passions. We become sticky with sweat and fall asleep with the covers off our bodies. Sometimes I feel that Henry my cat is watching us and I feel embarrassed and somehow wanton. When I make love with Henry the man, I have to close my eyes to enjoy it. I am afraid that if I open them, I will see Henry my cat staring at us, his eyes glowing in the dark.

It is a morning like other mornings. As usual, Henry my lover is ignoring Henry my cat. Henry my lover sits on the couch reading the morning paper. Henry my cat is sitting in the other corner staring at Henry my lover. They are so ridiculous looking, that pair of Henrys. Especially Henry my cat. He looks positively furious, twitching his tail at Henry my lover like that.

Softly I say, teasing, "Henry."

Henry my lover looks at me and says, "Why do you talk to your dumb cat like that? It's abnormal and unhealthy. Stupid cat."

He is not usually so touchy.

Henry my lover has never stroked Henry my cat's beautiful sleek head. He does not like cats. They make him uncomfortable. Perhaps he sees Henry my cat staring with amber eyes at us when we make love at night.

Henry my lover is asking me a very important question, one he has asked me several times before, one which I have never yet answered.

"Crystal, will you marry me?"

"Maybe."

"When?"

"I don't know." I always answer like this. It makes it sound like I do not care. But I do.

"When will you know?"

Jonathan is getting angry. I can tell. He is trying to control his anger. Why doesn't he just swear at me or something? I do not know what to tell him. How should I know when I will be sure? I do not even know if I really love him. What does it mean, to love?

"I don't know when I will know."

A pause. Jonathan looks at me with a suffering face.

"Do you love me?" he asks.

"Yes," I lie. I cannot stand that hurt look in his eyes. I wish he would talk about something else.

"What more is there?"

"It's not that simple," I say.

"Why?"

I pause, feeling the panic in my stomach spread. Sometimes Jonathan makes me feel cornered. He is always demanding that I explain myself to him.

"I don't know you," I say. I feel miserable. I wonder what put these particular words into my mouth. I wish that Henry my cat was here so that I would have something to do with my hands, and something to look at besides Henry my lover's face and my feet. I say things that I know will provoke Jonathan. I say things that will hurt him. Is it because these things are true? I say again, "I don't really know you."

He laughs a short bitter laugh. It is a hard, unpleasant sound. Softly he says. "You don't know me." He is incredulous. I am sorry I said that. Now it is his turn to hurt me.

"You say you love me when you don't even know me? You sleep with me without knowing me. Come now, surely you can marry me too without knowing me."

I cannot stand his sarcastic tone of voice.

"No!" I say. "No. You don't understand."

"I don't think I'll ever understand you, Crystal."

I start to cry. I want to scream at Jonathan. How does he know that he loves me? But I am afraid that he will say that he really does not love me.

Jonathan holds me gently in his arms.

"I think I love you, Crystal. But if you don't love me, I'm just wasting my time . . ." his voice trails off and he sounds so sad and tired.

I wish things were nice and perfect. I wish I could say yes and make things simple. Sometimes I wish Jonathan would leave me alone. Sometimes I wish I never got to know him this way.

Henry my lover has left me. I do not like to think about the reasons why he left. I suppose I have driven him to it. Ever since he first started coming at night, in the dark, I have been slowly pushing him away. I was not really aware of what I was doing. Maybe I was just fooling myself into thinking that despite all the trying things about me, Jonathan would still wait for me to make up my mind. Now he is gone.

There was no big quarrel at the end. He was so damn tactful and nice about saying that things had gotten to the point where he did not enjoy being with me. I never meant to irritate him. He told me he thought we should get to know other people who might be more suited to us. He said it would be better for me. I did not cry until he walked out the door. His last words were so trite I would laugh if it did not hurt so much. "We can still be friends," he said before he left. Standard farewell lines. "I'll be seeing you," he said, as if nothing at all had ever happened. I never want to see him again.

Do I love him?

I talk with Henry my cat. I caress his head and tell him silly things. "Oh Henry Henry Henry. You'll never leave me will you?" He miaows at me. I miaow back at him and laugh. I spend the night watching television with Henry on my lap. Nothing I watch makes much of an impression on me. I talk to Henry while the television goes on. I predict the eventual outcomes of each situation comedy and each serial. I laugh at the commercials. I tell Henry my cat what a lady-killer he is. I tell him what a handsome handsome tiger he is. I get tired of the television. I take Henry my cat with me to my bedroom. I want to lie down. I find one of Jonathan's socks on the floor by my bed. I start crying. I miss his dark shape and his breathing by my pillow. Henry my cat just looks at me. He purrs and rubs his head against my hand. What would I do without him?

Instead of going to sleep, I play some more with Henry my cat. I cannot sleep. I run through the silent rooms, breaking the stillness with my running feet while Henry my cat chases me. Laughing, I run over the chairs and tables in the living room and the dining room. I leap on the kitchen counters. I laugh as I cavort all over the house with Henry my cat at my heels. It is three o'clock in the morning as the sound of my laughter fades. The house becomes very quiet. I pick up Henry my cat and cradle him like a baby. I think I miss Henry my lover. Suddenly I feel very lonely.

I think I hear noises in the parlor. I go cautiously with Henry my cat to check. It is only the curtain billowing with the breeze and scraping against the lampshade.

Three days later, I come home to an empty house after shopping. Henry my cat is gone. I do not know how he could have left. I am always very careful to secure all the windows before I go out. I open all the cupboards and all the closets. I call for Henry. I run around the house calling for Henry. I wail for Henry Henry. I run around the block calling for him. I walk back to my place, telling myself that Henry is alright and he will come back.

That night I wait for Henry my cat. I try not to think about cars and cat-nappers. I try not to think of how empty the house is. I do not want my Henry to be squashed to death beneath the wheels of some car. I do not want him to be dissected in some biology class. I do not want him to end up as part of some woman's fur coat. I have kept him so carefully. And now he is gone. He has left me and I am alone.

I hear cats crying nearby. Henry? I run outside and start calling again for Henry my cat. I see the cats but Henry my cat is not with them. I go back inside the house, listening for Henry. There is a faint rustling noise outside. Henry? "Henry!" But it is only the wind blowing the leaves in the trees.

Who would think the night could be filled with such sounds? I hear all the leaves that move with each passing night breeze. I can hear the crickets that are rubbing their wings together and vibrating their dry little bodies.

I fall asleep waiting for Henry. I have a dream. I dream of a black panther who comes near my bed, who comes with the night. His fur ripples over his big panther bones. He glistens in the dark. I am afraid of him. I touch his head. It is smooth. I lose my fear of him in his beautiful head. His fur is thick and seems to perpetually flow over his skull. His eyes are brown, like the eyes of Henry my lover. But this is not Henry my lover. This is a strong panther. He stands by my bed as I stroke his perfect head. His ears are rounded at their cool tips. The fur on his body is also cool. It makes me think of mountain springs, and of dew on grass. He is so still. He stands patiently while I run my fingers through his rich black fur.

Henry my cat walks into the room. He is light and glistening. He is so small next to this panther. He is so tiny, the panther could probably kill him by simply stepping on him. The panther and Henry my cat start stalking each other. I do not know whether this is a game or not. I watch them gliding in their circles. I watch their immobile cat faces as they slide their soft paws over the smooth vinyl floor. It seems that they will forever glide and slither in their circles on their padded feet. I remember that their velvet feet hide claws.

The panther raises one paw. He raises it like a club. I think that he is going to club Henry my cat senseless; he will beat Henry my cat to death. I see the claws coming out of hiding. They gleam and flash. Cats are very clean. I see now that the panther is going to take the life out of Henry my cat with one clean and neat swipe of his claws. I want to save Henry my cat. I cannot move or scream. I am helpless as the panther's paw begins its descent towards Henry my cat. I cannot even close my eyes.

Suddenly, I see that it is the panther who is the victim after all. Henry my cat is under the panther. His tiny claws are moving upward in an arc. He is going to scratch the belly of the panther. I am afraid that I will have to see the panther's guts spill out. I am afraid that the pink guts will fall on Henry my cat and suffocate him. The big panther will fall on Henry my cat and crush him. I do not want Henry my cat to die. I do not want the panther to die. I want to save them. Henry my cat's claws flash like little mirrors as they continue upward. The panther's claws look like curved jewels, gleaming with the light of a hundred suns and stars, as they continue downward. I want everything to stop now. I want everything to start over again and end differently. I want everything to stop. Stop. Stop.

When I wake, I hear myself saying Henry Henry Henry. I reach for Henry my lover but he is not here. I want his arms around me. I want him. Why did I lie to him? I told him that I did not love him. Maybe I did not lie to him after all. Maybe I really do not love him. I do not know. Henry Henry. Maybe I mean Henry my cat. I miss Henry my cat. Where did Henry my cat go? How did he go? Henry my cat, if you will come back I will feed you good tuna every day. I will let you play outside more often. Henry. Henry my lover, if you come back I will even marry you. I will love you. I will be a good wife. And I will always call you Jonathan instead of Henry. Please come back.

The next morning, over a solitary cup of coffee, I consider an ad I could put in the classified section of the newspaper. "Lost: one cat and one lover. Call --------." People would only snicker. I would be plagued by obscene phone calls all hours of the day and night. Besides, neither Jonathan nor Henry my cat ever reads the classified ads. I rip the ad into little flakes of paper.

I wait for Henry.

Gail N. Harada

The Shell Gatherer

I never spoke to Manuel, or he to me.

But whenever I came across him in our lane, I would stare curiously at him out of the corner of my eye and deliberately slow my pace to match his.

With his wizened frame and long scraggly whiskers, he looked to be at least a hundred years old. He always wore a faded cotton shirt, a torn tweed cap, and baggy khaki trousers that seemed too heavy for his spindly legs.

His burlap bag was slung over one thin shoulder. It contained the shells which he would later paint and sell to the tourists on the beaches.

Manuel never looked up. On one occasion, grandfather had scoffingly told me that Manuel had gotten stooped from picking too many shells along the shore.

"That's the Filipino for you," my grandfather had said, "not intelligent enough to find a better job. Kiyo-chan, remember that good little Japanese girls never speak to Filipino men."

I had heard grandfather say this many times before. There was supposed to be something mysterious and sinister about Filipinos. I was told that they winked and whispered naughty invitations to young girls. They raised evil fighting cocks and watched the birds slash each other to gory bits with their flashing spikes.

It was no wonder that I stared wonderingly at Manuel.

Grandfather himself seemed to be everything Manuel was not. Now I realize that he and the frail shell gatherer must have been close in years. At that time, my grandfather seemed so much straighter and stronger.

He was lean with a wiry kind of strength and, like a soldier, he always sat ramrod stiff in his light summer kimono. I could easily imagine that he had been a brave captain in the Russo-Japanese War.

There was one person whom grandfather was unashamedly proud of. This was my older brother Takeo who was an army lieutenant stationed in Korea.

When Takeo had come home on a leave of absence the fall before, grandfather had insisted on having Mr. Taba and Mr. Shirai over, his cronies from early lumber-contracting days in Hawaii.

137

"Wear your uniform," grandfather had instructed Takeo.

He and his friends had sat on the cool straw mats on our porch, toasting my brother with rounds of *sake,* the heady rice wine.

"How proud you must be to have such a fine grandson," Mr. Shirai had said.

"Spitting image of you in your younger days," Mr. Taba had added.

Takeo had been embarrassed by the old men's admiring gazes and compliments, but grandfather had sat up very tall. He thrust out his narrow chest and said in a low but firm voice, "The American army is fortunate to have our Japanese young men fighting for them."

I remember sitting on the steps of the porch listening idly to their conversation. The shadows were gathering in the lane and I saw Manuel slowly making his way home.

Soon he was passing in front of our house.

Apparently I wasn't the only one watching him because I heard grandfather say:

"That one," jerking his head toward Manuel, "has a son in the army. Watch him come home AWOL someday. One Japanese soldier is worth a hundred of his kind."

The old men laughed secretly into their cups.

That had been last fall.

Now in the heat of the summer afternoon, I longed for the crispness of October again.

On the porch, grandfather was setting up the smooth white and black discs on his *go* board. Mr. Shirai would be joining him soon for a game.

He brought the round pieces down on the polished surface with smart little thwacks.

"Yaeko," he called to my mother, "bring the *sake* out as soon as it's heated. Today is indeed special."

He was referring to the telegram we had received earlier that morning. It had come, special delivery, yellow and important-looking. Mother had trembled when she had taken it in her hands. A sixth sense told her it concerned Takeo. She had cried with relief when she had read that my brother was hurt, but not critically so.

The part in the telegram that had caught grandfather's

attention, however, had been the ending of the message: ". . . conducted himself valorously in battle."

Mother had translated it into Japanese for him and grandfather had looked even prouder than he had that fall evening when Takeo had sat fidgeting under the approving scrutiny of the three old men.

Now it was the hottest part of the day. I sat on the porch steps cracking lichee nuts between my teeth, making the hard prickly shells give way to the juicy white flesh inside.

From where I sat the heat seemed to send shimmering waves up from the ground. Even the leaves on our mock orange hedge were shrivelling along their tips.

In the distance, Manuel appeared mirage-like in the lane. His pace was even slower than usual.

An eternity seemed to pass before he was plodding past our front yard.

Perhaps it was the special excitement of the news about Takeo. Or perhaps it was the heady effects of the wine he had started to sip waiting for Mr. Shirai. But for the first time, grandfather actually hailed Manuel in broken English:

"Too hot for shells, Manuel. Go home, rest."

The old shell gatherer took a few more steps before he seemed to realize that someone had addressed him. Like a marionette, he jerked to a stop. His head sagged lower. His bag of shells touched the dirt.

My grandfather continued, "My grandson, soldier. Fight brave. Get shot. Your boy . . . how he doing?"

I watched Manuel, beads of perspiration gleaming on his brown forehead and falling tear-like to the ground. Slowly he raised his head.

I realized then that I had never really seen his face before. It was an ascetic's countenance with hollowed cheeks and thin, flaring nostrils. It was his eyes, however, that struck me most. Large and dark, they appeared at once to be shy, suffering. They saw and yet seemed not to see at all.

A minute went by before he spoke in a voice barely above a whisper.

"I get letter."

There was a pause.

"My boy die yesterday. He stay back. Enemy kill him."

For an instant, his cracked lips trembled.

That was all.

He lowered his head and resumed his journey, expecting no words of comfort or sympathy and receiving none.

There was a brief silence on the porch. Then with a sharp thwack, grandfather brought another white disc down on the board.

He muttered aloud in Japanese, "Just like a Filipino for you. Too scared to move when he actually saw the enemy. Eh, Kiyo-chan?"

I did not answer.

My eyes were following the hunched form of the shell gatherer as he crept like a ghost around the bend and disappeared.

Violet Harada

Excerpt from *Teapot Tales* _____

Editor's Note: The following are excerpts from the biography of the author's mother, Iku Kubojiri, now age 89. The biography provides sketches of Mrs. Kubojiri's life in Japan, as well as her experiences as an immigrant homesteader in Glenwood, Hawaii, from 1908-1925.

II. Snatched From The Fire: Her Life Course Set

She was thirty years old and was entertaining thoughts of travelling next to Kobe, the gateway to the outside world. She was independent and educated. A liberated woman, you might say. But deep within her there were stirrings of a longing and a yearning for fulfillment as a woman. But she had cast all hopes aside of ever becoming a wife and mother. She was a scarred woman.

When she was about a year old, she had been left in the care of her older sister while her mother went to work in the barn. It was autumn, and the family was busy threshing the rice. Her older sister being only five years old soon forgot all about her charge and ran out to play.

The family cat was asleep in the straw nest the family had arranged upon some planks above the open fireplace. She went crawling up to grasp the sleeping animal. The planks tipped over and fell into the fire. The cat leaped out, but as a babe, she had no such reflexes to pull herself out of the fire.

Her mother, suddenly sensing an urgent need to check, entered the house and found the baby with her head stuck in the fire. Rushing up, she snatched the babe from the flames. The baby's crown was charred. The only sign that she was still alive was from the piteous cry that came from her burnt lips.

No doctor was available. In those days the country people had to go great distances to get any medical help. Her mother quickly put some ladies' hair oil on it, which should have been sufficient. But the neighbors began to come and advise her of all sorts of remedies.

Her distraught, desperate mother, already filled with self-condemnation for her negligence, tried them all in an effort to prevent scars from forming on her daughter's face.

Infection then set in and the condition worsened. The entire head was so blistered and swollen that it was impossible to locate the eyes and nose. Only a small hole remained where the mouth should be, and her mother squeezed her milk into it.

No one could conceive of this child ever surviving. And even if she did, they conjectured, she would surely be blinded in her left eye because there were severe burns there and above her left ear.

The neighbors then concocted the most hideous remedy of all. It was called *tomo*, a paste made from a dead man's bones, charred and ground to powder.

The bones were dug up from some grave, probably one belonging to a grandfather. The paste was made and plastered on the burns.

At first it did seem to help. The burns dried up and seemed better. But the paste worked its way into the burnt flesh where it festered. Soon her entire head and face became a mass of pus.

Yet, miraculously, she survived. Her burns healed. Even her eyesight and eyebrows were restored, much to the astonishment of all. Except for the crown of her head, which was bald because the roots of her hair had been burned away, her facial features were spared of unsightly scars.

Her hair was carefully brought down over her forehead to hide the bald spot. She passed for an ordinary child. But her life was destined to take an unconventional path.

Her first three years in school were happy ones. She loved school and excelled in her studies. But in her fourth year, life in school became unbearable because of the teasing and taunting of the city boys who called her Burnt Scar Face.

In Japan all girls in the fourth grade changed their hairdo from the bangs to one where the hair was drawn back from the forehead. Because the Japanese observe tradition so religiously, it never occurred to her mother to make an exception in her daughter's case and allow her to wear her bangs.

Hurt beyond endurance Mother refused to go to school. No amount of pleading and threatening by her parents or the school authorities could compel her to attend school.

Compulsory education in Japan ended after the fourth grade. The school authorities were finally able to persuade her to return to school for the remaining three months of the year to receive her diploma and graduate.

What was life to hold for her? She was told and overheard

people saying that she would never be able to marry because there was a stigma imprinted upon her life.

Her guilt-ridden mother felt she had lost her right to discipline and direct this child because it was due to her negligence that her daughter had been burned. Therefore, Mother was allowed to do as she pleased at home.

At about twelve years of age she did baby sitting for a neighbor. Then, at thirteen she went to a childless relative's home as a housemaid. During the summer months for three years she went to work at a silkworm farm unwinding the silk threads from the cocoons. Then, at seventeen she tended an aunt who was hospitalized for a long time. In those days, people lived and cooked for themselves in the hospital.

There she heard about another girl who had been more severely burned than herself who had received corrective surgery at Yamashita Hospital in Aichiken, Japan. Mother sought this girl out and found her healed and already asked for in marriage.

Much encouraged, she had her mother take her to the hospital in Aichiken. There they were directed to a good surgeon who did a skin graft operation to bring her hair line back to normal. Only a slight pink scar remains by her hair line.

III. The Call to Hawaii: A Chance to Get Married

About this time Father's older brother, Soske, received a letter from his half brother, Umetaro, who had emigrated to Hawaii 16 years before. He had written that he had purchased 200 acres of land there and would like to have Soske find a wife for him and send her to Hawaii. He specified that she should be a country girl, but educated, and not too ugly.

Soske found this to be a very big order. Country girls were not very educated, and the pretty girls were in the city. Also, it seemed hard to believe that Umetaro, who had always been the black sheep, could really be doing so well that he could have bought 200 acres of land.

Since he was not sure whether it was true or not, he felt he could not ask for a bride from the village or from among strangers. So, he decided that it would be best to find a bride from among the kinfolk.

Thinking over the qualifications which had been specified Soske thought about Umetaro's first cousin, Iku Hayashi. She was not too homely and was a country girl. But she could be considered educated since she had studied in Tokyo and had been travelling around trying to be a nurse.

Soske wrote to Umetaro asking what he thought about his choice. Umetaro wrote back that he would trust in Soske's judgment and accept whoever he decided was best. If he considered Iku to be a suitable bride for him, that was fine with him.

So, Mother was notified.

If you want to go to Hawaii as a bride, come home immediately, she was told in the letter from Soske.

As she read the letter, Mother was not very much excited by the prospect of marriage. But the thought of going to Hawaii was enough to entice her to head home immediately. No one from her little village had ever travelled abroad.

Soske was only a farmer, but because the government had run a highway through his rice field and rebated him 20,000 yen, he furnished Mother liberally with money for her trousseau.

"If you're going abroad, you should go in good style. Buy the very best," he advised her.

So, Mother went shopping in Nagoya and bought the best of everything she thought she needed. She purchased her kimono, her *montsuki* (bridal garment with the beautiful *obi* or sash, her *haori* or outer garment, and her *jiban* or slip), her gold wedding ring, her Wittnauer gold watch, her umbrella, her *zori* (slipper), and her *geta* (clogs). She had never owned or worn such fine things in Japan. . . .

Finally the day of departure came. It had been about two years since she had decided to go to Hawaii. She was thirty years old, and felt fully prepared for the life before her. Of course, she envisioned Hawaii to be a place like Nojiri where you could buy all the things you needed.

She was handed a three pound Crisco can of *ume* by Umezo Kongaki, a well travelled friend of Umetaro. The sour pickled plums were from his trees and were given to soothe the sea sickness en route. "Give the extra ones to Umetaro," he told her.

Umezo accompanied Soske and Mother to Yokohama harbor where she boarded the Taiho Maru. Last words were exchanged and a few tears shed. Then the men returned home. Mother was on her way.

The ship was full of other brides on their way to Hawaii. Most of them were women in their thirties. They were from various places and backgrounds, and all hopeful about a new life in Hawaii.

Many of the women had come well stocked with toothbrushes and tooth powder, evidently items which they felt could not be purchased in Hawaii. As Mother heard about all the different things the other women had thought to bring, she began to wonder if she should have done the same, although she did not see the necessity for it since she could buy them when she got to Hawaii.

The trip to Hawaii was hardly pleasant. Most of the passengers were terribly sea sick throughout the entire voyage.

On board was a young man who had gone to Japan to fetch his bride and was returning to Hawaii with her. During the course of the trip, he fell ill and died. He was buried at sea. The unfortunate young bride was left in a quandary as to what she should do. She decided to return to Japan. Whether she did go back to Japan or whether she found a happier life in Hawaii is not known. . . .

IV. Arrival At The Homestead: The New Life

The disembarking from the Taiho Maru in Honolulu was one of relief for the weary, sea sick passengers. The immigration center was a place of confusion and loud activity.

Very prominent there was a large, talkative man of about sixty from Niigata by the name of Katsuno-san who was a sort of manager for the immigrants coming in and had some official position at the immigration office. Katsuno-san was loud and spoke very coarsely, joshing the women with his crude remarks.

The identification time at the immigration center was a joyful time for some and a shocking crisis to others. Some brides who knew their husbands only by the photographs sent them, many of which were very deceptive, were so shocked at seeing their mates that they fled from their husbands.

When Mother's name was called, she was startled to see a tall, ferocious looking man with overgrown hair and an unkempt, bushy beard coming toward her. Could this man really be her cousin, Umetaro, she wondered. She had not seen him for over sixteen years.

Mother heard the word, "kau kau" being hollered to all the people. It was the first Hawaiian word that she heard in the islands. Wondering what it signaled, Mother followed all the other people who were heading somewhere. She came to the dining section where some food was laid out on long tables.

Mother thought it proper for her to serve her husband. She was surprised to see the men, not waiting to be served, but helping themselves. Their manners were crude and self-reliant. She then noticed the disproportionate ratio of men to women. There were so many more bachelors than women there.

When it was time to leave the Center, Mother remembered that she had left her handbag where she had first been sitting. Umetaro took her back there but the place was deserted and no handbag was there. So Umetaro took Mother by horse and buggy to the lost and found office. There she saw rows and stacks of other people's bags and purses. She looked for hers but could not locate it.

No money had been in the bag. Only Umezo Kongaki's three pound Crisco can of *Ume* had been in it. . . .

_____ *Clara Jelsma*

Excerpt from *Who Da Guy?* _____

ABOUT THE AUTHOR

He is the one pebble on the beach.

Have you seen a habitat of ants? Thousands. If the author was an ant, he would be one of them.

Have you seen the thousands of spectators in a sporting event? One of them in that crowd could be him.

We stand in line to be served. At the fast food counters, the banks, the supermarkets. The line moves faster at some counters and slower at others. He would be the one standing in the line that doesn't move.

Have you seen some boxing or judo tournaments? The victor would be standing; the other flat on his back. This writer would be the one that would lie comfortably on his back.

Did you notice some cars stalled in some heavy traffic or driving slow to hold up traffic? He could be that driver.

Football team plays eleven men. Baseball nine. Basketball five. You would most likely find him cheering his team along at the sideline.

Throughout the history of mankind, myriads of men just came and went. Existent men and men still unborn. Some carved a dent. A mark in history. This author is one of them, the one that stands unnoticed. A fallen petal, floating in the stream adrift, bopping in the ripples. Just a somebody that is a nobody.

The only meaning he had was to his pet dog, who showed mutual compassion and love.

A VISIT TO THE VET

When people meet, unavoidably there is conversation. Perhaps by age, hearing gets less keen. It is better to nod with agreement, with a smile than to say, "What?" and let them repeat. Usually, I get by with this. But not always so.

I went to the vet to get my dog innoculated. Like humans, the nurse asked me questions to fill out her form.

Owner's name? Dog's name? Age? Address? Etc. At one point, she asked, "Boy?" But I heard it as "Poi?"

I admitted with all honesty, "I don't know." She lifted his hind leg and slanted her head for a view. I thought, how in the world can she know if it is a "poi" by lifting the hind leg?

"It's a boy," she said.

At that instant all the dog owners sitting in the waiting room burst into laughter. As if to say, "What a stupid old man!" Like a fool, I had no chance to explain. I carried my dog and sat. Humiliated.

The lady next to me would occasionally slip a glance towards me, put her hands across her lips to suppress her rude laughter, adding insult to injury.

In such a predicament, the sensation is unique. I want to explain but I can't. That would be like making a speech. I want to laugh, but I can't, they are all strangers. I want to hide, but I can't, that would make me look more stupid.

So, what else can I do, but to suppress my own laughter. When you do that, you can feel your own stomach muscle contract. I sort of hold my breath so that I don't explode at the hilarity of the theatrics.

It is best not to get yourself into this kind of predicament. If only life's process can be reversed.

If at all possible, aging should be avoided.

MY PET DOG

I have seen obedience training for dogs. They do wonders. It is unbelievable. They can almost train their dogs to the likes of being human.

I trained Shaggy too. He can do a few things at command. I can train him not to jump on me when he sees and greets me. That is easy. All I have to do is step on his toes every time he does that. It can be awfully messy if the ground is wet. But why should I? That is the compassion I enjoy of him. Nobody else jumps, leaps and hugs me the way he does.

What I should do is to train my family to be like Shaggy. But at this age it is too late. If only I did that earlier.

I like Shaggy for what he is. Why should I train him to be other than what he is? Besides he barks at all intruders. Isn't that enough? He knows his job. A dog is a dog. That's good enough for me.

So you think my dog stupid, eh? Untrained. Not so. Untrained is the way I trained him to be. To be what he is. A dog.

I AM A DOG

I am a dog. I respond to the call "Shaggy." The earliest I can remember, I was in a cage. I don't know my heritage. Outside our cage there were strange animals. I understand now, they are called "humans." They have fur only on their heads. Few, on their faces. They are of the same species. We can sense their feelings by their faces. Unlike us they don't have any tail. They walk erect on their hind legs. I don't suppose they can run as fast as us.

I am pitch black. My fur is longer than short, but shorter than the longer ones. A male, I am not pretty. Here in this cage, I am alone most of the time.

One day this elderly man came. He did not look around. He just came directly towards me. He had a look of determination. He stood there just looking at me. I can sense his lack of joy. He wasn't a happy man. I don't know if he had domestic problems or if it was because of me. But then, as I recall, when they saw me, most of them reacted the same.

After a while, I was put in a box, with a load of things. Leash, chain, shampoo, collar, flea killer, etc. I was pushed out on a cart. When he opened his car door, it hit the box, and I fell with a thud. Frightened, I ran for my life. Around people, under cars, around. I heard him yelling. Finally I was caught. That was the first time I sensed him happy. He said something like, "Sun-u-va-gun, you rascal, you." Humans don't bark.

I suppose this is my new home. I am comfortable with a long leash. I have a shed, but I'd rather sleep next to the door above the steps. When the lady of the house comes out, she always calls me, always smiles and strokes me. I reciprocate. These humans, they want to be loved. They are very passionate. They must be lonely creatures.

Then there is this guy with a huge midsection. He enjoys teasing me. He turns my ears over, picks me up by the skin of my neck, grasps and closes my mouth, much to my discomfort. I suppose I have to live with this.

What can I say about my master? He feeds me. I cannot survive without him. I see cats around. They run faster than humans. Of course, they are motivated. When I chase, their lives are at stake. So there you can see, I am dependent on my master.

He taught me words like "sit," "come," "stay," "fetch," and rewarded me with snacks. Now, he just sits. He doesn't seem as happy except when he sees me. He seems to blossom. He enjoys my going over his lap. He always strokes me.

During the course of the day, he frees me in the back yard. I am free! I can run! I can bark! The first thing I do is to comfort myself. That pleases my master. Rather than my doing it in front.

I lowered my hips to urinate. I hated getting my toes wet. The lower I went the less it got wet. One day I lifted my leg. Lord behold! That was the most comfortable position. I further discovered that if I did it on objects, I didn't get my toes wet at all. Living with humans, these are the things I must learn on my own.

While walking with my master one day, I felt this sudden urge. By the force of this newly formed habit, I lifted my leg over his ankle. Wow! Was my master furious.

As you know, we dogs have good judgment on human sensitivity. We don't read them by their tails. Only by their faces. They tell a lot.

I never did that again.

DOG SENSE

I have heard of "Horse sense." I suppose it means common sense. But "Dog sense" is simply amazing. He can sense when I come home way beforehand. When I go in the kitchen to prepare his milk, he can sense that too. He sort of cries, and he is at the front porch.

I let him free in my back yard. He enjoys his freedom. But as soon as I make my move towards the gate he is there before me, ready to be chained.

My neighbor's dog cries when her master leaves home. My dog, Shaggy, joins into a duet. It is a melody of sadness.

I recall my son playing his trumpet. My neighbor's dog would cry. "Wooooo—," then her neighbor's dog, then the dog in front of us and their neighbor's dog. Before we knew it, all the neighborhood dogs. "Woooo—," what weird sadness. My son had to stop playing. We all had a laugh.

At that, I did not discourage him from practice. Who knows his hidden talent. Someday it can express itself. A possible Chopin or a Beethoven.

The dogs should know.

GOLD

I heard so much about this rare metal. How the dollar will devaluate, but gold will maintain its value. I am convinced it is a rare metal. You find it around as jewelry. When you buy it, the price is fabulous. The added cost must be for the art and the craft.

I thought of getting some gold coins. Maybe I can get rich. Deak-Perera, the broker, is located in mid-town near the waterfront. There was no parking space. I ended up parking on the Smith Street parking lot. It was quite a walk.

I bought two. They were the size of a big, half-a-dollar. When you buy them, it is with the green paper money and all the numbers are marked 20. You give them a handful, just to get two. It seemed ridiculous. I felt shortchanged. But that's what I wanted and that's what I got.

Walking back to the parking lot, I held the two pieces in the palm of my hand and the whole hand in my pocket. It got sweaty. The people I passed looked like hoodlums, pimps, prostitutes, lesbians, punks, you name it. Hardly any police. It is funny how the world can change its looks depending on the mood and situation you are in. I reached home with no incident.

Now, where do I put it? It is not something you sit on or use. It is something that you sell later. Hiding it here, hiding it there, it was never mentally peaceful. Finally, it went into the safety deposit box. A rare metal is a rare thing. It is so precious even our government has it buried in Fort Knox. It is not for use. It is to hide.

It is like Shaggy with his bone. He'll cherish it. He will walk with it in his mouth. You touch it and he will growl. Then it is hidden. I cannot find it. Even he cannot find it. It is forever hidden.

A POINT OF VIEW

The bitter wind of Hurricane Iwa. There was quite some damage. I picked up a torn off branch, kept it in the shade to dry. A year later, I peeled off the bark. It was a branch of a Hawaiian koa tree.

I got my handsaw, file, sandpaper and carved out a *boken*, wooden sword. It took a week. It was like carving a toothpick out of a tree trunk.

I went to pick up some kukui nuts, took out the meat and used them as polish. It was a time-consuming endeavor. You oil it, leave it to dry and repeat it, day in and day out. The longer you do it, the prettier it becomes.

It is now a month. The curvature of the *boken,* the natural dark spots, the grip of the handle, oh, it turned out beautiful. What it turned out to be, even the tree wouldn't understand.

In nature, death is not a tragedy. It is a fact of life. If given a choice, whether to be a decorative carving, to be admired or to stay in the wilderness and sway with the wind and bathe in the warm sun, which do you think the branch would have preferred?

In spite of the storm, cold, lightning or thunder, "to be alive in the woods," of course.

With my hands, I carved a beautiful *boken.* I wonder why I couldn't carve myself out to be a somebody, like an art object to be admired?

A tree has no wisdom that is analytical like man. It is just there being alive. In simplicity. It wants to live. Perhaps we are placing too much importance on ourselves. We may not be as important as we think we are. We give importance by our own choice, by our own ego.

Given a choice, to be other than what I am, to be highly esteemed, honorable in every respect or to be "me," just a plain "me," a nobody, I'd still prefer to be "me," of course.

Shaggy, too, he cannot talk. He cannot use his hands the way we can. He is chained like a prisoner. Yet, I bet given a choice, he would still prefer being himself. Just to live because life still remains.

Sitting on the mat with food spread out, to enjoy the cherry blossoms, this guy says, "Hana yori dango kana." Rather than the flowers, pass me the dumplings. Instead of flowers, pass me the food. Let's eat.

A down-to-earth saying. With your belly full and contented you can enjoy the beauty more. You can't enjoy anything on an empty stomach.

Imagine, all these nonsense thoughts with so many thoughts. Just a point of view.

When the wind blows, the branches sway. If I am hungry, I eat. Ummmm, the dango tastes good. How beautiful the blossoms.

Hey, life is simplicity. We choose to complicate. Why complicate simplicity?

_____ *Hiroshi Kawakami*

In Search of Girls' Day _____

Her name was Baby Teardrop. I remember Girls' Day because of her. Because my grandmother gave her to me wrapped in Christmas paper, and it wasn't Christmas and it wasn't my birthday, and because that March 3rd we were having our house fumigated and I insisted on taking her with us to Camp Kokokahi despite my mother's prediction that I'd lose one of her accessories. Which came true. I lost her teething ring. I remember that as clearly as her name.

I remember that Girls' Day at Camp Kokokahi because it was there that I discovered my first real fireplace, with its lethal-looking pokers and the battered wire shield that was supposed to protect us from flying sparks. I remember that we sang about a strange white man named Jack Frost who nipped children's noses off and how we roasted chestnuts on that open fire and how they came out rather dry and tasteless.

I remembered how my father found oysters when we waded along the rocky shoreline laying crab nets, how he sent me back to the house for something to pry them loose with and how I flew, so full of the gravity of my mission that I ran into someone's clotheslines full of sheets drying in the cold air. I returned with butter knives and I remember that we bent quite a few trying to separate rock from rock.

When it started to rain, cruel hard rain, and he sent us all back, I was the last to go—I always felt I had to protect him, I don't know why—and I remember turning back one last time to see him crouching by the rocks, a small gray figure knee-deep in the windchopped water. I ran to the house through a landscape turned suddenly hostile by the rain, the billowing sheets on the clothesline now limp and dejected as I left them far behind.

Perhaps I had always wanted to be a son, another son, to my father. To watch him hang a third koi on the bamboo pole on our front porch on May 5th, Boys' Day. *Tango-no Sekku,* when he would proclaim to all the world and Palolo Valley that, like the koi who swim upstream, his sons were strong, his sons were powerful.

One year he made a kite out of one of these koi. There was a big contest, and all the cub scouts and their fathers participated. My father went to the mountains to cut the bamboo for my brother's kite. He soaked and stripped and split it to make the bones of the kite, tying the crosspieces with string. Then he took one of the huge paper koi from its storage place in the basement and cut it up, gluing it to the frame with a paste made from old rice. As a finishing touch he cut out the eyes and, chuckling to himself, glued them on cock-eyed.

It was the most beautiful kite in the sky that day—a rainbow-scaled diamond looking down on all of us with those laughing eyes: my brother looking up, squinting a little, too intent on directing its course to smile back; my father watching him, too proud to smile; and the rest of us urging it higher with our own eyes, heads thrown back, throats aching with the effort. As if it were our combined breath that kept it airborne. It became my koi too, then, transformed as it was. And we were all strong koi, swimming upstream together into the blue sky.

* * * * *

"I'm writing an article on Girls' Day," I tell my friend as we pause beside the chocolate eclairs and cream puffs, row on sticky row behind the sterile glass cases at King's Bakery Coffee Shop. "Do you remember it?"

She smiles, her eyes thoughtful. "Yes," she says slowly, "I remember the dolls."

She looks past me at the tables, most of them occupied even at this late hour by young couples, after-the-big-game bowlers, a half-dozen or so policemen sitting in the THIS SECTION CLOSED section, looking uncomfortable and defensive without their hats on.

Have I said the wrong thing? I wonder as she motions me ahead of her to an empty table. We sit silently, watching the waitress clear away the previous party's meal. Someone has left a dainty last piece of French toast. Someone has eaten his beef stew and rice separately—no rice in the stew bowl, no trace of stew on the half-mound of rice left on the plate. Someone doesn't like green onions. I try to find a pattern in the flotsam beached along the rim of the saimin bowl before the waitress takes it away. My friend watches her wipe the table in slow semi-circles.

I feel frustrated. Other people I've talked to have not told me much more: the special food, the dolls. I feel as if I've been looking for some great revelation in the pages of a cookbook, under the subtitles FESTIVAL FOODS or CULTURE. As if knowing what people eat or how they eat it or why they eat it would tell me who they are and how they think. As if a multi-ethnic cookbook could ever bring about racial equality.

The waitress brings our menus. We order coffee and watch her leave.

"I don't remember really," my friend says, looking up from her menu almost shyly. "I seem to remember a photograph. I'm being held up in front of tiers of glass boxes, all larger than me. I am in a kimono—I don't know what color—probably it was bright, red or pink, the kind young girls wear."

She laughs apologetically, looking down again. "I hardly remember the dolls even, just that they had very white faces and very skinny hands."

The hands holding the menu are strong, tanned, the nails cut straight across. She is perhaps 50, a little younger than my mother. I try to imagine her as a child, soft and bewildered among the glass cases, a doll herself, propped up by someone else's strong hands. Her mother's hands perhaps, peeking out from the long sleeves of her daughter's kimono. Hands cut off at the wrist, the rest of her body swallowed up by a black page in a photo album, pieces of her tucked into the small mountings at each corner of the photograph.

Our coffee arrives. We both order french toast.

My own mother has no pictures like this from her girlhood. "We couldn't afford the dolls," she told me when I asked her about it. Yet she knows them all: the emperor and empress, the samurai and retainers grouped around them, the delicate ladies poised at their feet. Each case dusted off lovingly for *Hinamatsuri,* each carefully stored away again when it was all over. I also know of people who burned their dolls during the war, fearing for their own children's safety in the racist hysteria of the times.

"I never got a Japanese doll for Girls' Day," I say, watching the cream spiral down then swirl up again like smoke in the darkness that fills my cup. "Except one Girls' Day, I remember my grandma gave me a regular doll, a baby doll with her own teething ring and bottle and diapers, *you* know."

"Yes," she says stirring her coffee slowly, "I know. I didn't have too many regular dolls."

A regular doll. A non-Japanese doll.

I think of the harlequin doll I had once, its plush body

half-red, half-yellow, its face cool and plastic, friendly, soft. I named it after the first black child I ever met, a boy named Paul.

We were washing clay-working tools in a bucket outside our kindergarten classroom one day when two 6th grade boys came by and called him Black Sambo. It was a book I loved, a story I could hear over and over again and not get tired of, especially the way my mother read it. So I couldn't understand at first why he cried.

Then I reasoned that it was the way they said it. Like it was the worst name imaginable. Like you could get mean lickings if your father ever heard you say it, even though he might have said it himself just the other day.

Paul left sometime after that and I forgot about him, until it was time for class pictures and I insisted on holding my clown doll when the photographer came to arrange us in rows.

"It's Paul," I explained, and Mrs. Shimizu let me hold him next to me.

Maybe I did it just to get my doll into the picture, but either way, the irony was lost to me then. He was no substitute for the living child.

I am about to mention it when our food arrives. *Perhaps mercifully* I think; we are grown women after all—all this talk about dolls is embarrassing. We speak of our latest projects, of love, inflation, war, redress. It gets later. Our hostage emotions drift irresolutely along safer tangents. The waitress stops coming after delivering our check, and our half-empty coffee cups get colder.

We finish everything on our plates and leave.

* * * * *

I am holding a picture in my hands, an unsigned oil painting I found one day in a Salvation Army store in my unending search for old hats to add to my collection and old clothes full of other people's histories. A picture of a girl and her doll.

The girl is small, Asian, the familiar chawan-cut of my childhood framing her very determined eyes. She is sitting on a curbing somewhere, wearing t-shirt and jeans, knees together, one slippered toe barely reaching the ground, the other foot dangling. I hear the impatient sound of her slipper, flapping against her bare heel like a small bird taking flight.

She is looking down the street toward a future I can only guess at, holding an open umbrella—the smelly oilpaper kind—bamboo handle crossing over one knee. The doll is propped stiff-legged on her other knee, ice-blue eyes staring in the opposite direction. It is wearing a white dress with red specks, a white bonnet, black shoes.

It is a crude picture. Neither of them have clearly defined hands, for instance, and the umbrella is out of proportion—it seems flat although she is holding it at an angle. Perhaps it is the composition of the piece, the strange incongruity of the subjects, that drew me to it more than anything else. An Asian girl and her Caucasian doll. As strange to me as the photograph of my friend among the mythical figures of her past. Yet somehow just as real, just as familiar, as my own dolls.

To *be* that girl, holding her doll, waiting for something to happen. And, to watch her, paint her, photograph her, write about her, order her life into something whole!

I have decided that she and her doll will be rewarded very soon by beautiful *pa'u* riders in flowing skirts and fragrant leis and wonderful hats. That there will be marching bands and baton twirlers and beauty queens and floats. Maybe a few clowns, but no politicians. And not a funeral. And *certainly* not a formation of soldiers young enough to be her brothers, who will march past her, bayonets flashing, who will look straight ahead and not see her, perhaps mercifully.

As if I alone had the power to decide her fate.

_____ *Jody Manabe*

158

Pele's Own

The road which battled its way across lava flats from the main highway leading to Mauna Kea and town was a desolate, dusty road. Farther on as it neared Winona's shack, the road twisted and squirmed its way along the craggy coasts, slowing to a pleasurable crawl only when it hit the sandy inlets which speckled the barrens.

Shading her eyes, Winona spied the wastes ahead of her. The road was disgustingly empty. Angrily, Winona scratched her head. She shook her shoulders indifferently. She wished Julian would make it snappy. She was dreadfully anxious to see the new movie. Julian said it was a real hot love story.

That was typical of Julian. He knew so much about a lot of things. Maybe it was because he had gone to college. Anyway, he was different from the guys she knew. When she thought about that oaf, Kamaka, whom she had agreed to marry not a week ago, she wanted to scream. How could she have been so stupidly blind, so . . . so . . . so completely taken over by that scrubby fisherman whom her father employed. It made her shudder to think about it. If she hadn't met Julian at the county fair last Saturday, she would have been stuck forever. It was sure funny the way things happened.

Bending over, Winona lifted her skirt and wiped the dewy drops of sweat which glistened on her forehead. The air was a stagnant sea of heat. Delicately pursing her lips, Winona touched them with her tongue. She remembered that first night she had met Julian. He had kissed her, laughingly telling her that it was an old custom among civilized people. She wished she was as smart as Julian. Her lips suddenly felt full.

Ma called her. She went into the shack. Ma glanced at her, standing as she was over the sink savagely kneading the poi. "You going out tonight?"

"Yeah, Ma, I going out wid Julian."

Ma's dark forehead wrinkled as if she were trying to recall the name, "Who dis Julian?"

"Oh, Ma," Winona cried excitedly. "He da handsomest guy I eva meet. He going take me show tonight."

"And wat samatta wid Kamaka? I taught you going marry him." Ma put the bowl of poi on the table. "Wat you tink Kamaka going say wen him and Pa come in tomorrow? Wat he going say when he fine out you go fool aroun' wid this guy?"

Winona pinched Ma's cheek gaily. "No worry. Wen Ka-
maka come in, I going tell him dat us pau. I not going marry
him."

Ma swung around. "Wat you say?" she asked incredu-
lously.

"I not going marry Kamaka, 'at's all."

"You mean because dis udda guy, dis . . . dis . . . wat you
call him?"

"Julian."

"Yeah, dis Julian. You mean because you fall in luff wid
him?"

Winona nodded her head. Sure she loved him. There was
no use denying it. They were going to Honolulu where he
would work. And they would have a big house, a hundred
times bigger than the shack in which she was born. Julian
would give her a lot of servants and a swanky car too. And
they would have a lot of kids. And he would take her to the
movies, like tonight. And she would love him. And he would
love her. And maybe they would invite Ma and Pa and Ka-
maka to come—no, it would never work out if Kamaka came.
Kamaka would try to lick Julian. Anyway, she and Julian
would be happy forever and forever, and—

Ma was saying: "You dunno him, you sure you luff him?
He luff you?"

Did he love her? Of all the silly questions to ask. Didn't he
tell her the night he brought her home from the fair that she
was as lovely as a Botticelli angel. Of course she had no idea
what sort of an angel Botticelli was, but it really didn't matter.
The way Julian's eyes had suddenly become hot and glassy
told her everything she needed to know.

"Yeah Ma," she answered, "he luff me."

Ma sighed heavily. "I dunno. I dunno, Winona."

"Dunno wat, Ma?"

"How dis going turn out."

Looking at Ma's mountainous body, Winona thought: How
could you know what real love is, Ma? I mean the kind of love
which I feel for Julian . . . the kind that eats away at your
insides . . . the kind that gives you dreams which make you
weak just thinking about them. Nature gave you a wrong deal,
Ma. Maybe if you weren't built like a barrel, you would have
had the luck to have someone like Julian fall in love with you.
You never had the chance to love. You met Pa, and because he

was a good fisherman, a good provider, and probably the only guy who ever paid you any attention, you married him. Well, Ma, it's different with me. I'm pretty.

"No worry, Ma, I know wat I doing."

Ma shrugged as if she were too tired to go on. "I hope you right, Winona." Then in a burst of maternal indignation: "You betta go baiph. You sweat like Opunui's jackass."

"I went baiph dis aftanoon a'ready."

"Go baiph again." Winona knew it was useless to argue with Ma once she made up her mind. Ma was inflexible that way. Winona took another bath.

After bathing, Winona stood before the mirror admiring herself. Her hair was like a mass of black Spanish moss. She ran her hands over her hips, feeling a delicious tingle pulsate down her long, tan legs. Delightful, simply heavenly.

Ma came in, and watched Winona sort her clothes on the bed. She said, not without some pride in her voice, "I used to look like you befoa. Eveybody in da village use to say I was pretty." And then, as if to offer further proof to her statement, she added, "Ask you fada. He tell you."

Winona smiled tolerantly. Let Ma rave. Let her dream. She wasn't fooling anyone. In a way Ma's self praise was a crying shame. Winona was sorry for Ma. Anybody who begins to relive the past is admitting that he has been defeated in the present.

"Ma," she asked, "How I going hide dis ugly mole on my neck?"

"Wat for you like hide 'em?" Ma came peering closely, "'At's not'ing. In fact, 'at's look nice."

"Nah, Ma, you donno not'ing." Winona wrapped a forest-green scarf around her neck. "I tink I going use dis." Ma was silent.

Winona slipped on a purple blouse that had three-quarter sleeves lined with pink ruffles. Then she stepped into a dress which appeared as if it had been soaked in whale's blood. Pirouetting, like a ballet dancer with corns on her feet, Winona said, "Wat you tink?" She didn't really care whether Ma answered or not.

Ma didn't say anything. She looked at Winona, her face a blank mask, looking, just looking. Finally, Winona broke the spell. "Wat samatta, Ma?"

Ma put her hand on Winona. "You going wid dis guy all

dressed up like dat?"

"Sure, Ma. Julian not like Kamaka, you know. When you go someplace wid somebody like Julian, you gotta dress up. You gotta be high tone. You gotta show 'em you not ignorant."

Sadly, Ma shook her head. "You can wear one feather dress but dat no mean you can fly. Dat no mean you one bird."

"You no need worry, Ma, I know wat I doing." Winona smeared her lips with strawberry red lipstick. She hoped Julian would like its taste. She admitted it was a cheap brand, but for texture and color you couldn't beat it. "By da way, Ma, I need some money."

"For wat?"

"I like buy Julian one box candy foa present."

"But Winona," Ma tried to protest, "You no . . ."

"If you no like give me no need," Winona interrupted. She flung her lipstick into her purse and slammed it shut. Ma quietly left the room. Presently she returned. "Winona, heah two dollars. You tink des nough?"

Winona threw her arms around Ma. "Ma, Ma, tank you, you so sweet." She squeezed Ma.

When Julian called for her, Winona invited him in. She introduced him to Ma. They shook hands. Ma was politely reserved, almost shy. Julian acted as if meeting Ma was the most important thing that could happen to him. His effusive behavior seemed to annoy Ma, for she fidgeted uncomfortably, as if she had the itch.

Turning to Winona, Julian said, "I see now where you inherit your beauty, Winona," he winked.

Winona grinned. Julian was the perfect gentleman. Only a gentleman would say such nice things about her mother. And he was considerate of her own feelings too, otherwise he wouldn't have tipped her off with a wink. Julian said, "You've got a swell place here, Ma. But aren't you afraid someday Mauna Kea will erupt? You people are living in the path of the lava flows."

"Pele take care o' us."

"You believe in Pele, the fire goddess? I mean . . . well . . . do you really believe in Pele?"

"Sure. Wat samatta wid dat?"

"Why, I . . . I . . . I don't know. I'm an Episcopalian myself." He fumbled for a cigarette. "Mind if I smoke? Thanks."

162

He took a deep drag and exhaled. Behind a cloud of smoke he said, "I'm a Hawaiian, you know."

Winona blinked in surprise. Julian's skin was as white as the clouds over Mauna Kea.

"Wat part you Hawaiian?" asked Ma innocently.

"My father's grandfather was half. I suppose that would make me, let me see . . ." he wrinkled his brows for a minute. "I guess it would make me about one-sixteenth, wouldn't it?"

"Yeah," Ma answered, "You Hawaiian a'right."

"Getting back to this Pele business, I thought good Queen Kapiolani proved to our people that Pele was a fraud? You remember the story. She went up to the rim of the volcano and dared Pele to harm her. Of course nothing happened."

"And wat dat proof?" Ma seemed to have come to life. Winona was embarrassed. Why didn't Ma keep her mouth closed. She was only showing her ignorance. Julian was smart. Ma couldn't hope to hold an argument with him.

"It proves," Julian explained patronizingly, "that Pele is only a myth, a fairytale."

"You mean because Pele nevva keel da Queen, she no live?" There was a strange light in Ma's eyes. Julian puffed leisurely. "Yes, that's right, Ma."

"Who you belief?"

"I'm a Christian. I believe in Christ."

Ma rolled her sleeves. Raising her fists, she hollered, "Hey, Christ, I like see you keel me. I dar' you! I dar' you!"

"Good God!" exclaimed Julian aghast. "It's blasphemy."

A deep stillness descended upon the room. Julian's mouth was agape. Winona was confused. Ma had done something terribly, terribly wrong. She didn't know what it was, but she sensed it. At last Ma spoke. "You God one fairytale, Julian. He no do not'ing."

"I . . . I . . ." Julian fumbled, "I don't know what to say, Ma." He appeared dumbfounded.

"Julian," Winona said hastily, "we betta go befoa we late foa da show."

"Yes, yes, Winona." Hurriedly he killed his cigarette as if glad for the chance to escape. "You go ahead and dress, Winona, and we'll leave."

"Dress! Wat samatta, you tink I naked?"

"But surely . . ."

163

"Den let's go." Winona grabbed his arm, at the same time talking over her shoulder. "No need wait foa me, Ma. Maybe I come home late."

It was the morning after. The sun was shining, a perverse sun that streaked through the window and splashed all over Winona. It got into her eyes, and soaked through the covers, steaming her as neatly as if she were in a sweat box. Desperately, Winona dug her head under a pillow splotched with lipstick stains.

Somebody was calling. She pushed the pillow away from her head. "Winona! Wen you going get up?" Ma was shaking her. "Late a'ready, and us get plenty wo'k foa do today."

"Oh Ma," she groaned, "lemme sleep five moa minutes."

"We get plenty foa do. Pa comin' in today." Ma pulled the covers off the bed. Sleepily, Winona sat rubbing her eyes.

Ma was grumbling. "You go have good time, no come home til da frogs go sleep. Den wen time foa get up, you like sleep."

Stretching, Winona yawned. "You always squawking, Ma."

Ma snorted. "Who going do all da wo'k?"

"Wo'k, wo'k, 'at's all you tink about, Ma. Take it easy. We get plenty time." Again she yawned. Ma noticed the clothes Winona had worn the night before strewn on the floor.

"Why you throw all you clothes on the floor, Winona? You moa worse den one baby." Groaning, Ma stooped over with an effort and began picking up the clothes. "Who going do dis foa you wen you get married? I pity your husband."

Grinning, Winona patted Ma on the cheek. "No worry, Ma. When I marry Julian I going get servants."

"You mean he wen ask you marry him a'ready?"

Winona slipped into her dress. "No, Ma, not exactly."

"Den wat you mean?"

"Jest wat I say. He going marry me."

"But he nevva tell you he going marry you?"

Exasperated, Winona said, "He no need tell me. I jest know."

Ma shrugged. "I dunno. Maybe dis new style you get. Befoa, da boy use to ask da girl he like marry her. Now you tell me he no need."

"Look Ma," Winona said, trying to control herself, "you can tell if da boy luff you by da way he act, by da way he talk, by da way he look. If you know all dat, he no need tell you not'ing."

"I suppose," Ma replied sarcastically, "you fine all dis out last night wen Julian look at you, talk to you, and do something to you, eh?"

Winona felt herself blushing. She wished she hadn't introduced the subject. But it was true, every word of it. Somehow she felt she knew Julian better after last night. She didn't enjoy the movie as much as she had thought she would, but that was because Julian didn't seem to be having a good time. He had appeared embarrassed, self-conscious, not his usual self. He had tried, however, to conceal it by grinning most of the time, but she had noticed. Of course, she hadn't said anything to him. That would have made him more uncomfortable. It was bad enough with all those people staring at them. Why they were so rude, she could never understand. She wondered if all town people behave that way. She must ask Julian about it when he came in the evening.

It was funny, thinking about it now, how fast Julian had recovered. The movie had no sooner been over, and they were driving home, when he had swerved to the side of the road, doused the lights, and in complete darkness began to tell her how much he loved her. A delicious sensation came over her as she recalled his amorous advances.

"Okay, Ma," Winona answered moving toward the door. "I go eat breakfast den I help you wo'k."

And work she did indeed. She was so fagged out at the end of the day that she had hardly enough strength to bathe and dress and pretty herself before Julian would arrive. But miraculously, by six-thirty she was ready. Pa had come home by then, bringing with him a sack of fish and Kamaka. She was thankful to Ma for not mentioning Julian to Pa and Kamaka. Sometimes she suspected Ma of having a little common sense.

After dinner and another hour had passed, Winona decided that the thing she detested most, of all the things in the world which she could possibly dislike, was waiting. In spite of Pa's long talk on politics and fishing, which he had carried on throughout dinner, Winona couldn't remember a word he had said. Her mind was a seething turmoil. She was worried about Julian, and oblivious in a vague way, to everything that went on around her. Once or twice Kamaka had tried in his shy, unobtrusive manner to speak to her, but she had cut him short. She was sorry. Poor Kamaka, she hadn't meant to hurt him. He was so sensitive with women, that a harsh word or a cross look would immediately wilt him. Yet he was a regular bull with men.

Julian still didn't come. Kamaka had humbly said good-night to her and had departed. Pa and Ma had retired to their bedroom; and she, left alone, had gone out into the inky night with the chirping crickets and the eternal jewels blinking in the sky. A thousand questions tumbled through her mind, and there were a million answers, but none would satisfy the question: Why hadn't Julian come? She wept for a while. And then she must have sobbed herself to sleep, for Pa came out and carried her in.

Julian never returned. For months after his disappearance Winona never stopped looking for him. Ma never spoke of Julian, even to Pa. And Kamaka never understood what was going on, but sometimes when he'd visit with Pa, he'd quietly go out and sit with Winona, saying nothing, respecting silence.

Winona was grateful to him and one day as they were sitting together, she said, "Kamaka, you betta no foaget dat you and me was going get married."

Charles M. Kong

166

Nowadays Not Like Before _____

Danny stretched his massive body along the wooden bench that he often used as a bed. It was a windy night and he covered himself with an old shower curtain, feeling the warm plastic cling to his sweaty arms. He really did not mind the cold weather. The black coffee and the tin roof over his head provided ample warmth and security. What bothered him the most was the windy sound that stirred his imagination, keeping him awake throughout the entire night. He closed his eyes and wondered if the other men had the same problem.

Suddenly the wind disappeared, as if someone had captured it in a bottle, and the once churning white water lay flat and cold like the palm of a hand. Danny could sense that something was awfully wrong, the way the night birds started heading back to the mountains as if the black clouds that lay along the horizon were scaring them away. The dim glow from the lantern began pulsating like a heart beat, casting distorted figures along the concrete floor of the shack. Slowly the other men were climbing out of their sleeping bags, focusing their eyes on the angry clouds that were now rumbling right above them. Junior suggested that everyone tie all their shower curtains together. That way the eight of them could hide under one large plastic tent. Everyone worked at a frantic pace, collecting their gear together, tying shower curtain to shower curtain, and glancing every so often at the gloomy sky. No one, however, seemed to notice the changing tide—as it slowly rose over the ridge and completely surrounded the entire shack.

Danny could not recall ever praying so hard in his life, but the waves were hitting them with such a tremendous force he could not think of anything else to do but mumble the Hail Mary over and over again. The shack was close to fifteen feet high, so he could imagine how huge the waves were, the way they kept pounding on the corrugated tin roof. It was like being locked inside of a car trunk while someone with an angry fist kept beating down on him. He was holding on to Junior, fingers grasping three of his belt loops, while both of Junior's arms were hugging one of the wooden beams that ran perpendicular to the roof. Somewhere in the distance the men could hear the booming sound of a cannon—waves hammering the side of the cliffs. Then immediately in front of him, he saw their gear slowly float away. First the lantern, then the wooden table, then he closed his eyes and prayed a little harder.

Throughout the storm Danny could hear Junior's bellowing voice telling everyone to hold on to their positions. Danny himself thought it would be easier to make a run for it, but deep inside a little voice kept reminding him to trust Junior's decision. Over the past thirty years Junior had been caught in a number of sea storms and Danny remembered Junior telling him about the tombstones that lay scattered along the rugged cliffs. So many men had been swept to sea while trying to run away from the awesome waves. There was Gordon Pang in 1945, there was old man Harry in 1953, there was Walter Cobey in 1976 . . . the list seemed endless. All of a sudden the tombstones meant more to Danny than ever before. It was a strange feeling, like being close to someone that he always took for granted. He held on to Junior and tried to hide his fear like the rest of the men, patiently waiting for the sea storm to pass them by.

In the early 1920's an old Portuguese pig farmer often lent his donkeys to a handful of young Japanese fishermen. The men would back-pack their way across the steep lava sea cliffs on Southeastern Oahu until they reached Halona Point—their favorite fishing ground. The next day they would return to the farmer and provide him with enough fish for a month.

This bartering system continued until the coastal road opened in 1931. Soon, fishermen from all over Oahu began casting at Halona, and on a good night a multitude of bamboo fishing poles would line the perimeter of the point, which was given the name "Bamboo Ridge." And even today—some fifty years later—the men at Bamboo Ridge continue to tell the story of the old Portuguese pig farmer and the young Japanese fishermen.

In 1929 a group of fishermen founded the former Honolulu Japanese Casting Club, the forerunner of today's many casting clubs. In spite of their caution in fishing off the rocky lava ledges that are found along O'ahu's coastline, every year a number of their members and fellow fishermen were swept away and lost in heavy surf. In 1935 members of the club began a community service project to erect concrete warning markers at dangerous spots around the island. Each marker had the Japanese character "abunai," or "danger," carved on two of its sides. The markers were usually placed at a spot where a fisherman had lost his life; they can still be seen along the coast in Nanakuli and Kaena as well as the Koko Head area.

In addition to setting up the warning markers, the members of the Honolulu Casting Club pooled their money and sent away to Japan for a carved statue of O-Jizosan, the guarding god for people at all dangerous waterways and coastlines. When the statue arrived it was placed on top of Halona Point, overlooking the ridge and cove below. With the outbreak of World War II, however, O-Jizosan's head was broken off, because he was the god of the "enemy," and eventually his body was demolished entirely. The postwar cost of replacing the statue was too prohibitive for the club members, so they decided to have his figure carved into a large stone. This was done, and today O-Jizosan stands again in place, watching over the fishermen and swimmers near Halona.[1]

Freddy takes his fishing reel from his back-pack and attaches it on to his fiberglass rod. Ricky does the same, mentioning something about the advantages of being first. It is a very hot afternoon: the type of day when none of the clouds in the sky seem to be moving. Normally, no one would be at the ridge as early as one thirty, but both men are construction workers participating in the iron worker's strike. That gives them time to assemble their gear and cast their lines, long before the rest of the men. Freddy and Ricky continue to work silently, stopping every so often to study the movement of the changing tides and the blowing trade winds. Meanwhile an elderly couple wearing straw hats slowly work their way down to the ridge.

They turn out to be two red-faced tourists. One of them is an old man in Bermuda shorts lugging a Nikon camera strapped around his neck. His wife, dressed in a bright red muu-muu, seems to have a constant habit of giggling for no reason. He picks up one of Freddy's fourteen-foot fishing poles with authority and begins to examine it from butt cap to tip. He lets out a frown and says that back in Canada he does a lot of trout fishing, but never has he seen anything so ridiculous as this. Freddy smiles, then shrugs his shoulder, mumbling something about never having met a person from Canada before. Then the old man walks into the shack and begins to examine all of the fishing gear on the wooden table. He lets out a gasp of air as he picks up an ulua hook as big as his palm. Attached to the hook is a wire leader made from piano wire. Back comes his frown and he asks Ricky if he could keep the hook as a souvenir, so he could show it to his trout-fishing buddies back home. Ricky nods, telling the old man that he and Freddy never tasted trout before. By now the old man is practically shouting his disbelief. He runs outside again and picks up Freddy's rod. He tells his wife that no one could cast a pole as heavy as this. She giggles. Then he examines the ring at the end of the wire leader and demands an explanation. Ricky demonstrates how the ring can be snapped on to someone's line, enabling a baited hook to slide all the way down to the sinker. The old man thinks it's the craziest idea he has ever heard. He takes out his camera and starts clicking away at the ocean, the shack, and especially Freddy and Ricky. He stares at the poles for the last time, then heads back up the trail, shaking his head all the way to his car.

It's called the slide-bait method and is one of the oldest ways of fishing in Hawaii. And yet even the most experienced fisherman may not be familiar with its technique. You won't find it being used at Honolulu Harbor, or any of the sandy beaches around Oahu. Slide-baiting calls for a rocky cliff and a lot of guts to withstand the angry waves that constantly threaten you.

When fishing from a ledge, the slide-bait method will ease the physical difficulties that an ulua fisherman encounters. Enormous size baits—such as a whole octopus—make long distance casting with a fourteen foot rod quite difficult. The slide-baiter, however, avoids this problem by casting out a baitless line with only a sinker. Attached to the sinker is a wire hook which catches on to the nearest coral head. This enables the fisherman to keep his line in a taut position. When his line is finally set, he slides down a baited hook with a short leader. This is done by passing the line through a small connector, which is usually a split ring or a pigtail loop. There are several advantages to this type of fishing: a long distance cast may be made; with one cast several baited hooks can be sent down at intervals; the reeling in of the line to see whether the bait is still on is unnecessary; fewer sinkers are lost. And if you are a complete stranger to this type of fishing, like a trout fisherman from Canada, the usual response is that nothing short of a whale can ever be caught.

The sun is rapidly falling behind the mountains in Hawaii-Kai and Junior realizes that he does not have much time to work with. Standing on the edge of the ridge, he stares at the familiar blue water, patiently waiting for his body to relax. It is like watching a baseball pitcher. He takes a deep breath and waits; something is wrong with his footing and he knows he will lose control the moment he releases his line. He jerks his hip in a circular motion, then repositions his footing along the lava rocks. Once again he gazes at the horizon, timing his breath with the ebb and flow. Slowly he raises his left leg into the air until his entire body is balancing on his right leg. Then he takes a final dip to the right and his fourteen foot pole comes flying around his body in a powerful roundhouse fashion. It is a good cast, maybe eighty or ninety yards. But the rough current makes it difficult for his sinker to anchor itself onto the coral reef and he starts over.

The rest of the men are gathered around the wooden table, waiting for Junior to finish his casting. David glances at his watch for the second time in ten minutes and then mumbles something about not being able to wait any longer. A rumbling noise vibrates through his stomach but no one takes him seriously. David himself knows that he can really wait, even if Junior takes another hour; time is not important here. Their pot luck dinner has always been a tradition; a time of relaxation and the sharing of home cooked meals: Japanese, Chinese, Filipino, Korean, Portuguese style.

The table is filled with a number of local delicacies. Junior provides enough Portuguese sausages and shoyu chicken for everyone, Howard brings a bottle of homemade kim-chee, and Allen opens a plastic container filled with fresh bamboo shoots that he picked in Tantalus. Everyone has something to contribute and for the time being the men forget about their daily problems, engrossed in the good food and warm conversation.

"Eh, David, you went Tamashiro Market? Man, that's what I call scraping the bottom of the barrel." Everyone laughs at Junior's jeering remark but the cardboard container—filled with raw fish—is empty in no time.

"Da sashimi was on sale," David replies, "And anyway, you guys all know—nowadays not like before."

Almost twenty years ago, men like Junior and David could make a few dollars on the side by selling their daily catch to the fish markets around Honolulu. Today, however, they find themselves depending on the fish markets to provide them with their bait. Over the years, they have watched a number of Hawaii's fishing grounds turn fallow. Yet, in spite of all the drawbacks of shore casting, they continue to fish, season after season.

Freddy seems to put everything in a nutshell when he talks about "finding his God at Bamboo Ridge." Like the rest of the men, he realizes that the ulua is "very, very scarce." But through the years he has learned to enjoy the simple things in life, like the sound of the blue ocean and the brown sea birds. "Besides," he adds, "where else can you find a group of guys who can sit down together, every weekend, and still find something interesting to discuss? I mean, I can't even do that with my wife . . . I just run out of things to say to her."

Allen nibbles on a piece of chicken and tries to visualize David's favorite diving spot off Punaluu. The two men—sitting directly across from each other—exchange questions, then David draws a map with his finger on the wooden table. Allen studies the invisible map for a while, then suddenly his face lights up with understanding. He nods his approval, then takes another bite from his chicken.

At the far side of the table, Ricky holds up his left arm to show Tiny a small gash under his elbow. Tiny lets out a roar of laughter and so do the other men who are familiar with the "peeping Tom" antics of construction workers. Ricky stands on the bench and pantomimes the entire event: how he hides his body behind a slab of dry wall then cuts two holes big enough for his binoculars. Feeling brave enough, he decides to move a little closer "to get a better look," only to trip on a piece of scrap lumber. "A serious injury," he jokes, "but all in a day's work."

Freddy tells about the conflict he is having with his wife. How she cannot seem to appreciate his constant fishing habit. Allen pats Freddy on the back and stresses the importance of "wife training." Ricky nods his approval, telling everyone that long before he got married he made an agreement with his wife-to-be: if she had any nights off from work he would stay home, other than that, nothing would interfere with his fish-

172

ing. Ricky remembers getting married during the peak of the ulua season: "I wuz so excited I neva no what to do. So I figga, I get married, but I skip da reception. I went throw all da presents in da back of my jeep, and me and Val went spend our honeymoon right here at da ridge."

Howard picks up a dog-eared section of the Star Bulletin that someone has tossed on the concrete floor. He mutters something about the rivalry between Ariyoshi and Fasi and before you know it—it's election time at Bamboo Ridge. Surprisingly, everyone seems concerned about Hawaii's political future.

"Ariyoshi going lose," says Freddy with authority, "I bet you any much."

"How you know?" asks Danny, "You no like him cuz he Japanese right? Well dat not good enough."

"I no care what nationality him," Freddy replies, "I just know he not going get as many votes from the Japanese community cuz da obligation is over."

Freddy explains the obligation the first generation of Japanese (issei) had for John Burns. "And that's how Ariyoshi got in, but the obligation is over, and Ariyoshi is out!"

The friendly argument continues until Danny throws in his two cents which seems to touch home base with everyone. "I no like vote, because da state always jam up everything at da end. Dey always do dat." Danny mentions the mongoose; how it was brought into the Islands to control the rat population in the cane field. "Dat ting went eat everything but da bugga, and now we get one problem trying to control da mongoose!"

"And what about the Talapia and the Ta'ape?" shouts Howard. "That's another mistake. I tell you, those two fish are eating everything in sight." To his understanding, both fishes were brought in as a source of food. "But they're disturbing the natural cycle, especially that Ta'ape. None of the other fishes have a chance to spawn anymore. I tell you, in five years Hawaii will be in big trouble, all because of that stupid fish."

"And what about over population?" gripes Junior. "It's just not fair to us shore casters." He explains what the Ridge is like during the day. How the water is filled with weekend divers and commercial trappers. "My neighbors, they always ask me why I'm not catching any more ulua and I just shrug my

173

shoulders. But I know why, it's those trappers catching all of the small fish. And when you don't have small fish, none of the bigger fish come around."

"Dat's right, and more worse, dey like fool around," grumbles David. "Da other day I had one big strike, but when I pick up my pole I no feel nothing fight back, just something real heavy. So I figga I get one big eel and I all happy cuz dat good bait for ulua. But when I pick up my line, I find somebody went tie six beer cans to my hook. And den I see all the divers out there waving to me, like I suppose to wave back and laugh too. I tell you, if I wuz Governor, da first ting I do is make one restriction. Tell all those divers dey gotta stay two hundred yards from the shoreline. I mean, if dey get aqualungs dey get da whole ocean . . . why dey gotta bother us?"

All night long, the conversation flows as smoothly as the waves. And in many ways it is an ideal society. No social ladder exists: the youngest man holds equal weight with the eldest, and everyone is entitled to his share of compliments as well as criticism. The men realize that the fishing will never be the same, and the future looks as bleak as ever. But still, they continue to fish and wish at Bamboo Ridge.

[1]John Clark, *The Beaches of Oahu*, (Honolulu: University Press of Hawaii, 1978), p. 28.

Tony Lee

Beer Can Hat

You know, Bobo stay lolo in da head. Mental, you know. But he good fun sell newspaper and he smart fo' go by da cars when get stop light and sell to ladies, old ladies . . . and to da mokes who tell stink kine stuff about he belong in Kaneohe Hospital la' dat but in da end dey buy newspaypah and tip too! Most times dey give quartah and tell, "Keep da change," but sometimes dey give more.

Bobo he smart fo' time 'em good, him. He take long time get change fo' quartah at red light, bumbye da light change green and da guy tell, "Ay, ass okay, keep 'em," and step da gas. Bobo smile big and tell, "Tanks, eh." He time 'em real good. Me, everytime I get da real chang-kine guys and ho-man, dey wait 'til da light turn red again fo' get dey ten cents change.

Coming-home-from-work time is da bes' time. I go after school sell papers wit' Bobo—supposed to go straight after— but I stay fool around school little while 'cuz Bobo always stay dere and watch my papers fo' me. Mistah Carvalho, mah district manager, get piss off but he no can do nutting, nobody like work fo' him already. He get smart wit' me I would tell 'em, "Ay, no make la' dat. I know one time you went dump all da inserts inside one big garbage can 'cause was late and nobody came fo' help put 'em inside da home deliveries." Ass what I would tell 'em. Yeah, you know.

One time I went ask Bobo what he do during da daytime when I go school. He tell he go by da supermarket and wheel da cart around. Used to be he wheel 'em around inside da store but da manager tell him no can, so he wheel 'em around outside in da parking lot.

I ask him what he saving up fo' and he tell, "One Motobecane, jes' like motorcycle dat. Tired pump my bike." Bobo's bike stay all junky, old style gooseneck and one-speed and one old newspaper bag hanging on da handlebars. Was shetty.

Me, I saving up for one skateboard, Cobra kine with heavy duty trucks, and one college edja-kay-shen. Ass what my fahdah tell me.

So me and Bobo, we stay together pretty good. Plenny guys tell, why I stay wit' Bobo. Dey tell he talk crooked, his mouth funny kine and sometimes drool lil' bit. I tell, "Watch out bra—he know kung fu and make like da wrestlah, da Missing Link, 'Whoaaa . . . yeah!' " But I went show him how fo' wipe his mout' before he sell newspaper to da custamah. I went buy him hanka-chief too. I wanted da kine wit' initials on top, "B.B." for Bobo. But I couldn't find, so I went buy one with "W" I tink, at sidewalk sale. Make 'em feel good, boy—I feel good too, though. He learn good, wipe his mouth first before he go to da customer. He no talk too good. Everytime guys tell, "Hah? What you talking, stupid." He only can try his best but no come out clear, "Heef-teen sants, pay-pah." But me, I used-to to it already.

Chee, one time one guy went run over his toes. Good ting he strong, boy. My fahdah said good ting he was wearing his rubber shoes, stay all had-it but it save his toes or maybe da guy went go so fast that never have time fo' smash his feet. But Bobo never tell nothing jes' like no sore, but must've been, yeah? One time he go show off, he tell, "I show you one trick," and he go poke one safety pin through his skin, you know da thick part by da thumb? Suckin' weird looking, safety pin through his thumb skin and him smiling up wit' his bolo-head. My fahdah said dat his fahdah no like him already and like throw him out of da house but da social worker say no can. Bobo no tell nothing about his fahdah but my fahdah tell, "Ass why he bolo-head everytime. Da fahdah no like when he bring home little bit money, he tink Bobo go spend 'em or lose 'em on da way home so he give Bobo lickin's and shave his head." Ass why I ask my muddah fo' make him one, da kine, beer can hat. I go ask Bobo what his favorite team and he say, "Mah-keen-lee Tikahs." So I tell my muddah, "Can make 'em yellow and black? . . . For McKinley Tigers?" Tough man, da way my muddah can make 'em. She fast wit' da needles for knit. My fahdah laugh and tell, "I help. I help you Mama. I drink four beers right now so you can have da empty cans fo' make hat."

"Here Junior," he tell me, "You like taste beer?"

"Daddy!" Mama come all mad, not real mad, just mad voice, "No give da boy beer, wassamattah you!"

"Mama, I can make 'em like one real present? No stay Christmas or berfday, but can make 'em like one real present please?" Mama look at me and tell, "Okay, go get da wrapping and ribbon box . . . No, wait boy, come here first." And she tell me I good boy and how she proud I tink of Bobo. She hug me and I tell her, "Nah," but I feel good. Den I go get da box wit' all da old Christmas and birthday wrappings. My muddah save 'em from everytime get presents and da ribbon too. She lemme pick da paypah. Never have black and gold kine but had one with tigers so I went pick dat one even though was pink. Mama put da hat in one box and wrap 'em wit' da paper and I went help put my finger when came time fo' tie da knot.

Bobo was so happy when he went open da box. Was little bit big but he put 'em on and went by one car and tell, "Pape?" and da guy tell, "No tanks," and Bobo stay by da car and use da mirror on da side fo' make da hat good on his head, you know, so get one beer can label straight in da front.

"Tanks, eh. Tell you mama tanks eh. You sure fo' me? Tanks eh." Ass all he say over and over. And everytime when get green light, he take 'em off and look at 'em . . . make sure no mo' dirt on top. Me, I feel so good I miss couple customers at da red light.

So had me working da sidewalk and Bobo walking between da cars (my fahdah no let me go between da cars), and one shaka van went come: fat tires, mag wheels, teen-ted glass. Was just some mokes playing da tape deck loud and smoking pakalolo. I know 'cause more skinny da pakalolo cigarette and dey share 'em. One time I saw Cummings brother guys smoke dat.

Da mokes tell, "Eh, look da guy. He nuts yeah? Eh, go call 'em. Eh paperboy. Eh paperboy, where you get so nice hat? I like borrow. Ay, fit me good yeah? Ho man, perfeck dis. Eh try look, he stay bolo-head. Whoo, whoo, Kojack, man!"

Bobo he only stay try grab back da hat but da mokes only pass 'em around inside da van. Bobo try say, "C'mon, no fuss around," only ting he coming excited and no can understand what he saying.

"What you said lo-lo? You give us your hat? Okay, chee tanks eh?"

Bobo stay crying already and stay hitting da van, da side part. Pang! Pang! his hand stay slapping da outside and inside only get da guys laughing. I tell, "Bobo nevamind dat, dose guys no class. Bobo, come already!" I like go get him but my feet stay stuck by da curb. I no can go inside da street cause my fahdah said no go but I like help Bobo.

177

"Eh, paperboy, paperboy. Here, I like one paper," da driver went call, and Bobo went stop hitting da van and go give 'em one newspaypah.

"No give 'em, Bobo," I went tell him. But he went give 'em and den hold out his hand fo' da money and da driver guy only laugh and drop his cigarette butt inside Bobo's hand.

"Fucka, you fucka," Bobo go swear at him.

Da light went change and Bobo he stay standing in da street yelling, "Fucka," until da cars behind start tooting their horn and da van driver only laugh and spit and den burn rubber away.

Oh yeah, da guy on da other side went throw Bobo's hat out da window. Bobo almost went run into da street without looking fo' grab 'em but I went hold him back and den one car went run 'em over and Bobo he turn and look at me jes' like was on purpose dat I went hold him back for see his hat smash. Bobo tell me fucka, too. I get piss off and I call him dat back but little while more I come sorry I call him dat cause Bobo no can understand dat good.

Bobo no tell me nothing after dat. He go by da wall and scrunch up really small into one ball, you know, and only cry. He cry so hard he begin to hit his head on da wall . . . his head bang da wall, but no sore fo' him. But I get mad 'cause jes' like my fault but not my fault, you know, and I know dat but I get mad at him anyway.

"Shaddup already," I tell him, but he no hear nutting. "Shaddup, I tell you! You no mo ear? You lo-lo? Wassamattah wit' you? Mo' bettah send you Linekona School, da school fo' da mental guys!" And more he cry and more I get mad.

Good ting had one car went stop, green light and all, and toot his horn fo' one paypah. I tell, "Go Bobo, you go . . . ass Mistah Kim . . . he give big tip everytime." But Bobo still cry, so I go.

"Wassamattah wit' Bobo," he ask me. I tell some mokes went swipe his hat and tease him den dey went throw 'em away and da car run over 'em and den he cry and hit his head. He no can stop.

"Why no pick 'em up from da street?" Mistah Kim go tell me. "Ass da one in front da car?" I never tink of dat so I go get 'em. Look kinda had-it but still can wear.

"Eh, what about my paper?" Mistah Kim tell me.

"Oh, sorry eh."

178

"Here, you share dis wit' Bobo, go buy something nice."
And he gimme one dollah tip.

I went by Bobo and try give him da dollar but he only push my hand away and cry and hit his head mo' hard. So I went put da one dollar undaneath da rock dat stay holding down his paypahs. I went put da hat by his paypahs too. I went go back by da street and little while more, Bobo go real quick by his paypahs and grab da hat and put da one dollah inside his pocket and den go back by da wall. He nevah hit his head no more but he still went cry little bit. I knew bumbye would be pau.

So me and Bobo stay fren's again. He still wear his hat, smash and all and sometimes I go sell in da street wit' him (I no listen to my fahdah *all* da time). Good fun. We only laugh when da cars come close. Sometimes when he tink I not looking, he take da hat off and try fo' make da smash part mo' smooth. You know, he try bend da iron part back so no mo' wrinkles on top. Sometimes I tink though, what going happen to Bobo. He been selling paypahs long time . . . before me and still going sell bumbye even after I quit (when I get my skateboard and my college edja-kay-shen). I hope Bobo be all right. He gotta have somebody take care him. Maybe mama make him one 'nudda beer can hat . . . I go ask her.

II

One time after dat, one small kid went come by us when we was selling paypahs. He went put one box down by our newspaper pile, right next, and den he went pull out sweetbreads. Da stupid kid try carry four sweetbreads all one time. One under one arm, one under da uddah arm and one inside each hand. Da stuffs stay slipping down so he go smash 'em wit' his elbows. Cheez, I wouldn't buy da smash-up kine bread, man, besides must get all his B.O. on top. He go come by us and tell, "You like buy sweetbread?"

Bobo's eyes came big. He like sweetbread, you know. He jes' look. I stay tinking he better wipe his mouth, look like he stay drooling over da sweetbreads. Mo' worse, da small kid tink Bobo like buy.

I ask da kid, "What you selling fo'?"

179

"Fo' school, fo' raise money fo' go feel' trips and fo' see feel-ums."

"Fo' what?"

"Fo' go feel' treeps, you know, escursions. And fo' see feel-ums, movies."

I went tell him, "I gotta sell carnaval scripts fo' my school too. You like buy?" I nevah sell nutting yet. Everybody in my class went sell ten dollahs worth at least. Even da smash-face, Shirley, went sell almost two hundred dollahs worth. She tink she hot. I tink her fahdah went sell 'em for her. But I nevah sell nutting so far. So I went tell da kid, "I buy one sweetbread if you buy my carnaval scripts."

"I like see your scripts," da kid went tell me.

I went show him my pack.

"How much all dis?"

"Ten dollahs."

"You crazy," da kid tell me, "sweetbread only dollah half!"

Bobo came for look at the scripts too. He tell, "I know what dat. Dat carnaval scripts, yeah? Good yeah, carnaval. Get anykine, yeah? Good, yeah?"

"Yeah. We go carnaval, Bobo. You go ask your fahdah fo' let you have some money fo' buy scripts from me and I go ask my fahdah too. Den Saturday after pau newspaper, we go see if my fahdah take us." I went make 'em sound real good so da small kid would like go too and buy scripts from me. Me and Bobo was jes' having good fun talking about carnaval stuff. Da kid was jes' looking at us, his head going back and forth, wishing he could go wit' us. Make him jealous, boy. But he only went by the cars fo' try sell his smash sweetbreads. I no tink anybody went buy.

Bobo, he only stay talk about going carnaval. He really thought he was going go already. I was jes' trying fo' get da small kid fo' buy some script but I no mind going carnaval too. So I was real nice to my fahdah and tole him I would help him wash and polish da car if he buy da scripts from me and take me carnaval. I tole him dat Bobo was going ask his fahdah if he can go carnaval too. Daddy just rough up my hair and tell, "Shoot. Wash and polish, eh?"

Saturday, we went pick up Bobo, he was waiting outside his house. He said he no like go carnaval, dat he raddah go sell newspaypah at da baseball game. "My fahdah gimme da bus-fare. See, twenty five cents fo' go, twenty five fo' come back."

Bobo said dat and den he just stand by da car scraping da dirt with his rubber shoes. My fahdah look at Bobo, den at da apartment building where his house stay. He look long time den he breathe long and sad and tell, "C'mon Bobo. You come carnaval wit' us. You help Junior wash and polish my car bumbye and I treat you to carnaval."

Bobo came all happy. He smile up. When Bobo smile he make everybody like smile 'cause he stay so happy.

Had anykine, man, at da carnaval: plenny people, plenny rides, plenny food booths. My fahdah took us cruising all around da carnaval first. He tole us which ones we could ride (some was too dangerous he said, so no can). And he tole us which games was gyp (too hard fo' win, he said). And den he said he wait for us at da Beer Garden. No stay one real garden, just get folding chairs and one man stay selling beer. He said dat me and Bobo go half half da scripts.

Me and Bobo went cruise da carnaval again fo' decide what one we was going play and fo' see which ones had da good prizes. Bobo everytime wanted to go back watch da guys chrowing baseball, but dat was da one my fahdah said was too hard fo' win. Had some guys chrowing, trying for win one big doll. Dey was making big noise and never let anybody else play 'cause everytime dey lose, dey pay again for play somemore. Da guys could chrow real hard but fo' win you gotta knock down six heavy iron stuffs, dey call 'em milkbottles. Dey jes' like bowling pins dat stay stack on top each other. Get three on da bottom, den two on top and den one on top. Dey must be real heavy 'cause even if you crack 'em square, dey no all fall down sometimes. Da guy dat was chrowing was getting little bit piss off 'cause he couldn't get 'em all. After he chrow his three balls, he tell, "Sucka, gimme tree more, I get 'em this time." I stay getting tired watch da guy but Bobo no like go yet. So I had to stay and watch da guy somemore wit' him. Anykine stuff I went watch . . . how he hold da ball, how he aim, how he chrow da ball. He had one tattoo on da back of his uddah hand. I seen dat before someplace, three daggers tattoo. Pretty soon I went remember dat dat was da mokes dat went steal Bobo's hat. I went pull Bobo and tell, "We go Bobo, dry ovah here already. We go eat something."

"Play dis. Play dis," Bobo tell me.

"Nah, Bobo. Junk dis, we go."

One nudda guy was trying fo' chrow now but da guy wit'

da tattoo was razzing him up. "You plug, you chrow like one panty. You call dat good? C'mon. You no can chrow bettah den me. Give up. Me next, me next." And he went try give da worker somemore scripts for play again, but Bobo went already give da worker scripts for play next so da worker told da moke dat he had to wait until Bobo was pau.

Bobo no can chrow hard. I know 'cause sometimes we play chrow-chrow with tennis ball but he jes' like me, not so hot. Only can chrow soft. So Bobo went try chrow but he only could knock down one bottle with his three balls. After Bobo went chrow da three balls, da moke guy went try pay again but da worker told him, "Dis guy went pay fo' three dollahs worth." I never know dat and I went tell, "Bobo, why you waste your money. We go already." But Bobo hard head. He only like stay and chrow da balls. Da moke guy get more piss off 'cause Bobo take his time and he only chrow soft.

"Yeah, why you waste your money. Pau already," he told Bobo. I no tink da moke went recognize Bobo. Could tell he was getting piss off though 'cause he had to wait and watch Bobo chrow.

Me, I went give up. I no can change Bobo's mind so I jes' watch him chrow. Jes' like he no aim. He jes' chrow as hard as he can, but still yet soft. Da most he ever hit down was tree, I think. And he take long time watch da worker guy stack up da bottles. I thought he was jes' slow but little while more, I catch on. Bobo sly, da bugga. He stay watching for when da worker line up da bottom row of bottles little bit crooked so dat get more space between da bottles on one side. Den he aim for da space 'cause da bottle fall down more easy on dat side. Bobo he pretty smart. Couple times when Bobo went crack da right space, everything except one went fall down. But Bobo went miss with da other two balls and couldn't hit da last one down. I was figuring dat my fahdah was right, dis game was gyp . . . no can win.

Bobo had his last chance for chrow and he went crack da space right-on again. Only had one bottle left and he had two more chances. He was sweating real plenny and he nevah care about nothing but da last bottle. He went warm up real plenny and make plenny form and chrow real hard but da bugga went crooked and never even come close. He only had one left and da moke went tell him, "You like me chrow 'em for you. I can crack 'em you know." Bobo jes' went look at da moke and I thought he almost was going give 'em his last ball. Almost I went tell, "Bobo no give 'em, das da guy!" But funny, I never say nutting. Bobo finally went say, "Nah," and wipe his mouth with da back of his hand and chrow real fast without warming up. I seen da ball hit da table right in front of the bottle and bounce off and knock da last bottle down. He went win. Bobo went win! "Bobo you went win!" I went yell. And Bobo was jes' smiling and clapping his hands.

Even before da worker went ask him, Bobo went point to the biggest stuffed tiger hanging from da string.

"I like dat one," Bobo went tell real slow and real clear. Was gold wit' black stripes and was almost as big as me. Was one happy tigah, had big smile.

Bobo went hug da tiger and went show 'em off to me and he let me hold 'em little while. Bobo wanted to show my fahdah right away so we went to da beer garden place and my fahdah went listen to me tell da story about how Bobo went win da tiger. Bobo never even like leave da tiger wit' my fahdah for hold so he went carry 'em all around wit' him, even on da rides. And everybody went look at him. I bet dey was wondering how he went win 'em.

Going home, Bobo was talking anykine. Real fast. I couldn't even understand da stuff he was talking about. Only when we came by his house, he went stop. My fahdah came quiet too and went ask him, "You like me talk to your fahdah and explain dat I took you carnaval?" Bobo only went shake his head. He went get out of da car and tell, "Tanks," to my fahdah and den he went push da tiger back inside da car window.

"Fo' you mama. I win 'em fo' you mama. You give to her?"

"You sure, Bobo?" I went tell him. But he jes' keep telling, "Fo' you mama."

My fahdah went start da car and I went say "tanks" to Bobo. Bobo was waving to us from da sidewalk, smiling up. We was smiling up too.

_____ *Darrell H.Y. Lum*

Primo Doesn't Take Back
Bottles Anymore _____

"Four cases, that's one dollar and seventy-six cents, Rosa."
Harry of Receiving Bottle Empties wrote up the ticket for Rosa
and made change from the register. Rosa K. dropped his load
of empty Primo bottles on the counter and figured out his
profit. If he walked home he could save a quarter busfare. Rosa
used to list his occupation as "construction laborer" whenever
he got picked up by some rookie cop for being a "suspicious
person" rummaging through garbage cans. But now that he
only collected empties to turn in at the brewery, he figured
himself to be a "collector." It was forty cents a case, even more
for the bigger bottles.

"Tanks eh, I see you," Rosa said and shuffled out of the
brewery, the money carefully folded into his handkerchief and
jammed into his front pocket. He hoped that Harry wouldn't
check the last case until he left. It was short three bottles. The
three unbroken ones he should have gotten if that old lady
hadn't caught him.

Harry checked the cases and smiled as he filled the empty
slots in Rosa's last case with some extra bottles he always
saved for Rosa. He remembered the first time Rosa had come
in all shabby and ragged, a pair of tattered jeans buttoned
underneath his pot belly and a silken aloha shirt with hula
girls and Diamond Head and "Honolulu-Paradise" written all
over it.

"Sorry man, read the sign, can't refund any amount less
than three dollars. Come back when you have seven cases,"
Harry had said.

"Look Bruddah, I no can carry all dis back home, I nevah
know about the rules. C'mon give a guy a break. As means I
no mo' busfare home."

"Okay, look I'll cash in your three cases now and add 'em
to the next guy's load. But just this once. My boss finds out
and I'm in trouble, you understand?"

Rosa had smiled and had given him a little thumb and
pinkie wave. "Thanks eh," he had said. Since then Rosa had
been coming in every week with his pickings in his arms,
catching the bus to the brewery and walking home to save the
quarter.

Sometimes he brought something for Harry, some seaweed, a small bass, a little opihi in a smelly shopping bag along with his empties.

We used to have kick haole ass day in school. One time this one kid, little ass buggah with one big mouth, his fahdah was one manager of someplace or something, he went come inside the bathroom, cocky and smart mouth, went push Willy so I went kick the shit out of him. Nothing on the face so no can see the marks, just in the balls. The little shit started cry. He say, "I going tell my father . . . I going tell my father . . ." So I tole him, "Look boo, you tell your fahdah and you going get somemore." Yeah, we used to think we was big stuff. Go smoke in front the teacher for see what she do. She no can do nothing. One time she call my muddah though, and my fahdah beat me up bad. He tell I gotta get one education. I nevah go school for one week. The social worker had to take me hospital. Willy, he just one mahu. The kids used to tease me that my bruddah one tilly, but I take care of them. Willy, he wanna be one mahu, he be one mahu, as okay. One time Willy and his frens go make one mahu day in school, come all dress up. Whooo, make the girls jealous.

Rosa peered through his dark glasses out at the large metal garbage bin of the apartment building. He had to squint because the flimsy lenses did little to cut the glare. He had found them outside the theatre about two months ago when there was a 3-D movie. It was a good pair with plastic frames and looked like regular sunglasses except for the small print at the top of the frame which said, "For 3-D Panavision only. Do not use as sunglasses." The garbage bins looked a funny shade of white, the glasses cancelling the green paint of the metal. Large bins rarely held empties because only places like business offices and schools used them. But this was an apartment building and it was sure to have at least a case or two of empties. If someone asked him he could always say that he lost something in the bin. Rosa figured that apartment building garbage was surely anybody's. No one could tell whose garbage was whose. His search yielded a case of Miller, two six-packs of Schlitz, and only one six-pack of Primo. "Fucking haoles only drink shit," he muttered and stuffed the Primos into his shopping bag.

185

I used to think all the haoles look at me funny so I kick their asses and they still look at me funny. I wasn't that bad though. When I make "search take" on one guy, I everytime give 'em back busfare. Bumbye they gotta call their fahdah for come pick them up after school.

The entry on the police record said, "Assault and Battery, Petty Theft, Item—Bottles, empty, six dozen; Bottles, unopened, approximately one dozen; Location—Jay's Bar and Grill, suspect apprehended boarding Municipal bus (Aala Park) 10:55 P.M., owner James Nakayama reported prowler in back of premises, scuffle ensued; Damage—Two dozen empty bottles, broken, one dozen unopened Primo brand beer, approximate cost $3.50; Previous Record—Rosario Kamahele, A & B, Central Intermediate School, enrolled student, grade 9, 17 years old, charged as adult on request of school authorities and referred to Department of Social Services; Present Occupation—Unemployed laborer." The sergeant at the desk had said that he was an unemployed laborer when Rosa was brought in and booked. The lady at the welfare office had also told him that after he got kicked out of the ninth grade of his third and final school. He was just a kid then, a smart ass kid who beat up on anybody who didn't pay protection money. He was the bull of the school and ruler of the second floor lavatory. Some haole kid had told his father and the judge had sent him away to the Boy's Home for three months. When he got out he joined the union and was a laborer. He almost became a carpenter's apprentice when he and half the crew got laid off. That was when he started collecting bottles. For awhile the money from empties was all he had to live on until the welfare came.

After I come out of the Home, the judge tell me I join the army or go work, 'cause I too old for go back ninth grade. The judge he say I can go night school with older people so I no beat up people no more and then he assign me one social worker, one haole lady, Miss Pate, for check up on me. I tell Miss Pate that I like live with Willy, that I gotta take care Willy. She say I no can, that mahus, that home-saxtuals like live with their own kind. I tell her, ". . . but that my bruddah." She tell I gotta get one healthy family relationship and atta-tude. So Miss Pate she find me one place with one Portagee family and man, they thought I was one servant. Rosa do this, Rosa do that or we going tell the social worker for cut your check down. So one time I get fed up and I say, "Shove it," and I split.

The sticky smell of stale beer at the brewery always made Rosa thirst for a "tall, cool one." A dollar seventy-six was enough for a six-pack and still leave extra for busfare. Almazon, the Filipino bookie expected his ten bucks today. Almazon sold everything from lucky number chances to a "social worker home," a place where guys like Rosa could claim legal residence in a respectable home for the social worker's visits. Ten bucks a month to Almazon kept the family quiet.

The one time that I was scared for beef one haole after school was with this six-foot guy from California. He was in the smart class. I went tell one of my guys for let him know I wanted for see him, to tell him who was the big shit around Central. He was one show off too, that guy. He had his driver's permit and drove one car to school everyday. The day I was supposed to beef 'em I went skip class and went send Willy for steal some booze for me. Willy come back with Mama's bourbon inside one empty jelly bottle. Willy say the guys was talking that the haole's fahdah was a Marine. I tell, "So what," and drink the liquor down real fast and started for punch the wall of the lav for practice. The wall was hollow cement tiles and the pipes inside 'em went make one "tonk" everytime I punch the wall. I thought of all the haoles in the whole world and I went punch the wall somemore. Willy, he come scared and say something about Mama and I say to him, "Fucking mahu!" and Willy come real quiet. Ass the first time I call Willy that and he come real quiet. That make me more piss off and I punch the wall somemore until my hand it start for bleed and I no can feel no sore but I still punch the wall and then the teacher come and tell me for stop and I no can stop and my hand it keep making one fist and keep going and then I cry and Willy, he cry too, but Willy cry easy. I no cry, I no supposed to cry, but I cry. And then the teacher he take me to the dispensary and I try punch the nurse and get blood on top her nurse dress . . . They say that the haole was looking for me after school for beef me and I wasn't there . . .

Rosa got off the bus with a stinking paper sack and one case of empties under his arm. He had spent most of the week picking opihi from the rocks at low tide and only had had enough time to collect one case of empties. But he had a mayonnaise jar of opihi to give to Harry.

Workmen were painting over the old red brick of the brewery when Rosa shuffled up with his load. The "Receiving Bottle Empties" sign was painted over and the old smells were replaced by those of fresh paint and turpentine. Harry had acted brusquely last week and had mumbled something about bums who trade in bottles below the minimum refund amount and get employees in trouble and new management and aluminum cans but Rosa had just smiled and walked out quickly because his cases were short again.

One of the painters noticed his empties and said, "Eh man, you can't bring back empties anymore. The new man doesn't want them. Ought to just throw them away."

Rosa felt an old rage and the tight clenching of his fists, the punching feeling. He turned to the painter and said, "Why you paint over the sign, why you no want my bottles, why you do that, I bring something for Harry today, and you do that, where Harry my fren', Harry my fren' he no do that . . ."

The painter shook his head and said, "Not me fella, why don't you talk to the boss." He turned and left. Rosa walked around in little circles, clenching and unclenching his fists, finally stopping before the blanked-out sign. A brush and paint can sat on the ground before him. Rosa grabbed the brush and in several quick motions wrote "F-O-C-K" on the sign. The paint was the same color as the sign but the work was visible as the sun glistened off the dripping letters. Rosa crossed the street and sat at the bus stop watching his word dry in the afternoon heat. The painter never came back and the word disappeared as the sun dried the glistenings and the streaks melted away.

Darrell H.Y. Lum

Paint

Sometimes I feel mean. I like go bust something. Some guys like bust car antennas but I only like go spray paint. I donno, I feel mean and I feel good at da same time, you know. It bad, but still yet I like spray paint. I donno why. Make me feel mean when I stay painting but feel like I stay doing someting. Someting big you know, so dat I stay big, too. I no paint swear words la dat. I paint my name and make um fancy wit curlicues undahneat. Sometimes I paint my babe's name but I no like do dat too much, bumbye everybody know, you know. Sometimes I paint one surf pickcha. One real tubular wave with one guy jes making it . . . cranking through, you know.

When you paint on one new wall, j'like you stay da first one in da world fo spray paint. Even if you know get someting undahneat dat you went paint before, when da wall stay new, I mean, when dey jes paint up da wall fo cover da old spray paint, j'like, stay da first time you painting. You can feel da spray paint, cool on your hand. You can smell da spray, sting your nose but sweet, j'like. I no sniff, you stupid if you sniff, bumbye you come all stoned and you no can spray good. But j'like it make you feel big. Make you feel good dat your name stay ovah dere big. Like you stay *somebody*.

Coco. Ass my name. "Coco '84" is what I write. I no write um plain, I make um nice, you know. Fat lettahs. Outline um. Wit sparkles. Da kine dat you can make wit white or silvah paint, like one cross or one star. From far, j'like your name stay shiny. I stay undah da freeway aftah school fo watch my wall. I watch um from across da street by da school parking lot. Everybody who pass look at my wall everyday. I try put someting new everytime so get someting new fo everybody to see. Only little bit at a time, like somemore lines on da wave or one different color outline on my name, stuff la dat. Jes about everybody look at my wall, even if dey pass um everyday, dey look. Sometimes when get some other guys by me aftah school I no can paint new stuff but da people dat pass still yet try look fo figgah out what stay new.

Aftah school I gotta wait fo my muddah pau work pick me up. Sometimes I stay by da guys when dey no mo baseball practice la dat but most times I stay by myself. Everyday gotta plan how you going paint. When you paint, you gotta plan um good. You gotta be fast. You gotta know what you going do. And you cannot get nabbed. How many times I almost got nabbed, man.

One time somebody went put "Rockerz Rule" on my wall. Was anykine way. Wasn't nice. Had some guys hanging around da wall and I went ask dem, "You went make dat?"

"So what if we did?" one of da guys went tell me. I told dem, "Eh I know da guy Coco, and he going bust your head if he find out you went spray on his wall. He big you know, Coco."

Dey went look around first fo see if I had backers. Since nevah have nobody, dey went ack like dey was tough. But finally dey went go away. Deh nevah spray nutting else except fo dis one punk kid went spray and walk. Had one crooked black line all da way across my wall. I would've beefed um but I nevah like. I would've given um lickins. I could've taken um.

Nobody know I spray paint. Nobody even know I stay Coco. If they knew, they would say, "Naht, dass not you. I heard Coco stay one big guy. You too runt fo be Coco." Funny yeah, but dass me. Ass me, Coco. One time I going paint one big mural and everybody going know ass me. Would be good if you no need paint fast and hide when somebody come. Could make um nice and people would even buy da paint for me. I would make da whole wall wit spray. I would paint faces, my face ovah and ovah and I would make um look mean and tough. And I would look *bad* and I would be feeling good. I would make sparkles and you could see dem shining in my eyes. I would use silvah and some black paint. People would tink, "Who did dat nice one." Dey wouldn't paint um ovah. Dey would buy me paint. Dey would gimme money for paint da walls all ovah da place. Wouldn't need to do work in school. Da teacha would gimme one spray can, not brush and paypah, la dat. Junk, when you paint in school. Gotta do certain tings, certain way. No can be big. No mo feeling. Ass why spray paint mo bettah. Make you feel mean. And bad. And good.

One time had one lady came by da wall. She wasn't one teacha or nutting cause she had long hair and had jeans and tee-shirt la dat. I had to hide my spray can when I seen her coming. I nevah like her bust me. But you know what, she had her own spray can and went look right at me den she went spray on my wall:

190

REVOLUTION FOR THE 80'S
MAY DAY.

Den she went little mo down and went spray out my "Coco '84" and went put, "WORLD WITHOUT IMPERIALISM, NO IMPERIALIST WARS," right ovah my surf pickcha.

When she was pau she went look at me and say, "You know what dat means?"

"No," I told her.

"Dat means we gotta tell people to fight da government. Gotta get da people together and tell da governments not to have wars. Gotta give da poor people money and food and power la dat."

"Oh," I said, "But lady, why you went spray um ovah da wall? You nevah have to spray um ovah Coco's stuff. You could've put um on da top or on da side or write smaller. Look how you went jam up my pickcha, I mean Coco's pickcha."

"Sorry," she went tell kinda sassy.

"Why you gotta paint da kine stuff?"

"Cause I like. So what, kid." She was coming little bit piss off.

So aftah she went go away, I went try fix my wall up. But she went use red. Hard to cover, red. She nevah have to put um right ovah my writing. I wanted dem fo come paint da whole wall awreatdy, erase um so dat could start ovah. I jes went get my can spray and I went stand in front da Lady's words. I was feeling mean. Not good kine, jes mean. I went write, "LADY— HATE YOU," not nice with fat lettahs or sparkles but jes any-kine way. I nevah care. Was ugly, jes like her's one.

When my muddah came pick me up, I seen her reading da wall. "Who went do dat?" she went ask me. I told her one lady with long hair and tee-shirt. I went ask her who dat kine lady was and she went say, "Dat Commanists dat. Not Americans. Hippies," she told me. "Dey good fo nuttings." I was looking out da window when we went drive away. Couldn't even see "Coco" anymore.

I couldn't tink about anyting except what I was going paint ovah da hippie lady's words. First I thought I could paint somemore surf pictures but I went check my colors and I fig-gahed would be too hard fo cover da words. Da lady, she went write big. I thought I could do "Coco '84" mo big but still couldn't cover da lady's words. Would use up all my paint.

Aftah school da next day, I went to my wall. Could see da lady's words from far away. I jes went look at her spray paint words. Ass all was, jes words. Ugly words dat nobody like read. Not like mines, not nice wit sparkles la dat or curlicules or one pickcha of one surfah in da tube. Jes words . . . anykine words. Everybody going say, "Whoo da ugly. Who did dat?" What if dey tink was me? Betchu da painter guys going come paint da wall fast. J'like the time somebody else went write "Sakai Sucks" and everybody knew dey was talking about Mr. Sakai, da principal. Dey came right away fo paint da wall dat time.

Nevah feel good anymore fo look at my wall. Wasn't mine anymore. Wasn't Coco's. Wasn't even da hippie lady's cause she no care. Was nobody's.

And den da next day had posters pasted up on da wall. Was somemore stuff about May Day and had one pickcha of one guy holding up his fist. Dey nevah only put one, but dey went line um up. Had maybe six or seven or eight all line up. Cover everyting: my surf pickcha, my name, even my "hate you" words. And dey went paste um on good. Dey went use someting dat stick real good to da cement and den dey even put paste on da top so dat da ting was stuck extra good. No can peel um off. Hardly can scrape um even. Only little bit. I seen da hippie lady aftah school looking at da posters.

"You went do dat?"

"What you tink?" she went tell me.

"I donno. You went do um, eh?"

"So."

"You shouldn't have done dat. Coco going come piss off, you know. Dis his wall. Maybe he might even call da cops or someting."

"Who's dat, Coco? Dat you? Betchu da guy no stay. If he so big, how come he no come talk to me himself? From now on dis is everybody's wall. Not only Coco can paint on dis wall. Anybody can paint. Me. You. Anybody."

She jes went keep on talking, "Eh, you no need be scared of Coco. He ain't so tough. What he going do to you?"

"Yeah but, not supposed to be writing on da walls . . ."

"Who said? Da government? Coco? Coco went paint first. He went li-bah-rate dis wall first time. But now he no can hog um. Dis wall is fo everybody I tell you. Uddahwise he stay making up anykine rules. J'like one nudda government."

"Hah?"

"Howcome you gotta watch dis wall for Coco? You jes being Coco's stooge you know. You shouldn't have to be scared of Coco. Dat's jes like da people who scared of da government. I mean you no need be oh-press by somebody else . . ."

Couldn't tell what she was saying cause one truck was going on da freeway and from far could hear one police siren. Da lady went stop talking and we went look up at da freeway listen to da siren coming closer. Went pass.

I jes told her, "No paint on top Coco's wall, eh. Or else you going be in trouble. Coco, he big, you know. He *somebody* you know." She nevah say nutting. She jes went walk away but I was still yet telling her anykine stuff, "You no can jes cover up my wall la dat. Was *my* surfah. Was *my* wave. Was *my* name! I hate you hippie lady!"

I went get my can spray and I jes started for paint one face right ovah her words. I donno who's face. Jes one face. Was black and red. Had plenny lines in da face. Was one mean and sad face. I jes went keep on adding lines to da face and came mo black and mo black until was almost like one popolo but wasn't. Jes was one face wit plenny lines on um. Da paint went run out when I was fixing up da cheek. Went drip. I couldn't finish um. I went cross da street and watch my face.

Had some guys in one truck, regular fix-da-road guys, went come and look at da posters. Dey took out anykine scrapers and some real strong kine thinner fo take da posters off.

"Awright," I went tell dem.

"Damn kids do anykine yeah," one guy went tell me.

"Naht, wasn't kids. Was da hippie lady." I went tell um.

"You know who was?"

"Yeah, da hippie lady who come around here sometimes."

"You not da one, eh?" da man went ask me.

"Nah, but da guy Coco spray."

"Coco spray dis kine words?" da man was pointing to da word "hate" between da posters. Could only see "lady" and "hate" left.

"Nah he make nice kine stuff. He no paint ugly stuff."

Dey went clean off all da posters and started to paint da wall.

"What fo you paint da wall awready. Da hippie lady only going paint um again? What fo?"

"At least going look nice fo little while," da boss guy told me.

"Eh, try look dis face," one of da guys went point to my pickcha wit his roller. "Not bad yeah? Look almost like somebody crying wit dis red drip ovah here. You know who went do this one? Pretty good artist. Too bad gotta cover um up."

I jes went turn around. I started for cry. I donno how come . . .

Darrell H.Y. Lum

Daybreak Over Haleakalā/
Heartbreak Memories
(A Two-Sided Hit)

"Are you asleep?"

A few seconds of silence. Then: "Yeah, You must be too."

Bud and I giggled like two children cheating on nap time. "Well," I said as I sat up in my sleeping bag, "no use lying around." Bud got up too. I gazed at the long row of sleeping bags stretched out across the sands of Hakioawa. It dawned on me at that moment that Bud and I were probably the only souls awake on the island.

He lit a cigarette and offered me one. I didn't smoke but I accepted. It seemed right. As I flicked ashes on the sand the moon appeared. I imagine Bud was watching too. He sat silent.

Crescent-shaped—the heart of it implied—, the moon had risen gloriously over *Haleakalā*, the house of the sun, over on the island of Maui. The ocean, the sand, the rocks along the shore, everything—shimmered.

"So beautiful," Bud said. "S-o-o-o nice."

"Yeah."

"Too bad I gotta piss so-o-o-o *bad!*"

Those words caused me to choke on my smoke. While I tried to suppress both my laughter and my choke-induced cough, to not disturb the others, Bud made gestures that suggested anguish, squeezing his legs together just to soak me for more painful laughter. All the while I thought: here we are on a serious journey to an island that is being bombed to dust and still we are being hopelessly irreverent. *Buddy boy*, I said to myself as the coughs subsided, *you'll never change*.

"Here," I said finally. "Use my flashlight."

"And go alone?"

As we walked slowly in our bare feet toward the kiawe thicket, carefully avoiding thorns, I found myself amused (and, to tell the truth, relieved) that this powerfully built University of Hawaii football player—a first-string linebacker—who was often cited for his ferocity on the playing field was afraid to walk into the bushes alone. But being on the island of Kaho'olawe did that kind of thing to you. Uninhabited as it was supposed to be, you couldn't help but wonder what lurked about.

We had been drawn to the "target island," the smallest in the Hawaiian island chain, on what was called an access trip by a mutual friend, Kaeo Perkins. Like Bud, Kaeo played football for the UH. And he and I shared a journalism class. He was also a member of the Protect Kaho'olawe 'Ohana, or *PKO*, a Hawaiian activist group who had fought the United States Navy in an effort to wrest control of the island from military hands and their alleged abuses—that is, bombing it for target practice. As Bud and I pulled up our shorts (I found I had to piss, too) and started back toward our sleeping bags, I recalled reading somewhere that when Hawaiian activists—nine of them—first landed on Kaho'olawe in 1976, all but two were quickly picked up by the U.S. Coast Guard. The two who stayed were not seen because—ta *da*—they had gone into the thicket to relieve themselves.

Back in our sleeping bags, we lay staring at the predawn sky.

"Ever notice how the unseen part of the moon blends with the sky?" Bud asked.

"Hmmm . . . yeah, no?" I wondered why I never seem to notice the obvious.

Knowing Bud, I also waited for the punch line. Or a discourse on the moon . . . and the stars . . . and black holes and white dwarfs and on and on. Bud was an astronomy major—an unlikely field for a jock—and often let us know. But all he said was, "the reason is . . . ah, forget it. It's just nice." Then he faded to sleep.

I felt like the only person alive in the universe.

I think it was raining that March morning when the subject of Kaho'olawe came up. I had met Bud and Kaeo for coffee at the University of Hawaii's Campus Center cafeteria. It was midterm time, semicidal burnout time, and the three of us— and a disjointed parade of others—retreated to "the caf" between classes for quick coffee fixes. Caf*fiends,* we called ourselves.

"But, like, what's there to see?" Bud was saying as I sat down on a cold seat. "Just one rock."

"Bud, you fricken babozo," Kaeo replies. "It's like any adda island. Like Maui, Kaua'i . . ."

"Oh, yeah, get hotels . . . rent a cars . . ."

"No. Jes' get da bes' beaches. Good surf, even . . . and no mo' traffic."

"Surf? How big?"

"Biggah dan you . . . at least three-to-four."

"Three to four . . . ?" Bud put his head down. "Shit, I just blew a fucking midterm." He looked up, looking somewhat serious for a change. "Three to four, eh? You better be right, Kaeo . . . 'cause I'm going."

Bud Newman was an avid—forget avid—obsessive body surfer, as are many who are raised in the Hawaiian Islands. He was a Hawaii-born haole who had hard blue eyes and dark brown, slightly wavy hair which he always covered with a green UH baseball cap. Bud also had a passion for rock and roll—Stones, Springsteen, Seger, and that's just the ones that start with an "S." Kaeo was part-Hawaiian yet full-on into the culture. Though he spoke English as well as anybody, Kaeo usually opted for his comfy pidgin. He wore wire-rimmed glasses which shaded his green eyes. And though he was as muscular as Bud, he appeared to be leaner.

Kaeo looked at his watch. "Get time fo' one mo' cup." He stood up, pulled Bud's cap off and put it on his head as he went for a refill. Bud swore at him. When he returned he addressed me: "Hey, why you no come too? You should write about da place. You can write."

"Bullshit."

"Just do 'om fo' da course."

"For my *term* paper?"

"Yeah . . . jes' tell da prof you goin' write about what it's like to go to Kaho'olawe." Kaeo held up an invisible frame with his hands. "The Kaho'olawe Experience."

"Why *you* no do dat." There went *my* English.

"I did, twice, last year. In fact," Kaeo now spoke in a whisper, "I used da same papah *twice*. And got A's both times."

"So," Bud interjected, "lend him *that* paper."

"Yeah. Lend me *that* paper."

"Not till I use 'om again."

"Nah, come on, go," Bud said, grabbing my shoulder. "I don't want to be the only new guy there."

"See," Kaeo jumped in. "You gotta come."

But they weren't convincing me. And they gave up trying. Minutes later, when Kaeo was leaving, he told Bud, teasingly: "Da ting about the island, boy, is dat nobody comes back da same."

"Yeah, I notice you comb your hair different now."

Still teasing: "You'll see."

I don't know if I was just bored with school, or just burnt out, or what, but I found myself muttering, "What if I go?"

"What do you mean 'what if,' brah?" Kaeo quickly replied. "I putting yo' name down." I sat back, took a deep breath, then knocked Bud's hat off Kaeo's head.

The access had been scheduled for the last week of March, during the latter part of spring break. Bud and Kaeo would be through with spring practice and I couldn't come up with any excuses to get me out of going. Instead I forced the situation upon myself by promising my journalism prof a paper. Part of the deal was I could miss class the following Monday. The Sunday we'd return would be my birthday, and I figured I'd want, if not need, a day off.

Bud and I had to attend an orientation session—mandatory for first timers. A woman named Susan conducted the session. She was a tall, part-Hawaiian woman whose beauty kind of crept up on you. She was well tanned, with waist-length black hair. And when she smiled she lit up the dingy YWCA room reserved for the occasion.

Sue gave us newcomers the rundown on the kinds of supplies the PKO recommended we bring: collapsible jugs to fill up at Ma'alaea Harbor on Maui—for there is no running water on Kaho'olawe; waterproof flashlights—waterproof everything, if possible; fisherman's tabis—the best footwear to deal with the kiawe thorns as well as to get a grip on things; no booze or pakalolo—leave that stuff on Maui.

Then we had to sign forms releasing the Navy from liability in case any one of us blew up in a million pieces.

After that we viewed some slides that allowed Sue to show as well as explain how the island had been devastated by the bombing once the goats ate up all the vegetation. How the goats got into the picture I didn't know, because I was focusing more on the conveyer of the information. Bud must have been tuned into the same wavelength. When Sue asked if there were any questions, he said, "Are you going?"

"Yes, I am," Sue replied.

"Good," Bud said. "'Cause I need somebody to show me the archaeological sights . . . or whatevers." There were rumblings of laughter all around.

Finally Sue talked about *ukanas*, Hawaiian for luggage, I presumed, and how we would be brought to the island on a boat that literally dropped us off—into the water—fifty to a hundred yards offshore. "Make sure everything you bring is wrapped in at least three layers of garbage bags—the 3 mils thick size—'cause *everything* goes in the water. *Ev*erything . . . cameras and other expensive equipment have been ruined because they got wet."

That night marked the first time Bud and I were together without Kaeo. Kaeo had told us he wouldn't come because, as he put it, "*I* don't need orientation." It turned out interesting. Like a couple of sailors on shore leave before sailing, we took on the city of Honolulu. Cruising in Bud's silver-blue Mazda *RX-7*, we obliterated joints while Bud continuously fed his tape deck with songs he wanted to turn me on to. And in between the short, frenzied drives there were stops at various bars and other night spots for equally frenetic moments and quick beers. Bars and joints, bars and joints . . .

And tapes, Bud had cassette tapes for every reason, season, rhyme and time of day dispersed throughout the car—in the glove compartment, under the seats, on the dashboard, next to the handbrake—Police, Doors, REM, Pink Floyd, Elvis Costello, you name it. We coasted on the H-1 to "San Lorenzo," blitzed down University Avenue to the feverish strains of "Layla," reggaed to Bob Marley on Kalākaua Avenue . . .

During the David Bowie song, "Changes," which we screamed along to *(Ch-ch-ch-changes . . . Turn and face the strange),* when we were wasted to the point that Bud's driving was affected, Bud said, "Change. You think we're gonna change?"

"Shit. Everything changes. We all change . . . even the light. Bud. I said the light. The *light* just changed."

"Oh."

All that evening Bud drove recklessly, often causing me to press imaginary brake pedals from my position in the "death seat," as well as shout Kaeo's favorite line, "Bud, you fricken babozo," around scary turns. But something happened that changed his driving style to slow and deliberate, something immediately sobering.

On the corner of Kapi'olani Boulevard and McCully, there appeared to be a roadbock. Bud quickly slowed down and sprayed his mouth with a breath freshener. As we neared the scene we saw the ambulance . . . police cars . . . a tow truck . . . a badly smashed late model Toyota *Celica.* One man lay on the ground. He was being attended to by medics who were placing him onto a stretcher. Another man, the driver, was pinned in his seat in the upside-down car. People were trying to free him. He wasn't moving. As Bud drove me home I'm sure he was thinking what I was thinking: *It could have been us.*

Suddenly, Kaho'olawe loomed as a much safer place.

Change, we are going to change. That became the big joke. But as I lay awake on Hakioawa sands, gazing at the first rays of sun, it was already clear to me that Bud was not his usual self. He seemed somewhat subdued. Except for our brief episode on the beach earlier, I hadn't heard a wise remark from him since we had landed.

Still I had no doubt that this was temporary—once we had returned to O'ahu. Bud Newman would be his old self again.

The sun had begun to ascend over Haleakalā, hot on the trail of the fading moon. I had thought that the daybreak I had witnessed twenty-four hours earlier at Mā'alaea was breathtaking, with its deep pink and orange glow edging over the verdigris and into the soft blue. But from Kaho'olawe . . . the lights over on Mākena—tiny rectangles of blue and orange—were still visible. Seven miles away it looked like Sleepytown. The ocean, from periphery to periphery, burst into color—rippling waves of orange-lavender melding and bending over into this blue and that blue in gold and silvery light. Those sleeping on the beach began getting up from their refreshing slumbers like clockwork. Or like mercury lamps in reverse. I stood up and stretched too, and began folding my sleeping bag as the others did. After everyone had gone to wash up or to the cooking area I nudged Bud a few times. "Hey, Bud, get up. Beautiful morning."

"Eh, come on . . . I just fell asleep . . ." he turned over. ". . . have mercy."

After nudging him a few more times and listening to his moans, I began my tired trudge away from him to join the others. At one point I turned around and looked at him—the only object on the entire beach—with his cap on, sewed up in his sleeping bag. A funny sight—if it weren't so corpselike.

On the way to the island, Bud kept ribbing Kaeo.

"Okay, get surf . . . and sand . . . but like, ah, what's there to *see?*"

"Lotta tings. Betta dan Disneyland."

"Oh. You mean . . ." Bud snickered. ". . . the damage." Kaeo grabbed him by the shorts and made like he would throw Bud overboard.

The Constellation, a seaworthy craft with a skyworthy name, skipped past Molokini, a crescent-shaped atoll, obverse to the silvery moon above. I began to feel ill from the diesel fumes and sought out a section of the boat where I could find relief. At one point I leaned over the edge to feel the spray and to fill my lungs with fresh air.

"Hey. No jump yet." I recognized the voice. It was Susan.

"Hi." I felt stupid.

"Hi . . . Better in the front, you know. Less sway."

"I'll be all right." Sue smiled, then headed toward the bow. I went back to see where Bud and Kaeo were. I found them in the pilothouse, still going at it.

"Looks like a rock to me," Bud was saying to Kaeo. The "rock" turned out to be a pretty large island.

"I goin' rock you, man," Kaeo replied. Then he turned to me. "No get your papah wet, eh? Lots to write about."

"I forgot my pen."

"I get. Papermate, Bic, Flair, whatevah you like. Black ink, blue ink, red, orange . . ." I covered my ears and backed away. "Green ink, purple . . ."

Minutes later it was "JUMP!"

We had gone from *The Constellation* to the small, maneuverable craft that was called a *zodiac.* I thought it would be easy. *Wrong.* Fifty yards out, we were told to jump, and everything and everyone but the steersman went overboard. We threw the *ukanas,* the plastic water jugs, and ourselves into the water.

So there we were, pushing our luggage in, trying to time our thrusts to flow with the three foot (and surfable) waves. I guess it hit me then that there'd be no room service.

Ashore, we dragged everything and everyone in.

Slowly we settled in. We unpacked our *ukanas,* reserved our camping spots, hung out to dry the things that, in spite of the garbage bag wrappings, still got wet. Wet clothes. Wet paperbacks. We ate some of Kaeo's soggy cookies . . .

Instead of exploring the shoreline like the rest of us newcomers, Bud chose to stay at the base camp at Hakioawa with

Kaeo and the regulars who worked either on the traditional *hale*—a planned meeting house; the hula mound—to be used for traditional dancing and other cultural ceremonies; or the garden of indigenous plants. These were all symbols of the Protect Kahoʻolawe ʻOhana's efforts to make valid their claim of a Hawaiian resettlement of the island.

After I got used to the feeling of kiawe thorns accumulating on the underpart of my slippers (I chose not to try the tabis yet), I walked alone along the shore. We had been instructed to not stray inland and to watch out for unfired shells.

When we gathered together early that evening for dinner, we were first treated to a lecture by military personnel, an officer and two Explosive Ordnance Disposal (EOD) experts on the dangers of picking up anything that looked like it could blow up in your face.

Then we gathered to *pule.* We prayed standing in a circle, holding hands. And then we ate. Afterwards, some of the people hit the sack to get a jump on the next day. Others, Kaeo, Bud, and me included, sat or stood around the kiawe wood campfire and told or listened to stories till way past midnight.

It had been Kaeo's suggestion that we "rough it" with about two dozen others on the beach. It sounded like a good idea then, but the next morning . . . the exhaustion I felt made it hard to be cooperative and helpful *ʻohana style,* which was defined by Noa Kekipi, a PKO member, as "if you see dirty dishes, you clean them."

I did manage to clean some dishes—in pots of varying degrees of clean water, and I rinsed pots in the tide pools. I also helped gather kiawe for charcoal fire, hoping at times that somebody would notice and tell me to take a break. But they were all too busy.

Everyone except Bud was up and about, and plans were made to take us newcomers on a hike to the top of the island, a spot called *Moaʻula iki.* Sandwiches and drinks were packed and we were told to be ready at ten a.m. sharp for an all day hike.

Before we left, I tried a few more times to awaken Bud, without success. I even mentioned that Susan was leading us on a tour of the "archaeological sights or whatevers" and it only elicited a "leave me alone" groan. So off we went without him.

Sue and I walked side by side for a good part of the trek. Apparently, she had heard that I was writing an article or something—this "writer" business was getting out of hand—and made the extra effort to sort of "be there" as someone who could explicate things for me along the way.

There was little she needed to say; it was all there to see. Much of the island was stark, barren, just as one would imagine. The red, hard-packed ground—top soil all gone—ran aslant for miles, it seemed, in every direction. The little vegetation we saw was usually found in the gullies, especially those that were washed out into ravines. Occasionally, we'd see in the smoothed surfaces of rocks, and on the polished edges of harsh slopes, like they were clay, an array of colors. This was caused by smooth cylindrical objects scraping against them—objects like missiles.

At one point we came across a dead goat. Killed by gunshot, apparently.

It had been dry and hot for most of the trip, but when we neared the top we were suddenly treated to cool, steady winds. And just as suddenly there were hundreds of trees, a wispy, willowy sort I didn't recognize that leaned almost horizontal in the wind. Sue told me that the Navy had agreed to plant them in compliance with a court action and after some negotiating sessions with the PKO. The Navy had also agreed to eradicate the goat population. The success or failure of the U.S. Navy in these matters was debatable . . . and debated.

At the top we formed a circle and prayed. Then, like pilgrims at the designated shrine after a hard journey, we each wanted our quiet moment and either stood in the *pali* wind or sat on a rock or wandered about. Everyone seemed taken by the view, a lei of islands and mountains—Lana'i, Moloka'i, West Maui Mountains, Haleakalā—that seemed to surround the target island. Like they did, I'm sure, I experienced moments of cutting serenity.

At the topmost point of the island there were two boulder-sized slabs of rock. One lay atop the other. And one could only speculate as to how the gigantic slabs got up there. Sue told those of us standing around that these slabs were a communication device the ancient Hawaiians used to relay messages across the channel. She said that a *kahuna*, a priest, would strike the top slab with a hammerlike object and chant. She pointed to a long, straight crack on the top slab. The crack, she said, pointed a straight line to a similar set-up many miles away on Moloka'i, where the message would be received and sometimes relayed. Other times it would originate there and go the other way. I didn't believe all this . . . but I didn't doubt it either.

As we headed back I felt somewhat moved, yet cautiously distanced in a way that made me feel sure that a Bruce Springsteen concert would more likely change me than Kaho'olawe would.

Still, I couldn't wait to tell Bud what he had missed . . . and what I had seen.

When we returned, I was hit by some riveting news. Noa came up to me. He said Bud had "flipped out" and had to be *Medevac'd* to Maui.

"What do you mean, 'flipped out'?" I bit real hard on the corner of my lower lip.

"He just . . . couldn't handle. He got emotionally distraught."

"What . . . ? How . . . ?"

"I'm not sure what happened. He and Kaeo were together. Kaeo was showing him some *heiaus,* and I guess they came across some petroglyphs, some that even the archaeologists hadn't come across . . . I guess. . . . Man, he must be on some kind of guilt trip."

"He going be all right or what?" None of this made any sense to me. I left a sleeping Bud, and returned to some kind of madness.

"Oh, yeah. He'll be all right." Noa took a deep drag from a cigarette. "He's not the first . . . well, now the Navy's got another excuse for us not coming here . . . too many Hawaiians flipping out. Fucking assholes . . . but how the fuck are we supposed to react?" He took another deep drag then flicked his cigarette down and mashed it into the sand.

"It's ironic, though," I said, "'cause Bud's not Hawaiian . . ."

"What do you mean, he's not Hawaiian?"

"I mean . . . I know he was born here and all that . . ."

Noa looked at me like I was an idiot. "What do you mean he's not Hawaiian?" He must have noticed my confusion. "He *is* . . . Don't let his haole looks fool you."

"You mean Hawaiian . . . as in blood?"

Sarcastically: "No. Sugar." Noa shook his head. I was embarrassed. "His grandfather—hey, you get some blood on your mouth—" I wiped it and sucked on the cut on my lip. "Anyway, his grandfather was pure Hawaiian. Well known. One of the first territorial judges. His great-grandfather, now get this, his great-grandfather was one of the Royalists who tried to put Queen Lili'uokalani back on the throne. He was one of the young ones and he got thrown in jail. . . . Lemme clue you, Bud may not *look* Hawaiian, but . . . now what?"

Noa didn't finished his statement. Someone was yelling for him and he left in mid-sentence.

I wanted to be alone for a bit, to try to digest the sudden strangeness. I walked along the beach and around a rocky bend. Instead of solitude I found Kaeo, sitting alone on a rock, facing the inscrutable surf. When he saw me, he knew I knew. I sat on the same rock, my back to his side.

"Was my fricken fault . . . I wen' lay too much guilt shit on him, telling him he was too haole, li' dat."

"I didn't know he was part-Hawaiian."

"Ev'reday. . . . Da ting is, no show, eh? I nevah know until I went his house one day and saw his mom. When you see her, you can tell." Then Kaeo snickered. "He got pissed off when I wen' ask 'om if he was adopted." I almost laughed, picturing Bud. We both fell silent for a minute.

"You know," Kaeo said, "just today he was telling me all kine tings about himself, about how he got into one classy school like Punahou on one at'letic scholahship, how he wen' fool plenny people by getting heavy into da academics . . . den he started hanging out wit only haoles—he could fit right in, eh? . . . said he figured da only way he was goin' get anywhere was by being full-on haole . . . an' dass true, right?" I nodded to affirm that I got his drift. "Da problem is, kinda hard fo' fo'get tings like eating guava and liliko'i off da tree, picking limu wit grampa, goin' net fishing, eating poi wit da fing-ah—" As Kaeo said this he gestured, dipping his finger into an imaginary bowl. "—an' all dat. Hard fo' get into all da competition shit."

"Yeah," I muttered, realizing at the same time that my right hand covered my forehead. Again we fell silent.

After some long minutes Kaeo said, "Eh. No tell nobody, but, ah, we wen' stumble across . . . some bones."

"Bones?"

"Yeah," he said as I turned to face him. He looked distraught. I thought: *Oh, no. Don't you flip out, too.* "Human bones . . . had part of one skull . . . Buddy wen try pick 'om up . . . wen' sorta crumble in his hands . . . look like da bones was used fo' target practice . . . had lotta shells . . . an' I no mean *sea*shells . . ." Kaeo appeared to be fighting tears. He hid his emerald green irises by closing his eyes. Then he pressed his palms to his forehead. ". . . oh, fu-uck."

After our third silent spell, this time a brief one, Kaeo said with a sudden shift in mood and tone, "So, you writing all dis down o' what?"

"In my head."

He pointed an index finger to my chest. "Yo' heart, brah. Record it in yo' heart. Bettah dan *Memorex.*" Then he got up and said he was heading back to the camp area to haul kiawe and help prepare the evening meal. When he was about thirty feet away he turned around and faced me. "One-fourt' Hawaiian," he said. "Dass plenny, you know."

I headed back slowly, feeling very much alone. At times I stopped and gazed at the distant slopes of Maui's seemingly twin mountains. "Flipped out" could mean anything. I wished Bud could climb up one of those mountains and pound out a message on large boulders, a message declaring his condition. And if I thought he could do it, I'd billygoat up to Kahoʻolawe's barren slopes to receive it. But I seemed to know better. Molokini loomed in the distance. Its name means "many ties," I recalled someone telling someone on the boat. Funny name for a cut off piece of volcanic moon, a perpetually crescent anomaly as "severed from—" as I was at the moment. No ties. Incommunicado. You walk around in a smooth groove for years and years, then one day you *turn and face the strange.*

Along the Hakioawa shoreline up ahead I saw a figure pulling something out of the water. A minute closer I realized it was a woman struggling to pull in what appeared to be a fishing net. I ran to help. The woman turned out to be Sue. Though I began pulling with her she seemed oblivious to my presence. I noticed she had some mean scratches on her arms. Her veins were popping out. The wraparound garment she wore was wet up to her waist.

"I'm not sleeping on the beach again," she said, finally acknowledging my presence after we had dragged the net ashore. "No way. This is our hammock."

Our hammock? By the way she smiled, easy-like, I didn't want to refuse. So this is how they get those makeshift hammocks, I figured. I had seen some of those comfortable looking things set up in the camp area. After we found a suitable spot, a clearing between five strong kiawe trees, I helped Sue set up the netting, tying many ties around the gently bending trees.

That night, after dinner and hours of conversation with whoever was around, conversations that centered on Bud or on me and my "planned article," I found my way to the hammock and climbed in.

Just as I was dozing off, I was shaken awake by Sue climbing on. "Hi," she said. "You sleeping?"

I groaned.

"Still worried about your friend?" I sat up a bit and shrugged my shoulders. "He'll be all right, you know."

"I hope so." Sue sat facing me in the darkness. The lack of light gave her beauty an ethereal tinge. *Oh, my God,* I thought.

"I heard you guys laughing last night . . . on the beach. And I heard you coughing . . . you guys really—"

"So you were awake."

"Couldn't sleep. I tossed and turned all night . . . I saw you guys walking into the bushes . . ."

"Well, when you gotta go . . ."

Our conversation continued that way. Light, insignificant banter. A much needed respite, actually. And while Sue and I first sat opposite each other, our talk—as if by mutual strategy—drew us closer together. Finally we lay side by side.

When I felt it was well past midnight I told her something that had been on my mind: "It's my birthday."

"Oh, wow." She slapped her forehead. "Well," she added, turning toward me, "happy birthday." She kissed me on the cheek.

"It always works. Actually, it's two months away."

"You *ass*hole . . ."

"Nah. It is. It really is . . . really. . . . Gee, I'm a quarter of a century old—"

"That's a funny way of saying you're twenty-five."

"—and a failure."

"Has it been that bad?"

"Not really, I guess. Just uneventful."

"I wouldn't worry. You'll probably live to be a hundred. You've got three whole quarters left."

"Yeah . . . it's kinda sad how the future, the unknown and

unseen stuff is the stuff I look forward to."

"Well, you're a sad optimist. At least *you're* an optimist." Sue did not elaborate. She just snuggled up to me while saying this, placing her head on my chest.

"Funny, I, ah, I thought for some reason that you . . . were married . . . or something." Sue pulled away from me. A momentous silence began.

After an eternity, after my thoughts had again turned to Bud, Sue whispered, "I'm separated."

"From what?" I said, without thinking. "Oh, shit . . . sorry, I'm really slow today." Sue said nothing. She just stared at me. Everytime I looked at her I had to quickly turn away from her penetrating eyes. Finally I was able to return her gaze and whispered, "I love your eyes."

"I love *yours*." Sue again placed her head on my chest. I shifted and let her head rest on my arm. In minutes she was asleep. I lay awake for hours, my mind racing and retracing the day's events: the sleeplessness, Bud's crashing out, the long hike, the news of Bud "flipping out," the conversations with Noa and Kaeo . . . and Sue . . . and her crashing out . . . maybe *that's* how people change on Kaho'olawe—in their sleep. *Invasion of the Body Snatchers* . . . the kiawe does look sort of pod-like in the darkness . . . God, I was tired.

As morning approached and I lay still awake, I found myself stroking Sue's hair and face with my free arm. (The other one was hopelessly numb.) Her face looked impossibly tender in the zodiacal light. *Jesus. If she's been snatched, I want to be snatched, too.*

At daybreak, *The Constellation* rocked gently in the waters a hundred yards offshore. Perhaps crew members brought with them news of Bud's condition.

I was among the first sitting on the shore awaiting our return trip to Maui. I sat next to "Uncle Leo," an elderly PKO member, a *kupuna* whom the largely youthful PKO membership sought out for advice. He chatted endlessly.

"Dey shoulda been here one hour ago. Already da tide coming up. Da surf getting rough. Stupid. Dey no listen. Wheah evrebody, anyway? Still sleeping, I bet . . . mo' bettah I take on da Navy myself . . . I wen' tell one of da EODs, when I was lighting his cigarette, I said, 'Take one good look at dis face. One day you goin' be hunting me down on dis island . . . we friends now, now is a time fo' peace, now we bury the hatchet. Laytah on, we pick up da hatchet, dass Hawaiian style . . .' " Uncle Leo went on and on and I lost track of much of what he said. Then, when the *zodiac* was being steered in, he said, "Damn fools. Dey not watching da waves, dey not going wit da flow. Da damn boat goin' sink." Just then a large wave came and overturned the *zodiac* and its two man crew. Uncle Leo laughed. "Stupid . . . dey no learn."

The *zodiac's* motor wouldn't start. Though we had dragged the inflatable boat ashore and wiped the motor dry, our attempts to render it useful were fruitless. We ended up forming a human chain in the ocean, passing the *ukanas,* the water jugs, and anything else we were handed as those of us in the deeper parts tread water for what seemed like hours. At one point the two EODs who had gone on the hike with us jumped in to join the human chain. *'Ohana style* at its fullest expression, it seemed. Or, rather, *felt.* And this wasn't just something *Hawaiian.*

Bud would've got off on the whole scene. But I guess he had already created quite a scene of his own. He must've put Kaeo, Noa, and the others through a lot of shit. His "flipping out" was unreal to me, surreal, if you will. Like reading a newspaper. Like not being there.

I tried and tried to imagine the scene. Maybe to soak it for all the heart-bending drama it seemed to offer. But I wasn't there. Still, I imagine it this way:

Helicopter landing. Man on stretcher, or walking with the help of others. Loud, whirring noises. FLAP-FLAP-FLAP-FLAP. . . . Men in army fatigues jump out of helicopter and help carry the victim in. Dirt flying, people sheltering their eyes from the dust. An exchange of words, people yelling to be heard above the din. Helicopter takes off. More dirt . . . and dust. Nothing but dirt and dust . . . and a green cap flying around.

That fucking vague. A fucking MASH episode.

I want to remember Bud for the brief—but intense— moments we both shared . . . afterwards. 'Cause this is too fucking vague.

I saw him only three times after . . .

The first time was him standing at the dock at Mā'alaea harbor. Bud had walked out of Maui Memorial Hospital without a release just to see us return. He was all smiles, looking healthy as ever, hugging everyone, helping us unload, downplaying his own little episode.

And of course he was wearing his green cap.

It did seem that Sue disappeared fast that day when we all returned—tired and browner. By the time we were unloading she was gone. I didn't even know *how* she left, if someone had picked her up, or what. She had squeezed my shoulders and kissed me on the cheek as I lay awkwardly comfortable on the front deck of *The Constellation* with the other tired ones and sea sicklies. I did not open my eyes but I knew it was her. Nets of sunlight warmed by skin. Her lips warmed my soul.

Before we left for our plane flight to Honolulu, Noa came up to me. He came to say goodbye, and also to tell me (without my asking) that Sue was going through some bad times, and though she seemed to like me a lot, it would be better on all hearts involved if I kept some distance. I nodded, and before he could leave I asked him if he sometimes thought that what the PKO was trying to accomplish on Kahoʻolawe ever seemed futile to him, the stuff for dreamers. "All the time," he said. "But if you can't dream, forget it, yeah?"

Then there was the time Bud came to meet me many months later, one cold, Mānoa evening. I sat shivering on a bench outside Hamilton Library on the UH campus, trying to warm up my insides with a cup of bad coffee. From afar, I heard—and others heard too, unless they were deaf—someone singing, out of tune and real loud, "BORN . . . in the USA, BORN . . . in the USA. . . ." A Bruce Springsteen song. Then, out of the darkness, Bud appeared, wearing headphones attached to a portable cassette player. A far cry from Kahoʻolawe, an experience I still struggled to convey on paper. Bud probably didn't realize how loud he was singing. Or didn't care. "I'm a COOL ROCKING DADDY in the US of A—."

And he was. Unhindered, unaffected, unassuming . . . *strange. If America can produce guys like this,* I thought, *it can't be all bad.*

Kaeo, Bud, and I—and countless others, I guess—always found ourselves wondering where being Hawaiian started and being American left off and how the two blended and why they mixed like water and oil sometimes. Kaeo continued to re-use term papers while trying to figure it out. Bud had moved to Maui, dropped out of school—Coach Tomey's dreams of a pro football career for him notwithstanding—to deal, perhaps, with his reorganized confusion, and had, in his own words, "just happened to be in Honolulu and thought I'd meet with the writer who can't seem to get over his writer's block and give him some scoops to get him going." By scoops he meant his looking into the Navy's plans to detonate unexploded ordnance at a safe place, the place being Molokini Atoll. Of course it meant destroying the coral reef and thousands of fish but who cares.

This was all serious business to Bud, yet he still expressed things in a way that made it clear that he hadn't lost his comic edge. In other words, he was still crazy.

The last time I sort of saw Bud was when his ashes were being scattered at sea. Not really scattered, rather dropped into the ocean off of Mākena at sunset in a *pu'olo,* a ti-leaf container. It was beautiful. Sue and I returned the next morning at daybreak to find that each ash had become a sparkling light riding the crest of waves forever. We threw all the flowers we had gathered—plumeria, 'ilima, hibiscus, the others I don't know—and red, orange, and yellow bougainvillea leaves . . .

Bud had been killed in an auto accident. Kaeo called to let me know. It was as if he had struck a hammer on a cracked boulder fifty miles away, and the sound tore through the sky in a straight line with the speed of a missile right into my chest. Then exploded.

Bud was on the losing end of a head-on collision. A car full of teenagers, driver reportedly drunk, had swerved onto the wrong side of the road on the lonesome highway between Kīhei and Kahului. These joy riders, like Bud and I had been some eight months earlier, escaped serious injury. Bud did not.

Maybe Bud just wanted me to write. Or maybe he wanted to bring Sue and I together (I had confessed to him my lasting crush), I'll never know. But he surely succeeded.

Right now I am sitting on some pillows in a cabin on the slopes of Kula. This is where Bud lived his last days much like his first, as a Hawaiian. I'm typing on Bud's *Smith-Corona,* which is set on an upside-down cardboard box. Across the room, Sue leafs through his papers, laughing sometimes, smiling with tears in her eyes. I stop sometimes . . . to think . . . to rest, because my back and head hurts. At times I pick up and again skim through the police report, which we got a copy of this morning. The same words always leap out: *Laceration of the heart. Death instantaneous.*

It has been quite a day. The funeral was two days ago. It

was then that I saw Sue for the first time in months. It was a sad time to feel one's heart leap. It was then that I asked Bud's Hawaiian-looking mom if I could write about her son. She did not curse me or slap me across the face. She just stared into my eyes for one long moment. Then she handed me Bud's housekeys.

Today Sue and I tracked down Bud's car, the same Mazda *RX-7*. It had already been taken to a junk yard. *E*verything had been removed from it. There wasn't a cassette tape to be found. No rolled up match covers. No last words on a piece of paper. *Nothing*.

Then Sue and I searched out and found the scene of the accident. There we found skid marks, lots of tiny pieces of broken glass swept to the side of the road, burnt out flares, pieces of tire, thousands of cigarette butts, a Volkswagen hubcap, a flattened out *Gold Leaf* chicken box, a frisbee.

I still searched for something, anything, as Sue walked off in a sort of daze. Many minutes later, she found me, doubled over, clenching a green baseball cap in my hands. She caressed my shoulders from behind, letting her hair fall over my face. Then she whispered in a subdued sort of way, as if thinking out loud: "I see you found your bones."

After Sue had lifted me up and *Medevac'd* me to the rent-a-car, she drove us back to Bud's place. When we were both feeling better we walked around outside in the chilly December air. It was twilight. We gazed up at the sky for the longest time. The moon was three-quarters full. "Ever notice how the unseen part blends with the sky?" I asked her.

"Oh, yeah. Always."

"That's his Hawaiian part."

She turned to me and hugged me . . . real hard. It seems we were both a fraction of our usual selves, and became, in each other's arms, somehow whole. Afterwards, we walked back to the warm cabin.

And I began to write.

Between outpouring of words onto paper, Sue and I talked. A lot. She told me about her divorce, how she "zombied out" afterwards, took long walks, long hikes, cried a lot, tossed and turned in bed for countless sleepless nights, as if her bed were a cold barren beach, thought a few times about me and how I was doing. I told her how I pretty much fucked up in school, never could get my papers done, and wasted a lot of time just thinking about such matters. I told her I often thought of nothing but her. We discussed her cultural confusion, my cultural confusion, and we vented our sanctimonious anger at the greed of men who overfuck *every*thing. Great way to start a romance. At best, like dancing on ashes.

If we did dance, though, it was a gentle rock, back and forth, to imaginary music on 45 that some celestial deejay kept turning over and over. Joy . . . and sorrow. Joy . . . and sorrow . . .

And, as if the world wasn't fucked, we made love.

The Confession _____

> "A sacrament is an outward
> sign, instituted by Christ to
> give grace."
> —The Baltimore Catechism

The call came long and slow as if from a great distance.
Amy put down the pocket knife, scooped up the largest pieces
of wood and stuffed them into the back pocket of her jeans. She
had been shaping a panax branch into a sword. After testing
the tip with her thumb, she folded the knife and brushed all
traces of wood from the concrete surface of the survey tower. A
faint breeze raised gooseflesh on her arms and left faint inden-
tations in the California grass. She hated to leave. The tower
sat like a small fortress on the crest of the hill, and from this
vantage point she had an unbroken view of her surroundings:
the town strung out around the wide curve of the bay, then the
breakwater and the sea, behind her the two great peaks. There
was another reason the place held such an attraction. The
tower was forbidden. "You are never to go there," she had been
warned. Amy's mother often spoke in absolutes, yet these dic-
tums lacked the restrictive nature of other commands and fre-
quently enticed rather than hindered. To disobey mother was
venial. To disobey the church was mortal. The problem was
keeping the two separate, to know one from the other. Venial
and mortal. She had been struggling with such distinctions all
afternoon.

The call came again, sharper, insistent. She turned toward
it. "Coming," she answered to herself. Directly below were the
gabled roofs of the houses on her street. Beyond were cane
field, scrub forest, and because there was no rain, the blue
volcanic hills on the horizon.

She slapped the back pocket that held the knife and, sword
in one hand, climbed down the seven pipe rungs and dropped
lightly to the ground. Reluctantly, she hid the sword at the
base of the tower, then entered the shoulder-high grass. Long
blades whipped her arms and face. A Christmas berry tree
separated wilderness and garden, its branches reaching over a
metal fence into a well-tended back yard. She scaled this last
obstacle quickly, and once on the other side felt safe. Now all

she had to do was skirt the terraced bank, walk the lava wall along the side of the property, and cross the street. When she heard the call again she was turning into her driveway.

She stopped by her father's DeSoto to catch her breath. Bernice, the Portuguese woman who helped around the house, was waiting for her. "I'm home," Amy said.

"Your mother was worried." Bernice put an ample arm around Amy's shoulders. "Where'd you go? You're supposed to be home at five o'clock." When Amy didn't answer, she asked, "What's the matter?"

"Nothing, Bernie. Don't worry."

A somewhat troubled looking Bernice opened the back door, and Amy followed her into the house. A pressure hinge kept the door from slamming, and Amy heard it hiss before she was enveloped in the heat of the kitchen, the smell of food. Her mother was taking a large casserole out of the oven. She put it on top of the stove.

"Where were you?" she asked.

"I was up at Teddy's," Amy said, tugging at her sleeve. "In the eggroom. I came as soon as I heard." She turned to go.

"Amy?"

"Yes." She faced her mother, who regarded her with a raised eyebrow.

"Bernice called you three times."

"I know," said Amy, aware that her lie was surfacing. One more question and it would be out. But she was reprieved.

"Mrs. Freitas," said Bernice, "I have to go. My brother's here. He got the truck today."

"I'm sorry, Bernice. I completely forgot. Go ahead. I'll talk to you in the morning."

"You sure you don't need anything?"

"No. No, everything's fine." She turned to Amy. "Go get cleaned up. You're a mess."

Her father was engrossed in the paper. Sara, Amy's youngest sister, played at his feet. Maybe, thought Amy, she should begin with the sword. Yes, he would like the part about the sword. Then she could tell him why she made it. And he would understand. After all, he too was a soldier of Christ. But before she could begin, her mother called for help from the kitchen. From behind his newspaper, he said, "Go help your mother, OK?"

215

"I have to clean up," she protested, showing her hands.

"Well, then call Lizbet." He lowered the paper, smiled, then added, "For Daddy?"

Amy went quietly into her parents' bedroom. The large windows faced east toward the bay. She closed the blinds and turned on the light. A double bed covered in green was flanked by identical maple nightstands and two old pewter lamps her mother treasured. Three Japanese woodcuts were centered above the headboard. Amy's favorite showed a persimmon tree, the fruit bright orange against the black branches. Near the closet was her mother's uncluttered vanity. The alabaster jars were from Italy—Uncle Tadashi had brought them back after the war—and the tortoise-shell hand mirrors were a gift from Japan.

On the other side of the room was her father's dresser. A familiar assortment of his things lay on the bureau top—blue tin of Old Granger tobacco, pipestand, calabash for loose change, ashtray heaped with matches and discarded pipe cleaners. There was a photograph of her parents on their wedding day, and next to it a small gold-framed picture of Jesus holding open his robe to expose his heart. Amy read the words: "I will bless every place where a picture of my heart shall be exposed and honored." Amy opened the top drawer and laid the knife under a pile of folded handkerchiefs. Then, remembering her father's request, she went down the hall to her sister's room.

"Daddy says help Mother."

Lizbet put down her book. "I bet you went to the tower," she said. "The fence is bent. But I won't tell if you take me. Please Amy?"

Amy ignored her and stormed into the bathroom, slamming the door behind her. The tower was not her sister's place.

The face in the mirror above the sink was neither Asian nor Caucasian. There was little color difference between hair and skin; both were light brown. Her hair, cut severely, fit like a little helmet. The face was long, angular, with high cheek bones, amber eyes, and full lips. Dark brows met faintly over her nose in an almost perpetual frown. It was a face capable of, but not given to, animation. Amy did not like it. "Tiga-eye, tiga-eye," she said to her reflection. Once, for a whole month, she had slept with a clothespin clipped to the end of her nose because her mother said it looked like Grandma Freitas'.

216

Her ministrations done, Amy threw the towel carelessly over the rack. Hesitating, she studied the towel for a moment as if contemplating an opponent. Then, whipping it off and holding it lengthwise, the end under her chin, she folded it and draped it carefully back over the rack.

"Bless us O Lord and these thy gifts which we are about to receive from thy bounty through ChristourLordamen." Amy studied her father over the centerpiece as he helped Sara finish the blessing. "In the name of the Father, Honey, in the name of the Father, yes, and of the Son, no the left first, and of the Holy Ghost. Good girl, Amen."

Meals were an occasion. Amy put her left hand on her lap and picked up her fork with her right. She loved the circle of faces over the white tablecloth, the heavy feel of silver, the ritual of serving. Yet the attention to behavior both irritated and confused her. Surely meals in other homes weren't so formal. At Bernie's they just grabbed and ate, and whoever grabbed more got more. Everybody laughed and talked with their mouths full. At Grandma Kinoshita's house, they ate with chawan and hashi. Uncle Tadashi slouched on his elbows and made noises into his ricebowl, but no one said anything about manners.

She wiped her mouth with her napkin and thought about how to tell him. Maybe she should begin with the hard part first.

"Daddy?" she asked, "can only Catholics go to heaven?"

"What?" he said, a forkful of food suspended between mouth and plate.

She repeated the question.

"Well," he began, putting down his fork. He looked quickly at his wife. "Not necessarily."

"I told Harold Deikman he couldn't go to heaven."

"You did what?" Amy now had his attention.

"Because he's a Protestant, and Father Goodman said Protestants can't go to heaven."

"When did you say that to Harold?" her mother asked. Amy didn't want her mother to take the lead, but there was no way to avoid answering.

"Today."

"At school?"

Amy nodded. The truth was getting out of hand. She looked over at her mother's fingers, which were tapping gently on the edge of the table. Her mother's hands were fine-fingered but large enough to span ten keys on the piano. Amy tried desperately to remember the lesson on lies.

"Amy." Her mother again. "Is there something you're not telling us?"

Amy looked up at her father from under her brows. "I said it in Mrs. Dever's class. She was asking about what church everyone went to, and Harold bragged about his church, about the missionaries starting it and everything. So I told him."

"Right in class? What did Mrs. Dever say? Was she angry?"

Amy took a deep breath, the memory of the humiliation still fresh. "Yes. She said we have freedom of religion in this country. She made a face like this—"

Lizbet giggled, and Amy turned on her. "Shut *up*!"

"Don't speak that way to your sister."

"I'm sorry."

"Well, then what happened?"

"She made a horrible face at me"—Amy glared for a moment at her sister—"and said no church is better. Everyone can go to heaven. Even Buddhists!"

No one said anything.

"But she was wrong," Amy insisted. "I told her sin makes your soul look like a leper to God, all full of sores and no toes or fingers. Only confession can take it away. I was going to say about how good it felt, but she told me to sit down." Amy turned to her father. "We *are* the true church, aren't we Daddy? Daddy, *look* at me."

"Yes," he sighed finally. "We're the true church."

Amy felt a wave of relief.

"But you don't tell people they aren't going to heaven." her mother added.

"Father Goodman said only Catholics can go to heaven. He said it," Amy insisted, repeating the words she had memorized in preparation for her confirmation: "Unless you eat of my flesh you will not have life in you."

"Look," her father began, using the same voice he did with Sara, "Mother's saying you don't tell people that. OK? Not just anybody. You hear Daddy? Keep it to yourself."

Amy thought about that for a moment. Something was wrong. In the book of martyrs they gave her at catechism, Saint Dorothy died on the wheel for speaking the truth. And what about the missionaries and the poor pagan children?

"But if you don't tell them, they might go to hell. Shouldn't you tell them so they can do something about it? I told Harold if he came to our church he wouldn't burn . . ."

"That's enough, you two," said her mother. "Look at me, Amy. You don't have a monopoly on heaven just because you're Catholic. I'm not a Catholic. Grandma and Grandpa aren't Catholic. Are we going to hell, Amy? Is that what they teach you in your church?" Sara began to whimper. "Don't cry, baby. Mommy's not angry."

But her face looked as if it couldn't decide to cry or be angry. Amy had seen that look once before, and as she did at that time, she felt helpless and confused. Her mother had waited and waited, then cried after she got angry. That was when Daddy came home too late for a party. They said things to each other. Angry things. Amy had never seen her mother cry before, and she was mad at Daddy for making Mommy cry. The dress had been so beautiful, black velvet with long, wide sleeves lined with pale, flesh-colored silk. "Here, Amy-chan. Feel this. See? It's silk, Amy-chan."

Her parents looked at each other over the lilies. Lizbet left the table without saying "Excuse me" and no one said anything. Sara climbed down to the floor. Amy watched her mother's hands resume their quiet tapping. "You see?" her mother said into the lilies. "This is what comes of it. I should never have promised. It was a mistake. Sometimes I think I've lost her." She paused for a moment. "What on earth will Mrs. Dever think?"

The light from the street filtered through the venetian blinds, making pale stripes across Amy's bed. She held up her arms, and they were marked too. The brass chain on the ceiling fixture gleamed. Amy crossed her arms over her chest, turned on her side, and pulled her knees up close. The closet door was open, a great black portal that made her shut her eyes and think about something she had heard. About the darkness, the lights far away. The tower on the hill. Wild dogs in the cane fields. Grass against her face. Amy thought about the wind in the California grass. She had not had a chance to tell her father about the sword, about the name she had chosen for herself.

The house creaked and settled. In the next room Lizbet murmured in her sleep. Amy wished she could crawl in bed with her sister. She heard her father's footsteps and waited for the sound of the shower. Her mother had been quiet for the rest of the evening. Amy tried to think of something else.

"Fuck," she whispered, and felt the mystery of the forbidden, the pleasure it gave to say the word. Like the mystery of the mass. "Sanctus, sanctus, sanctus. Lord God of Hosts, Heaven and earth are full of thy glory."

The shower stopped, then a few minutes later her parents' voices reached her. They were arguing. "I'm sorry, Mommy and Daddy," she whispered. Thoughts crowded in on her, rustling like dry leaves. That word! "Oh my God, I'm heartily sorry for having offended thee, my Lord, who art all good and deserving of all my love." Her last prayer ended. "And blessed is the fruit of thy womb." And what was fruit of thy womb? Fuck, she thought sleepily, she would ask Father Goodman. He would know.

Susan Nunes

The Grandmother

She was ninety-five years old, Frances said. That was old, but she could have been one hundred and fifty for all the difference it made to me. I believed Frances. Mrs. Furuisato was the oldest person I had every seen, and in those years we lived on the hill, she never changed. Frances teaches school in Honolulu now. I hear she is married and has two children. Her grandmother is long dead I know. And yet I cannot separate the old woman from the place, and I think I do not want to go back and see the house and the garden because she will not be there.

Nostalgia tends to select. I have never forgotten how she looked that first time, before I met her granddaughter who would be my best friend throughout childhood before the frail bent figure had become a part of the place, a fixture both fascinating and terrifying, like the hothouse with its sweaty flasks or the cooking shed with its strange smells. We had only days before moved into the house on the hill, and because my parents were busy, I was left to wander about on my own, quite forgotten. A row of hibiscus bushes separated our yard from theirs, and I was sitting in this hedge near the cooking shed when the old woman walked past.

First I saw her feet, withered and veined, the color of dried shrimp, with chalk-white nails so long they grew into the flesh. She was wearing grass slippers. Through the hedge I could see her white dress, and moments later I could hear noises coming from the shed. Curious and a little scared, I emerged from my hiding place and on hands and knees crossed the narrow path where she had walked only moments before. Carefully I edged along the side of the hut and peered around the corner. There was no one there.

The room was small, windowless, just three walls and a dirt floor. Along the back walls were several shelves crowded with empty bottles and odd-shaped flasks. Just inside the open front was a small cooking pit lined with stones and covered with wire grating. Next to the pit was a low table and on it a wooden rice pot, a blackened water kettle, and a plate of dried fish with long wooden chopsticks laid across it. The room smelled of old things and charcoal burning.

I don't know how long I stood there, the old woman forgotten, but suddenly I sensed a movement behind me and heard a low laugh. That impression, in the moments before I ran, has never left me completely, and because of the strength of that impression I remain in awe of Frances' grandmother. She comes to me sometimes, even now, just as she was that first day, a shriveled-up shell of a woman standing sideways looking at me, her head sunk low into her narrow shoulders, her veined hands bent as if they clutched at something, her dress falling loosely from the hump on her back, hanging as if there were nothing underneath. And the low laughter.

"Furancesu," she called her granddaughter, enunciating each syllable, "Fu-ra-n-ce-su."

"She's calling you," I said. We were sitting in the old guava tree below the last terrace.

"I know," Frances said nonchalantly. "You want to come?"

We went up toward the cooking shed, and standing at the top of the last rise was Mrs. Furuisato, holding something in her apron. She didn't say a word as we approached but turned into the shed and knelt at the cooking pot. We stood behind her, watching as she emptied the contents of her apron onto a newspaper. They were little knobs, brown and wrinkled. I said to Frances, "They look like fingertips."

"Sweet potatoes," she replied. "She saves them for me. Watch."

The old woman poked at the ashes with her chopsticks and made a hole in the middle of the heap. Under the grey ash the coals glowed for a moment, then faded into pinpoints of orange. She put the potato ends into the hole and covered them with hot ashes.

"It doesn't take long," Frances said. She helped the old woman sit down. We waited there, the three of us, Mrs. Furuisato on her low stool, Frances and I on the floor close to the fire. I could feel the heat against my legs and face. No one said anything, but occasionally the old woman would murmur "Furancesu" and chuckle to herself. Frances watched the heap of coals. I tried not to fidget.

When we could smell the potatoes, Mrs. Furuisato reached for a newspaper, got up from her stool, and squatted before the fire. She thrust the chopsticks through the ashes and searched out the little knobs, now grey and steaming, and put them one by one on the newspaper. When she finished she handed the paper to Frances.

"Come on," said Frances, "let's go down to the tree."

We retraced our steps down the hill, Frances holding the newspaper in front of her with both hands. I looked back, just once, and Mrs. Furuisato was standing in front of the shed at the top of the last rise, old and bent in her faded dress with the white apron. Sitting in the tree, we ate the potatoes. They were sweet and earthy, but what I remember most is the lingering aftertaste of ashes.

Who can remember precisely when wonderment gives way to something else? Mrs. Furuisato was old—I could see that. She was also a grandmother. I knew that because Frances said so. But to me, grandmothers were different creatures. When they smiled their gums didn't show. They were tolerant people, closer to you than your own parents, easy to talk to, easy to love. Mrs. Furuisato *was* Frances' grandmother, and because everyone loved their grandmothers, I reasoned that Frances had to love hers. I had not pondered upon this logic. It was just so. Still, I saw that her face was more skull than flesh, and there was always about her the aura of old wood and charcoal burning.

Frances' family raised orchid hybrids, and their back yard was terraced. Rows of tree fern lined the flat portions. Each trunk had been shorn of its foliage and fixed to the ground. Tied to them with wire and twine were countless orchid cuttings. From some of them sprays of orchids shot out every which way, and we had to be reminded again and again not to run down the cinder paths or we would break something.

Our favorite place was the greenhouse. It stood in a corner of the yard sheltered from the wind and was partially shaded by a wall of giant tree fern. A red cinder path lined with azalea bushes led to an entrance framed with hanging wire baskets of maidenhair. Inside, all was transformed. Sunlight filtered through in patterned stripes, intensifying the greens and purples. The flasks glowed with a light of their own, and their air was laced with the damp smell of tree moss and the heady fragrance of cattleyas. The flasks contained hundreds of orchid seedlings in a water medium. They were particularly vulnerable to disease, so they lived in their sealed containers until they were old enough to be transplanted. I don't know how long it took them to mature and flower, but I believe it was a long, long time.

Frances and I often played there, but sometimes I came

alone, just to be in that otherness. When I left it would be quietly, aware of the cinder beneath my bare feet. It was at such a time that they found me there, Frances and her grandmother. I had not heard them approach, so the old woman's low laugh startled me. She brushed gently past, and I caught the smell of old wood and charcoal burning. A few feet in front of me she paused and reached among the clay pots and singled out one plant with three deep purple blooms. The roots had traced a complex pattern around the clay pot. She spoke something in Japanese I couldn't understand. I kept thinking that the cinder hurt my feet.

After a few moments of silence Frances said, "That's the oldest. All the others come from this plant." She stepped around me to join her grandmother. "My father says this one's older than he is." She took the plant from the old woman, placed it back on the shelf, and pulled at some bits of moss.

Again the old woman said something, most of which I didn't understand. But I didn't miss the last word.

"Purebred."

And Frances said again, "It's very, very old." I hardly heard her, though, because I was staring at her grandmother's face, at the toothless mouth, at the purple flesh. Something in the meeting of the word and the experience had alienated me. I was alone. Not like them.

That is all I remember. I don't know what we did after that. It might have been any number of things, all lost. But I do know that it was in the weeks after that chance meeting that I decided to destroy the plant, to deliberately crush each flower, to snap the stems and grind them into the cinder, to pull from the pot the moss that held the plant and sustained it, to rub from the pot all traces of the white roots.

They never told my parents. Never complained. Frances and I played together until we reached intermediate school and different interests pulled us apart. She was my first and only Japanese friend. But she is as alien to me as that part of myself which is like her. As alien as her grandmother was. Old Mrs. Furuisato.

_____ *Susan Nunes*

Guilt Payment

"If I'd had the right teacher, I wouldn't have failed in the Western Regionals," says Mira bitterly.

"But you've won the Hawaii audition," I point out. "Look how many competitors you had to put behind to get that far. John Singleton's daughter, Mary, who everybody said had a heavenly voice, placed only third. You hold the crown here."

"I'm no tractable Polynesian lass to be content with an island title. I want to go all the way to the top. I want to sing at the Metropolitan. I want to show the whole world what a Korean-American girl can do."

"There is always next year, and besides you have to learn to be content . . ."

"With a thousand-dollar cash prize? And end up salesgirling or teaching a bunch of tone-deaf kids, occasionally singing on the side at churches and ceremonies for a pittance? I don't want any part of it. I must go to Florence and study under Maestro Vincenti."

"Isn't Florence where he comes from, that Italian snob hanging around you all the time, Peter, Petro, or whatever his blasted name is?"

"Piero. I haven't seen a man with a worse memory for names. I really don't see how you could have become a professor of English, which presumably takes a lot of memorizing. Well, after all, it's only the University of Hawaii you are a professor at."

"Young lady, we are discussing this Piero fellow and your fantastic scheme of going to his native town at a great cost for no purpose at all . . ."

"What've you got against him? Anyway, Piero has nothing to do with it. It's just a coincidence that the world-renowned maestro happens to reside now at the place where Piero was born."

"Where his parents and relatives live, no doubt."

"Will you or will you not make this little sacrifice? When I get the big roles, the money you are investing now will seem like nothing. I will pay you back every cent with interest. I simply have to go to Italy."

"But what have the Italians got that this great country of ours hasn't? Go back to Julliard and take graduate courses or private lessons from Professor Bertram whom you used to think so highly of."

"He is old fashioned. Passe. Played out. He is old. Period. I have to breathe fresh air, learn new styles and techniques, receive new inspirations, get out of this old country."

"Since when has the U.S. become an old country?"

"Father, I respect your knowledge of English, but you know very little about musicianship, especially operatic singing and the training and discipline that go with it."

Haven't I paid full tuition for all her special lessons ever since she was three? But of course I hold my tongue.

"Trust my judgment, father. If it was avoidable, I wouldn't ask. This is the only way. I know Mother would see it my way if she were alive."

That vanquishes me for good. Oh, the burden of remorse and self-recrimination! It was quite by accident that Mira came by this infallible formula for neutralizing my resistance. She was about seven and wanted to go to a carnival at the other end of the island. She had been to a dozen already, and they were of course all such dreadful bores to me. Besides, I had an important paper to finish for a journal. I couldn't spare the time. Pettishly she remarked that her friend Joyce's mother was taking her children, adding that if she had a mother like everybody else, she would not be left at the mercy of a selfish father who did nothing for others and just read and read all day long. Life was no fun at this house of ours, she said. Her mother, whom she had never known, would see it her way, she was sure.

Silently, like a sleep-walker, I drove her 50 miles to the Haleiwa Beach Park carnival grounds. I had been her slave ever since. Not that she was reckless in the exercise of her power. Like a discerning monarch she let me, her subject, enjoy a degree of independence—even an illusion of sovereignty—in small things, but when it came to things that really mattered, matters of money and time, out came the mighty club to beat me flat. She must wonder at the efficacy of this weapon, for invariably she asked me, a smile twinkling in her eyes, what wicked thing I had done to her mother. But she never really gave me a chance to tell her, as she bolted away humming or singing merrily over the fresh reaffirmation of her supremacy. After all, when you have it good, why jinx it by looking into the whence and wherefore? But would I have told her if she really wanted to know? Not in a million years.

* * *

We had been married only eight months, Yoomi and I, when the war broke out, on Sunday, June 25, 1950. On Monday I went to the university as usual. We were to carry on our business as usual, Syngman Rhee told us over and over on the radio. The whole affair was nothing but a border skirmish, for which the provokers, rash North Korean communists, would be soundly thrashed by the South Korean army, backed by the U.S. with its atom bombs. The spring semester was winding to a close, and the finals were not too far off. The monsoon had started early and it rained dismally, incessantly. Neither the faculty nor the students could keep their minds on their books. I called on my class to translate some passages from Hardy but could not get their attention. When I called a student's name, he would look briefly at me with indifference, then turn away to resume his talk with his friends. There was no point in dragging on. When I came out of the classroom, I noticed the same restiveness had possessed all the other classes: students had poured out into the school yard, milling around like lost ants. The general assembly bell rang and the dean mounted the rostrum. The school was to go into recess indefinitely until further notice. I left for home, wondering whether the indefiniteness included the end of the month, pay day.

Hayhwa Avenue was filled with trucks of khaki-clad troops in netted helmets heading north up Miyari Pass. There was an intermittent distant boom like suppressed thunder, which got louder and more insistent by the minute. At nightfall cannon shells whirred overhead, freezing the blood. Shrapnel tore the rain-drenched, blacked-out air. Machine guns and rifles rattled. Grenades exploded. The terror-stricken populace, caught in the crossfire, ran blindly for shelter, getting maimed and mauled in the process. They had to get away, to run, no matter where. The artillery shells seemed to be aimed directly at their homes, the places they had known so long and well, and they sought refuge by running right into the hills where the shells pelted like hailstones. The next morning the sky opened and the indifferent sun shone, disclaiming all responsibility for the nightmare of the previous night. Russian tanks were already in town. Rhee had fled south after destroying the Han bridge, making sure that nobody, neither the invading army

227

nor his trusting people, followed him.

A wave of mass arrests swept through the city. All those who had managed to make a decent living were counterrevolutionaries, enemies of the people. Their houses, their jobs were proof enough of their treachery. The dregs of society rose to the top and banded themselves into Youth Leagues, Women's Leagues, People's Leagues. Armed with fixed bayonets, the gift of the victors, these upstart self-decreed legislators and justices, flaunting their red headbands and armbands of authority, ferreted out the enemies of the people who had committed the colossal crime of supporting their families with all the diligence their training and aptitude afforded. The Soosong Elementary School, packed full to bursting with such undesirables, was posted with armed guards. Other public places also served as collection and detention points. A percentage of the prisoners were taken out at regular intervals and shot at public squares, where their bodies were left to be spat on and kicked at, to rot for days. First to go were all government employees, however lowly: office clerks, guards, even custodians. But top priority was given to the so-called power sectors, policemen, tax officials, and soldiers. There was a whole division of Rhee's soldiers, stragglers and wounded, who hadn't gotten away before the bridge fell.

I went into hiding and managed to elude the first searches. We had just moved to the house a few months before, and nobody in the neighborhood knew about my teaching position at the university. But they caught on soon enough, and Yoomi, nearing her time and anemic from malnutrition, had to go to the district office to account with browbeatings and threats for my absence. With the intensifying American air raids, which did not distinguish between military and civilian targets, it wasn't too uncommon to be reported missing, unless there were witnesses to the contrary. There was no food in the house, and Yoomi had to drag her heavy body laden with clothes, utensils, and other valuables for barter at the nearest open market, until we had nothing left. Even the bedding was gone, and we shivered at night.

The only news we had of the war was what the communists gave out. The fall of the Pusan perimeter was imminent, the last holdout of the American running dogs. They would be driven into the sea to drown, and the fatherland would at last be one. As the days lengthened into weeks, I wondered whether there was any point in my continued hiding, which meant overworking Yoomi to death. I contemplated seriously giving myself up, but Yoomi wouldn't have it. Sangjo Kim, the historian, Wongyong Chay, the criminologist, and all those we knew had been coralled and marched away God knew where.

One day after carrying home a sack of barley for the last of my winter clothing, she collapsed at the gate. Since I could not go out and help lest the neighbors should see, she crawled on all fours, undid the latch, and came into the house. Her labor had started. The placenta had burst. It was our first birth, but I had heard that this was an emergency. Her life was at stake, but when I made ready to run for the midwife who resided in the neighborhood, Yoomi clutched my ankles with an unbreakable grip. She would not let me go. I watched helplessly, biting my lip as the pangs tortured and twisted her. Mira was eventually born. Yoomi, delirious with fever, lay unconscious for days. I hated the bawling lump of flesh, the cause of the impending death of my beloved.

I made barley broth and fed it to the baby, but she rejected the food after a few sips. She raised hell, her face turning red and blotchy. In spite of her delirium Yoomi heard the child, hugged it close and fumbled about her breast. I offered no assistance; either the baby had to survive on barley broth or perish. It would not further endanger its mother's health by leeching. With an uncanny homing instinct the little brute deftly sought out the teats. Then, gathering her lips into a snout, she cupped them over one with a flopping sound and sucked away voraciously, draining her mother's life blood. She sucked and sucked, until the previously swollen sacs sagged and shriveled. Then she bawled for more.

I was furious and could have strangled her. Marveling at my unnatural disposition, I wondered what the poets who spewed ardently about parental affection could have meant. The crying, wetting, misshapen, grotesque bundle of newborn flesh did not inspire me with anything but loathing. I resented her untimely intrusion. Already her birth could be kept secret no more. The neighbors had heard her cries and came officiously to assist and give advice to my half-dead wife, while I had to scamper away to my perch under the roof, erasing all traces of my latest descent.

Miraculously Yoomi survived the days of fever, near starvation, and constant suction by the little vampire. She was back on her feet to feed all three of us, now carrying the baby on her back. We had sold the stereo and records, the clock and radio, the guitar and accordion, even the harmonica and cymbal. The time had come to part with our wedding gifts, her half-karat diamond ring and my Omega watch, which we had sworn never to sell. I again proposed to give myself up. Surely the communists must have use for an English professor. Maybe I could be their translator, intelligence decoder, or what not, but again Yoomi prevented me.

It was early September and the food from our wedding mementos had lasted only a week. Yoomi hired herself out as a kitchen maid at a neighbor's, Char somebody, who was some kind of a big wheel with the new regime. We had been smelling his barbecuing beef all through the summer. The place seemed a Mecca for the Communist cadres to congregate and celebrate, their drunken, raucous singing lasting through the night. These communists didn't seem to know choral singing at all and everybody always sang in unison. The repertoire was limited to the Red Flag, the Glorious Leader Ilsung Kim, and other Party and Army songs which they never seemed to tire of, which were too sacrosanct to allow accompaniment by any musical instrument other than their own vocal cords. Occasionally they tried some traditional folk songs. At this point some rank amateur banged down on our Baldwin grand, off key.

One of the first things every citizen had to do was report to the authorities special luxuries such as the piano. Yoomi volunteered and contributed it to the cause to forestall its inevitable discovery by the search parties, which might keep looking to find more. Perhaps such cooperation might mollify their suspicion and antagonism toward our house, if not quite win their favor. The piano was moved to Char's. Yoomi's father had bought it on her graduation from college with top honors in her piano class. She had brought it with her when she married me. We had planned a recital sometime in September at the Municipal Hall with the Seoul Philharmonic. Of course none of the Communists had kept up with the musical scene of the south and nobody knew her. To them she was just another miserable housewife, a reactionary's deserted wife, with an infant child to feed. But when they seemed to murder the good music and ruin the piano, I felt an urge to show to Char and comrades what a good musician like Yoomi could do with it.

Even their musical travesty stopped altogether and the piano was never heard again. We learned later that the grand had been moved to some public hall for the Liberation Day ceremony on August 15, but the place was bombed and a piano was the farthest thing from anybody's mind.

Her pay was the burnt layer of rice scraped off the bottom of the pot and occasionally the leftover goodies from their tables. At that time, when a peck of rice was worth more than a piano, we had to consider this a generous remuneration. But the strain of work so soon after childbirth ruined her health despite the improved diet. She hemorrhaged continuously. Her shining eyes receded deeper and deeper into their bony sockets, and her skin grew sallow. Sweat stood on her forehead and dizzy spells forced her to steady herself by holding on to the wall or furniture. I told her to stop working; we could skimp, and the burnt rice, which we ate by soaking in water, would see us through a week. By then surely the Americans would be back. Witness the almost round-the-clock air raids by the American Air Force, completely paralyzing all daytime mobility of the People's Army.

But Yoomi wouldn't listen. She had to do it for her baby, who indeed prospered. Her cheeks filled out nicely, and her earlier formlessness gave way to a proportioned articulation of features. When she smiled and crooned in her contentment after a lengthy feeding at her mother's breast, there was even a hint of the innocence and beauty of the Raphaelite Christ child. While she was the epitome of health, her mother withered. I resented the little selfish creature and resisted my growing fondness for her.

September was drawing to a close, yet Seoul was still solidly in the hands of the Communists. The air raids seemed a mere surface irritation to the dug-in, deeply-entrenched ground forces. After what seemed to be a thorough devastation of anti-aircraft bunkers in a given area, the new formation of fighters and bombers the next day would be greeted with as vigorous salvos of flak as before from the same area. Time was said to be running out for the Communists. But it might run out for the Americans, too. After all, planes and bombs couldn't be inexhaustible. And time was definitely running out for us, our little microcosm of three, a nameless and lost speck in the vast macabre chessboard of indiscriminate death and destruction.

Whole streets were turning into honeycombs of pillboxes and bunkers. Naval bombardment had begun from American ships off Inchon, systematically erasing the city off the map. Fires broke out everywhere. A few houses down the block from ours got hit. What had been a sturdy concrete structure disintegrated, leaving a huge crater, while the ensuing fire spread and stopped just before our house. Yoomi and Mira had been moved out, and I was almost smoked out myself. We might absorb a direct hit ourselves at any minute. Wistfully I looked at the repapered walls of our main bedroom, how we had spent days looking for the right color and pattern, how upset we had been whenever a fly left a black spot and what meticulous care we had taken to remove the blemish without staining the rest of the paper.

Last-minute roundups of reactionaries were going on, which now included just about every civilian still left in the city who could not be positively identified as an activist in the new regime. As the first U.S. Marines crossed the Han, the detainees at various basements and temporary lockups, emaciated, bruised, mangled skeletons who had somehow survived the torture and interrogation without food, were led out and shot. Both banks of the Chonggay Drain were strewn with their bodies. Some were packed into abandoned air raid trenches and buried alive. Many were simply shot on the streets and left there to be trampled. Whole families, including the very young and old, were executed. The Communists became more vicious and wanton; if they were to die, they would leave no survivors to curse their memory and exult over their end. They killed anybody for no cause at all.

One night there came a loud knock at the gate. Our hearts were tight knots. Our legs wouldn't move. Mira started crying frantically, bringing us to our senses. Yoomi snatched her up and went to the door, at the same time motioning me to the attic. But there was no time for it. There seemed to be half a dozen of them and they were already through the gate, apparently having broken the latch. They were beaming their flashlights all over the house, especially toward the attic. One was going into the kitchen, another to the basement, a third to the back of the house. I had barely gotten into the outhouse latrine by the fence, when I realized one of them was coming toward it. In the three-by-five compartment I had no alternative but to jump into the tank, feet first, my hands pushing down the slippery sides. The thick mass on top closed over my head without a ripple. I was conscious of a flashlight overhead. The stamping feet on the creaky boards left and the door banged. I nevertheless stayed submerged as long as I could.

I heard Yoomi shriek. She thought they had found me in the attic when three of them vaulted into it through the access trap and turned over every piece of furniture stored there, poking into the corners with their bayonets. It was painful not to go out and reassure her of my safety. Mira went on screaming harder; probably Yoomi had dropped her. At one point I thought they were coming back to the latrine and was ready to duck again, but they didn't. About half an hour later, what seemed like an eternity, I issued out of the outhouse and ran to the inner courtyard. Hair disordered and face ashen, Yoomi was suckling Mira. She gave a start as if she had seen a ghost. She had passed out and regained consciousness only minutes before. She thought they had taken me away. Only then did we notice my odoriferous condition. We laughed like two lunatics. Thank God I had postponed installing the flush toilet. The cost of the new plumbing and septic tank system, there being no city sewage, had been prohibitive.

We had to leave the house. A shell had gouged a big hole on the street next to the stone fence, which had been blown off like dust. The roof had collapsed and we were squeezed between the sprung closet door frame and a fallen beam. A window slat dug into my calf, but Yoomi and Mira were unhurt. We had to get out fast. The dry wood had caught fire, and the smoke pierced and blinded our eyes. Shells were falling everywhere. The night sky was lit with a reddish glow that gave the illusion of soaking the whole city in blood. But the alleys were pitch dark, except for occasional flickering through the openings.

Just as I turned a corner, with Yoomi and Mira close behind, rifle shots rang out. Instantly I drew back. Pressing close to the wall we retreated into the alley we had emerged from. A patrol of the People's Army passed. They paused briefly at the corner to peer into the darkness, but apparently more urgent business elsewhere didn't allow them to tarry. We came out of the alley, rounded the corner, and swiftly went along the other street. Dry plane leaves crackled at our feet, startling us. We kept walking fast, backtracking and detouring whenever a shell crashed near, a roadbock loomed ahead, or a patrol was audible. We were going in the general direction of the Han to the south, but the topography, jumbled beyond recognition by dugouts and shellings, was thoroughly confusing. To the south the sky was bright with flares, probably attesting to the American beachhead. Only the Americans would try to expel darkness, and we had agreed that our hope lay in getting through the Communist battle zone to the brighter sky.

Sudden tommy gun bursts were followed by the noise of people shouting and running.

"Stop or we'll shoot," a voice yelled. The tommy guns burped. Instinctively we had crouched flat to the ground. Shots whizzed past. Cannonade continued with their booms and crashes. A highrise down the block tottered and broke up. Whole walls and floors flew overhead and dumped all around us. We got out of the alley and suddenly came to the broad Namsan Avenue, pale with the shimmer of flares and fires and explosions. The avenue was full of enfilade. We had to get away from this highway of flying metal.

"Let's find a trench, an air raid shelter," I said.

"They say they're filled up with bodies." Yoomi said.

My spine crawled. I shuddered at the thought of what must have happened to the man who had been fleeing in our direction a minute before. A half circle of grey was fanning slowly in the eastern sky, eroding the redness of artificial illumination. The chilly morning breeze buffeted our noses with whiffs of rancid smoke, the overpowering compound of burning gunpowder, wood, paint, earth, concrete, and human flesh. There was a flare right above our heads, disclosing our shapes. For the first time we looked at each other's face in the eerie light and were shocked at our skeletal haggardness, as if all the meat had evaporated. But we were not allowed the luxury of mutual scrutiny for long. A few feet from us lay a headless man's body, drenched in blood, still warm, kicking. The brains had spilt out of the bashed head a few feet away. Dark patches of blood stippled the whitewashed wall. Yoomi trembled and hid her face in my chest.

"Let's get into a trench before we get it ourselves," I said, pulling her behind me into an alley. There was a tearing explosion. The place we had just stood disappeared in a cloud of fiery smoke. More mortar shells rained upon the same spot. We could see fire spitting out of a machine gun emplacement a little distance away. Near South Gate we found and jumped into an unoccupied dugout, about four feet by ten feet. The floor was covered with a sheet of water. The walls were slimy. The smell of mildew, feces, and decay staggered us. Fresh pine trunks, their green-needled branches sticking up here and there, supported the ceiling of earth packed in straw bags. Where the bagging was torn, earth cascaded into the puddle of water on the floor with each ground-shaking explosion. Yoomi uncovered the flap of cloth she had put across Mira's face. She slept on soundly, quite unconcerned. One shell fell almost on top of the trench. The ceiling and walls shook, ready to cave in. The dust was suffocating. Instinctively Yoomi hid Mira's face against her bosom. The infant's nostrils fluttered, her eyelids quivered, her clenched hands waved uncertainly. Then she went back to sleep, her facial muscles relaxing, even hinting a smile. I was gripped with compunction. The little innocent life seemed the dearest thing in the world. I recalled how beastly my attitude had been toward this sublime being, free from taint and impurity. Her faint, still-lingering smile seemed the climax of all life, as if all previous generations had existed only to culminate in this perfection. So many lives had been plowed back into the soil to sprout this exquisite flower.

A hot puff of air, as if somebody had suddenly opened a heated oven, filled the trench, sizzling the wet floor. Flames darted into the trench from the opening. We gasped for breath. Our bodies were like burning brands. We doubled up and burrowed our heads into the ground, but the floor was aflame, too. Outside were rushing feet and loud voices.

"Napalms, napalms," shouted somebody running past our trench.

"Retreat to Position Two," another voice shouted, as the trotting feet scattered. Shortly afterward, there were other voices.

"Stop!" somebody yelled. Tommy guns clattered away, followed by screams. Cool air came into our trench and we could breathe. Mira let out a piercing cry. Her face was flushed like a ball of fire. Yoomi tried to comfort her but Mira kicked and thrashed, crying louder and louder. We heard footsteps approaching us. Yoomi bared her breast and tried to pacify Mira, but it did not work. The child dodged her head left or right, thrusting her hands mightily against her mother, and her face contorted with the effort, her cry growing louder. We didn't know what to do. Discovery by the Communist soldiers would

235

be certain death. Anyone other than themselves on this battle line would be enemy agents or undesirables summarily to be executed. At that moment, just as the detachment of troops were almost above our trench, more napalms fell around our trench, and the footsteps ceased. Hot flames hissed past the entrance, and some leaped in, almost licking us. I pulled Yoomi to the other end of the trench, our feet sinking in the mud. Mira expressed her disapproval of the jolt by doubling the decibels of her cry.

"Help, good people. Help!" said a voice at the mouth of the trench. Our hair stood up and our breath stopped. A young man of about twenty was crawling into the trench. He dragged one leg, his torn flesh showing through gaping trousers. His entire face was sleek with blood.

"I heard you, good people," he said. "I knew you could not be bad. People with crying children can't be bad. Give me anything to tie up my wound with."

Yoomi tore a strip from her skirt before I had a chance to protest and handed it to the wounded man. He hurriedly tied up his thigh, stopping the bleeding in his leg. He stretched out his hand for more strips of cloth and Yoomi was about to oblige, which would have left her practically bare. I stopped her. The young man noticed it. He tore off his torn trouser leg, split it along the seam, and wiped his face. There was an ominous gash in his upper left forehead from which blood kept oozing. He bound his head above his eye and just below the wound, which seemed to stem the bleeding somewhat.

"Can't you stop the baby's crying?" he said, looking at us with annoyance. "They'll hear us for sure, just as I heard you, and we will be done for. They shoot any civilian. It is their last vengeance."

"Do they really?" I said incredulously.

"You'll find out soon enough if you let the child carry on," he said, urgently, imperatively. He made a lunge toward Mira but stopped short when Yoomi gathered Mira closer to her and shrank from him.

"Don't you hear them coming this way? I'll be damned if I'll get shot in this stinking hole because of a crying baby," he said, crawling out of the trench. A few seconds later, amid the crashes of artillery and mortar, we heard the nervous chatter of tommy guns and a long scream, which could have been the young man's, but we weren't sure. There were more feet rushing back and forth, more explosions.

"He was right. We'll get caught if we stay here with her crying her head off like this. We've got to leave her and get out," I said.

"Leave her?"

"Yes. But we'll come back for her. They won't kill a baby."

Horrified, she backed away from me, holding Mira tightly.

"If you want to live so badly that you have to abandon your own child, then go away from us," Yoomi said in disgust.

"It's not a question of abandoning. It's a question of avoiding suicide. It's survival, survival of us, you and me."

"What about Mira?"

"A lump of flesh, hardly conscious of its own existence!"

"Why is she crying if she's not conscious?"

"That's precisely what I mean. If she was truly aware of her position, she wouldn't cry. We have perception, a fully-developed adult consciousness, but hers is not even human yet. It's not much different from that of bugs. Besides, we made her. We can make many more like her."

I heard another detachment of troops approaching, their voices growing louder. Mira seemed to time her crying for a crescendo. In immediate reaction I put my hand across her mouth.

"Get away from her," Yoomi shrieked shrilly above Mira's crying, at the same time bending down and biting my hand so hard that a bone crunched. I jumped back in pain. The detachment was unmistakably coming directly toward us.

"Get out! Get out! I don't know you. We have no need of you," Yoomi was shouting. I had no time to think. I bounded out of the trench. Tommy guns burped behind me. A giant had grabbed me by the thigh. I fell down. Something warm suffused my leg. There was a loud thunder that completely deafened me and knocked out my senses.

The next time I noticed anything, it was broad daylight. I was lying before the gaunt remains of a building. Down the street, on both sides, I saw crumbling pillboxes and barricades with machine guns and dead soldiers slung across the sandbags. Farther down the street, around the Taypyongdong Rotary, a motorcade of American amphibious tanks, armored cars, and trucks was approaching, followed by thousands of Koreans waving flags and shouting hooray to the saviors. Where had they all been? I thought they had all been murdered or starved and no soul had been left alive in Seoul. In between the shouts and the rumble of the engines I heard a

237

baby's subdued, hoarse whimpering. For the first time I re-membered what had happened. I stood up and tried to run, but the big hand pulled me down. My left leg was a useless stump. It was the very same leg from whose calf a splinter had been extracted earlier. The bullet, entering at a small neat hole, had departed on the other side after wrenching out a big chunk of steak, bone and all. The rest of my leg hung by mere skin. How foolish the Korean saying that one doesn't get hurt twice in the same place!

I crawled across the street to the heap of earth from under which the sobbing of the baby continued intermittently, inau-dibly. I started digging away frantically with my hands. Soon the nails broke off and the fingers bled. The crowd arrived. An American Marine walked up. To his surprise, I explained in English that my wife and baby were underneath. He had sev-eral of his buddies come with shovels. First came to sight a People's Army soldier with a broken back. Then, under a log, in a cubic foot of space, Mira was safe, although her legs were trapped in earth. The jagged end of a beam had rammed through Yoomi's chest.

* * *

"All right, Mira," I say. "I'll get the money ready tomor-row, and you can make the plane reservations and other prepa-rations. But please write to me when you get to Florence."

"Oh, Dad, you are an angel," she says, hugging me. "I'll remember this always and pay you back, all of it and more. I know what kind of a sacrifice this is to you."

Does she? Perhaps. Strangely, she doesn't ask this time the usual question of what wicked thing I have done to her mother. Well, no matter. It boils down to the same thing, me picking up the tab, sweating and toiling to fulfill her big deci-sions. I'll have to withdraw from my Christmas Club savings, which I have intended for my next sabbatical trip to England. I'll be signing a note at the University Credit Union to pay back within three years. I thought I had finally gotten out of all those debts, those eternal monthly salary deductions, for the car, the TV, the stereo, the piano, everything except the house mortgage, but here I go again, accepting more install-ment payments. Mira may indeed go on to sing at La Scalla or the Metropolitan, but even if she doesn't, well, she won't bring her mother into the picture again, at least not for a while. But why do things have to be so tough for Americans now? I remember the times when an average American income commanded princely accommodations abroad. It is quite the other way around now. Damn Arabs, damn Japanese, damn Italians, damn Koreans with their exports and favorable trade balances!

Communion

It was quiet, deathly quiet, and that was strange, for Morio Tamura's life had always been full of sounds. There had been the crickets and cicadas on the Tamura farm in Japan, and the rustle of canefields and harsh commands of foremen on the sugar plantation on Hawaii. Here, in Honolulu, the sheathed thunder of cars, buses and trucks from below his locked and heavily draped bedroom window merged with his everyday life. Sound and noises were taken for granted, like the air around him, yet now there was this depthless, monotonous silence.

Was it time to get up? He had to be at the delicatessen by four if he wanted the coffee and doughnuts to be ready by five. A few faithful customers always came early for breakfast. What time was it anyway? He tried to open his eyes but couldn't. He then tried to reach for the clock by his pillow and again he couldn't. He didn't even hear the tick-tock tick-tock that put him to sleep every night. Am I dreaming, he wondered. Then he fell into motionless sleep once again.

The next time he awoke he noticed not only the silence but the chill in the air. It was . . . it was . . . was there such a thing as antiseptic chilly? As if one were being preserved in a tub full of alcohol?

The tub reminded him of his iron vat with bubbling oil in which he made his doughnuts. How many more cases of oil did he have in his storeroom? And flour . . . should he order another forty bags? The newspapers talked about a shipping strike in a few weeks. But if the strike wasn't called, then he would be stuck with the flour and somehow the mice always got to the flour sacks. The health inspectors didn't like that.

Time . . . time to get up . . . what time was it? Surely it must be almost four. Why was it so quiet and cold? Where was Mama? Where was the alarm clock? I must be really exhausted, he thought, and fell asleep once more.

Two nurses entered the room in the morning, one with some towels and the other with a tray of thermometers. The first one said, "Mr. Tamura . . . Mr. Tamura . . . I'm going to wash your face, okay?" The second slipped a thermometer under Morio's tongue.

The first nurse asked, "How many days is it since he's been in a coma? Forty? Fifty?"

"More like ninety," the second nurse said, examining the chart at the foot of the bed. "Ninety-seven today, to be exact."

"You think he'll ever come out of it?"

"Hard to tell. He's a tiny man . . . only five feet tall and weighed 110 pounds when he was brought in. He's 76 pounds now. But he looks like a scrapper, a fighter. The other day I was giving him an alcohol rub and it seemed like he tensed his right arm. First time I felt that. So he could be coming out of it."

"Sad . . . being pistol-whipped for a few dollars. Honolulu was never like this. I can remember when we used to leave our windows and doors unlocked all the time . . . even at night."

"I know. Now I don't feel safe even in my own garage. And I lock myself in the car when I drive."

"Kind of a shame, isn't it, someone in a coma lying in this private air-conditioned room. He can't even appreciate it, yet he has to pay for it."

"I think the police wanted him here. Anyone coming here has to pass through two stations."

"Must cost the family a fortune. I heard a rumor Admissions suggested the family take him to another hospital, when they found out he didn't have any health insurance."

"You can't blame the hospital. But we took him, didn't we?" She picked up her tray. "Hey there, Mr. Tamura, brave man, you in your secret world, have a nice day, huh!" She left, followed by the other nurse.

Morio Tamura, in his secret world, faintly heard Mama calling him. Or was it his mother in Japan? No, it was Mama. "The paper cranes," he thought. "The paper cranes Mama's making for my 61st birthday party. What fool originally thought of making 1000 paper cranes for a 61st birthday party, and what fools made this into a tradition? Fools with time, that's for sure."

I wish we had a daughter, he mused. A daughter-in-law is okay, but a daughter is different. Now I understand why Mama used to say that if we're going to have only one child, she would have preferred a girl to a boy.

He thought of Tom, his son, and Evelyn, his daughter-in-law. They were good kids, kind and considerate, but somehow not as close to them as a daughter would have been. His friend Shoda had a married daughter and always on Sunday afternoons this daughter brought some food over for her parents . . . "so you don't have to cook tonight" . . . she said. Then she

241

cleaned the kitchen and bathroom and sometimes the inside of the refrigerator while her husband talked to her father. How lucky the Shodas were!

It must be time to get up and go to the shop. Must be close to four. What would the workmen say if the shop wasn't open by five? They depended on him for coffee, doughnuts and biscuits. Where would these truck drivers and construction workers have their large but cheap breakfasts? I must get up. But I can't open my eyes. Am I drugged? How could I be? Am I dreaming? Wake up, Morio Tamura. You don't have time to be sleeping. But he fell into another deep, unconscious sleep.

A few days later, Mrs. Tamura sat folding her paper cranes in the hospital room, as usual.

"*Oto-san*," she whispered. "*Oto-san*, papa, can you hear me? Wake up! Try! You've got to come out of this coma. You can't die without saying goodbye to us. At least to me. Wake up! Look, I already have 800 cranes. Only 200 more to go, and remember your birthday is only a few months away. You've got to be well by then. I sewed your red kimono for the party, and we have the guest list. So wake up, *Oto-San*, for how can we have your party without you?"

Mrs. Tamura sighed. After three months she was exhausted with anger and worry. What would happen to them now? Should she sell the shop? Maybe the new owner would hire her. After all she was still strong at 57, and she knew all the customers. Would she have to depend on charity in her old age when she had worked steadily for 35 years, minus 6 months before and 6 months after Tom was born? Thirty-four years of hard work in America, the land of the free and the home of the brave, Tom used to sing. The land of justice, of plenty, of love. And a land where someone wanted to kill her husband for a few dollars!

"What kind of country did you bring me to?" she asked. "I gave up a country where I had relatives and I could understand the language. In that country I don't think anyone ever pistolwhipped another person from the back, even in the feudal days of long ago. The Japanese fought man-to-man, from the front, with warning. Why did we come here? What happiness have we had, working from four in the morning to nine at night, every day of the week?"

She pounded her husband's body in anger, heedless of different tubes attached to his body. "They say this country has justice, but there's no justice. The police didn't even bother looking for the boy. They said they had no clues. They just wrote something down on a piece of paper, that's all. They just accepted it . . . it wasn't anything unusual to them to have someone almost killed by another. When I try to talk to them they just move away. *Oto-san,* how can you die now? You didn't have your party. You didn't see the 1000 crane tree. What about that trip to Japan? You said we would go back on your 65th birthday . . . when you retire. Lies . . . all lies! You aren't even trying to come out of your coma. It's easier lying in this air-conditioned room than working in a hot delicatessen and standing on your feet all day. You don't care about us . . . you're taking the easy way out."

"What? What?" her husband mumbled. "Four already? Time to get up, Mama?"

Mama . . . Mrs. Tamura . . . was so shocked she forgot to ring the bell to call the nurse. Instead she ran to the door and yelled, "Nurse! Nurse! Come quickly. My husband just talked to me!"

Two nurses came running. "Mr. Tamura, Mr. Tamura, do you hear us? Can you understand? You're in a hospital and we are taking good care of you. You have nothing to worry about. Your wife is sitting right here. Mr. Tamura . . . Mr. Tamura?" But Morio Tamura was back in his deep, deep sleep.

"Are you sure he spoke?" a nurse asked. "It wasn't a moan? Or a gurgle?"

"No," she answered. "He asked if it was 4 o'clock already."

"Four o'clock? Why four o'clock?"

"That's when he used to get up to go to work every morning."

"You're sure it wasn't wishful thinking? You didn't imagine it?"

"I'm sure. He spoke clearly." The nurses waited. But they had many other chores, Mrs. Tamura knew. So she said, "Thank you. Maybe I did dream it, after all." She picked up her bag from the floor, extracted some paper, and began folding a crane.

After the nurses left she leaned over Morio and whispered, "So! You make me look like a fool! Why did you stop talking? Listen, Papa, I know you can hear me. By the time I have my 1000 cranes, I expect you to be out of your coma. You understand?" She scolded gently.

When, several days later Morio next awoke, he felt his mother pushing him. "Morio-chan, Morio-chan, wake up. Wake up and work in the fields for a few hours. Remember your brother is sending you to high school. You must work hard before and after school since he's making this sacrifice. Be grateful to him."

Be grateful to his older brother? But Morio knew why his brother was sending him to high school. Ever since Morio had contracted diptheria when he was 12 he had stopped growing. Now he was 15 and still so small he was of little use on the farm where strong labor was needed. His brother was hoping that with more education Morio would go to some city and not be dependent on his older brother.

"I would be grateful if I hadn't heard my brother discussing this with my sister-in-law late one night," Morio thought. "They were talking of ways to get me off the farm for good. They made me feel so unwanted. I wish I had never heard them talking about me."

So he continued sleeping although he could feel his mother pushing and pulling him . . . maybe even washing his face? Now why would his mother wash a 15-year-old's face? He wanted to protest, but instead he fell into his deep sleep again.

Five days later Mama said, "Well, that's the 1000th crane. Now I'll have to tie them to the tree branch Papa got from a friend. We have the invitations ready . . ."

"Mama, did you get white print on red paper or red print on white paper?" Morio asked, as if he had been in conversation with Mama all along.

Mrs. Tamura trembled and dropped the crane she had been holding. It took her a few moments to say quietly, "White print on red paper."

"Good. It'll be easy to read. Remember we had an invitation once with red print on black paper and we had to hold it a certain way to read the invitation? Poor Mama, 1000 cranes! But now you can relax a little."

"I enjoyed making them," Mama said, hoping one of the nurses would walk in on the conversation. "Somebody come . . . somebody come . . ." she prayed.

"Come to bed, Mama. We have to get up early tomorrow morning, as usual. I had a long day, standing on my feet, and they feel like lead bars attached to my body. I can't even move them. You sleep early, okay?"

"Sure . . . sure . . . as soon as I put my things away."

She pressed the bell. When two nurses came in she said, "My husband spoke again. Right now. He asked about the color of print on the invitations we made for his 61st birthday."

The nurses looked at each other. "That's wonderful, Mrs. Tamura. That's a good sign he might come out of his coma. Now listen, there's nothing more you can do for your husband now so why don't you go home and rest? We'll take good care of him."

So they still didn't believe her. But it didn't matter. It was a matter of days or weeks before he'd come out of his coma completely. Papa was getting better and look what a clear mind he had. "Yes I think I'll go home and rest," she reassured the nurses.

It was a week before Morio spoke again. "Where am I? I dreamed I was in Japan with my mother."

"You're in a hospital, Papa," she told him. "Remember someone hit you on the head with a pistol?"

A muscle twitched in his face. "Oh, I remember. A boy . . . a man . . . came in and bought doughnuts. One-half dozen. He paid me and as I was going back into the kitchen I felt something hit me. That's all I can remember. How much money did he take?"

"All that I left in the cash register before I left. About six dollars in bills, nickels and dimes."

"Strange . . . he looked like such a nice boy. He talked so softly. I gave him two extra doughnuts because there were two left. He told me he wanted only six and I said the extra two were free. He said 'Thank you.' By the way, when can I leave here? I have to order some flour, in case we have a shipping strike later in the month."

"We already had a shipping strike, Papa, and it's been settled so don't worry about the strike."

"We had a strike? But it was supposed to begin June 15!"

"It's September 9 today."

"September! How can that be? It was June 2 yesterday."

"You were in a long coma, unconscious, Papa. But thank heavens you're okay now. Listen, I'm going to call one of the nurses. They didn't believe me when I said you talked the last time. Talk to them . . . the nurses . . . so they'll know you can really talk."

When Mrs. Tamura returned with one of the nurses, Morio

245

was again in his deep motionless sleep. The nurse sighed in exasperation, but with sympathy. "Hang in there, Mrs. Tamura," she comforted her.

For another long ten days Morio Tamura slept, like an empty sack with tubes going into and out of him. Mama talked to him, pushed and pulled him, whispered, shouted, scolded, whimpered. Had he really talked to her? Even Tom wouldn't believe her, so she herself began having doubts.

"You know, Mama, when we wish and dream for something, it seems true," Tom told her. "You wanted Dad to come out of his coma and you wanted him to talk to you, so you heard him. It had to be in your mind, because how come he doesn't talk when anyone else is around?"

But the very next day he opened his eyes for the first time, although he couldn't move his head or hands. "Mama, forgive me," he said. "I lied to you. Well, I didn't exactly lie, but I didn't tell you how short I am, when I asked my brother to find me a wife in Japan."

Mrs. Tamura was surprised. He was now talking about what took place 40 years ago. How his being short must have bothered him!

"I didn't want to tell you how short I am because I was afraid you wouldn't come to marry me. The white people on the plantation used to call me "shrimp" and the plantation boss told me to work in the kitchen because I was so small . . . like a girl, he said."

"So what?" Mama answered. "I lied to you too. I told the go-betweens not to tell you I'm 5'3" tall. At all my *miai* in Japan the mothers turned me down because they said I looked big and clumsy. They wanted a dainty daughter-in-law."

"Mama, remember when we were first married? When we took snapshots I always took them on steps. I would stand one step behind you so I would look taller. How it bothered me, being shorter, yet I was happy because I had a tall wife and I wanted tall sons."

Mama waited for his next words but he closed his eyes, sighed, and went back to sleep.

The doctor and nurse came in, just a little too late to hear Papa talk. By now Mama refrained from telling the nurse about Papa holding a conversation with her.

"How's my husband?" she asked the doctor.

"As well as can be expected," the doctor answered.

246

"When will he be completely out of his coma?"

"What do you mean . . . 'completely out of his coma'?"

"Well, sometimes when he talks to me he's clear about things, but then other times he thinks I'm his mother, I think. When will he not go back to sleep again for days at a time?"

The doctor and nurse looked at each other. "We've had cases where patients have been in coma almost ten years," the doctor said. "Then we've had patients who came out of a coma perfectly normal and patients who couldn't remember anything or recognize anyone. We don't know about Mr. Tamura."

"Papa's mind is clear, and of course he recognizes my voice."

"Remember, when your husband does regain consciousness, if he ever does, he may not remember much because of the brain damage and massive hemorrhage," the doctor warned.

"But he does remember," Mrs. Tamura insisted. "He even asked about the color of print I used on his 61st birthday invitations."

The doctor looked at his watch. "Fine . . . fine . . . let's keep working and waiting and hoping and praying. Miracles can happen. Now would you mind waiting outside for a few minutes?"

"What about this case, Doctor," the nurse whispered after Mrs. Tamura left.

"Damage was extensive to the brain area . . . plus the hemorrhage . . ."

"It's a wonder he's still alive, isn't it?"

"He got hit two or three times in the back of his head, at the nerve center. I think the paralysis is permanent."

"Poor man. Better if he had died right away. Now maybe he'll be a burden on his wife for years and years, and they don't even have health insurance. Personally I'd rather die than be a vegetable fed by tubes."

"Sometimes you don't have a choice. Sometimes the next of kin don't have a choice too. Unless laws are changed." They left, and Mrs. Tamura entered to find her husband sleeping peacefully.

Seven days later Morio opened his eyes and said, as if he had not been unconscious for more than a week. "Listen Mama, will you promise me one thing? Listen carefully, now. In case I turn out to be a bed-ridden invalid, if I'm completely

247

paralyzed, promise me you'll help me to die."

"No, how can I do such a thing . . ."

"Mama, please. Won't you help me?"

"Even if I wanted to help you, what could I do?"

"I don't know. A healthy man can die in a car accident or drown in the ocean or fall from some tall building. But if one is bedridden and especially if he's like a vegetable, how can he die when he wants to? I don't know, Mama. That's where I have to depend on you."

"What are you talking like this for, just when you're getting well. Every day you're getting better, you know. I don't want to hear anymore. Besides, visiting hours are over."

"Please, Mama?"

"No."

"It's my only request. From my only life partner. For the sake of my life partner."

"I don't know what you're talking about." But she reached out to him. His thinness pained her. How could a man's arm really feel like a stick?

"Mama, is it daytime or nighttime?"

"Nighttime."

"Could you open the window and please turn my head so that I can see out?"

"There's nothing to see out . . . only a few stars."

"Stars? Oh, I want to see the stars . . . I never had time to see the stars while I was working. Remember when Tom was in kindergarten and he had to sing 'Twinkle twinkle little star' all by himself for a Christmas play and we practiced and practiced together with him?"

"And the teacher scolded him because he sang 'Twinkoru twinkoru litoru star . . . raiki a diamondo in za skai.' "

Did he chuckle? Mama thought so, and she too smiled. But then he seemed to have fallen asleep again so she left.

Morio opened his eyes and saw the stars. As he gazed at their shiny brilliance they seemed to break into little pieces and slide earthward, together with his tears that slid down his cheek to the pillow.

The next morning the nurses called cheerfully, "Good morning, Mr. Tamura. And how are we today?" But instead of wiping his face, the nurse called the doctor right away.

"Too bad Mr. Tamura passed away without regaining consciousness. 136 days in a coma so he's really skin and bones," the nurse said.

248

"It's a wonder he lasted this long," the house doctor agreed.

"Kind of sad," the nurse said. "You know, there was such love between them, Mrs. Tamura is sure Mr. Tamura spoke to her several times. But that's physically impossible, isn't it? His throat muscles were paralyzed as much as the rest of his body, so he couldn't have talked, could he?"

"Most likely not," the doctor agreed. "But then there's a great deal we still don't know . . ."

The nurse pulled the pillow case from the pillow. Strange . . . it was wet, as if with tears.

Patsy S. Saiki

Intermediate School Hapai _____

just the other night
Val a junior at UH
me four years older than her and cruising

I was tuning up my car the other night when my sister Val
came up to me and asked, "Eh, Vince. You get some dope or
what?" Just like that, out and out, with no beating around the
bushes. "Eh Vince. You get some dope or what?" Usually,
when you talk to your brother or sister, you just make conver-
sation and you talk-story about really useless stuff like "Eh,
your turn for wash the dishes tonight," or "What you doing?"
or "You went play around with my guitar or what?" The other
night, not Val. She just came up to me while I was tuning up
my car and she asked, "Eh, Vince. You get some dope or
what?" What a little punk.

I was trying to get the distributor gear lined up with the
camshaft gear. Real pain in the ass business. Especially for
one GTO—Pontiac, that's why—the distributor stay way in the
back of the motor. I was lying on the fender, holding the Accel
dualpoint distributor, the one Duki got for me free so no can
complain, trying to keep the two sets of points at top-dead-
center open, while trying to match the two angle-cut gears.
Then she asked me that. I gave her a stink side-eye and kept
on with my business. She was probably only joking anyway,
and I wasn't going to let her pull my leg.

"Vince!" She insisted, "You get some dope or what? I
asked you one question." She was still standing there at the
front of my '64 Goat, obviously determined to get some kind of
answer from me.

I figured too-bad-for-you and shook my head while I kept
on with the distributor.

"Come on, Vince. You get. I know. Just the other night you
bought one O-Z from Duki for 90 cents."

I gave her a meaner stink-eye, looking straight at her this
time. And I went back to my work.

"Vince, no make stink. Come on." She was still standing
there at the front of my car, leaning against the nose of the
Goat.

Apparently she wasn't satisfied with the subtleties of non-
verbal communication. Goddam it. I put the distributor down

on the aluminum intake manifold and slithered backwards off the fender. I hopped to my feet and looked at her.

She was going out tonight. She was dressed, maybe not to "kill," but she was set at least on "stun." Tight, dressy jeans and a silkie top that wasn't too shiny in a semi-aloha print theme. Looking good. A white loose-mesh sweater was draped over her shoulder and this thin clutch purse was tucked under her armpit. The purse was supposed to be rabbit fur, but the poor skinned rabbit must have either been scrawny or just given a grunt crewcut.

Once I told her, "Eh, that's not rabbit skin, Val. Look more like cow fur."

She looked at her purse and then at me, saying, "Doubt it. Cow fur! Who ever heard of cow fur!"

So I told her, "What you think—cows stay bolo-head or what? You and me, we went go Lani-Moo Farm down Kahuku-side when we was small kids. We both went go pet Lani-Moo and her baby cow . . ."

" 'Baby cow!' Try 'calf'!"

She probably still thinks it's rabbit. She was standing at the front of my car, waiting for an answer. She was barefoot.

"Val, honey. If you going out, I think more better if you wear rubber slipper at least. How you figure?" I was talking sassy.

"Ne, later. I going back inside the house."

"Howz about the grease all over the ground?"

"Grease!" She looked down at the garage floor, stepping carefully backwards.

"Ne, I just kidding. Fool you, eh? So what you like again?"

"Eh! You think you wise, eh, Mr. Speed-Racer with the pseudo-fast car that no can catch up to one Z-28!" She was teasing me. I was sure about that when she started singing the chorus from the theme song of the old "Speed-Racer" cartoon. "Go, Speed-Racer! Go, Speed-Racer! Go, Speed-Racer, go-o!"

"Funny, funny, funny. You ever thought about getting one job as one knee-slapping comedian? And what's this about some plug Z-28?"

"Oh, yo! No make, Vince! Duki told me about the time you got dusted by the red '68 Camaro!"

"Duki? Fuck that shet! I gave the guy in the Camaro one chance and the bugga took advantage of my kind generosity. Never mind that. You went ask me something or what?"

251

She was singing again, "Go, Speed-Racer. Go, Speed-Racer..."

"Okay. If you going make like that..." I started to lean over the fender again.

"Ne-ne-ne-ne-ne! You no can take one joke or what? Shi, what a sourpuss."

I stood back up. "So what you like then!"

"Gee, no need get all piss-off."

"Okay, okay, okay. I not. What!"

"I just wanted to know if you had some dope."

"Ye, I get. So what?"

"I can have couple J's or what?"

"Magic word?"

"Shet."

"Oh! Sorry, you lose. That is definitely *not* the magic word."

"May I *please* have a few J's then, Vince-sir?"

"For what?"

"I was going clean out my ears with them."

"Well, in that case, why you no try the Q-tips in the bathroom? Mo' better."

"Come on, Vince."

I looked at her. Who does this junior-in-college child think she is? To ask her big brother for some rolled-up sweet cannabis buds? She's still yet four years younger than me!

"Ye, okay. Stay in my guitar case. You know where."

"Eh, thanks, ye, Vince." Val smiled. She has such a pretty smile with these cute tiny dimples. Her eyes sparkled in the glare from the trouble-light dangling from the raised hood of my car, and she kind of skipped off to the kitchen door.

I called her, "Eh, Val."

"Ha?" She turned before the kitchen door. Ye, she had her eyelashes on. I told her how many times before, "No need!"— her real eyelashes were long and thick enough—but she still alwayc wears those things when she goes out anyway.

Her hair is black touched with brown. I told her once that it was "almost 'ehu" and she said, "I doubt!" And her hair isn't the dried-out brown of peroxide or lemon juice or sun scorch. I have the same kind of hair but not as thick. Her hair is full and curling with soft waves, but it's not severe enough to be kinky or Brillo pad. She had it cut to just below her shoulders and it curled at her forehead, away from the sides of her face. She was always worried about the frizzies when she hardly had any.

"Ha?" She asked again from the kitchen door.

"Ah, nothing," I told her.

She gave me her "how bizarre!" look and turned back to the door. Val has a nice figure—she takes care of her body. She's almost slender but not skinny like a bony baby Bambideer. "Try 'fawn,' " she would probably tell me. Ye, ye. She opened the kitchen door and went inside the house.

Val's four years younger than me. She's a junior at UH, easing into an English degree, the same thing I was going to go into. But I quit UH, for a little while at least. I'm working at Times now—I got hired after I got turned down three times—the McCully branch, the one across from Washington Intermediate and Zippy's. I figure I'll go back to UH maybe next year—I'm doing okay, I guess. At least I have a full-time job. My friend Duki doesn't even have a job and he's older than me. I'm doing okay.

Inside the house, Mom called, "Val! No forget, your turn to wash the dishes tonight. And did anybody feed the dog?"

Val answered from my bedroom, "Mommy! Not my turn tonight! I washed 'em last night. Vince's turn now. And I think the dog was fed already."

Mom said, "I hope so."

I was going to protest this laying-on of the chores on top of me, but I figured, Whatevers. BD's. Val, what a liar. And Taro wasn't fed yet. I could see him from the garage. The old shaggy poi dog was sticking his head out of his doghouse, looking sad and starving. One paw was resting in his empty food dish, his way of hinting to us about feeding him. No worry, I going feed you. If Val was to feed Taro when she was in a rush, all she would give him would be the dry dog food, not the Kal Kan.

"Eh, Vince. You get some dope or what?" Just 'cause she's a junior at UH, she thinks she's pro-Joe grown-up mature. Tsa! She's still yet four years younger than me! She still has all her stuffed animals like the chubby snow-white bear with the red nose. She still goes to sleep with her Winnie-the-Pooh bear, the one I gave her for Christmas when she was in tenth grade.

five years ago
Val in ninth grade
me at UH

Back then even, she thought she was so grown-up. When she was in ninth grade at Kawananakoa Intermediate, she was going out with this senior guy from 'Iolani. Well, not really going out with. It was more like hanging around with—they weren't going steady or anything like that. I remembered the guy from high school—he was one grade below me at 'Iolani. I guess that's how she met him, through me in the school.

Was the summer after her ninth grade. She was all excited about going to Roosevelt come fall. Big duduz, ye? I had finished a harsh first year at UH-Manoa. Now it was in the summer, after most of the high-school graduation parties were pau. The guy from 'Iolani was taking her around to all the parties and sometimes he would bring her home real late at night, if not early in the morning. Mommy and Daddy, they were concerned about the late night hours of their baby girl. I told them, "Ah, let her. Stay graduation party time, that's why. Only for little while, going be. Plus the guy taking her around, he's okay. He just graduated. I know him—he's a good guy." The guy was really laters, but I said that just so that they could let Val go out. Val had begged me to talk to Mommy and Daddy. Reluctantly, they let her stay out late, since it would only be for a little while, being graduation party time, and since big brother seemed to know what he was talking about.

That summer, after the graduation parties were pretty much pau, I was moping around the house early one Saturday morning, thinking of what to do. School was pau for me and no way was I going to go to summer-school session. I had been turned down by Times Supermarkets and about five other places and I wasn't in the mood for going job-hunting again.

The sun wasn't high enough in the sky to make the morning hot. A tradewind easing down Pauoa Valley rustled the leaves of the mango tree in our yard. The weak drying leaves dropped off the tree's branches and scattered themselves in the yard, around the rose bushes along the back stone wall, onto the green onion and string bean patch in the corner, into the garage.

That afternoon I was going to go to Al's house to help him pull the motor out of his '66 Chevy. But I had nothing to do in the morning. I turned on the TV and clicked through all the channels couple times. I looked out the parlor window at the old gingerbread-type house across the street. The old haole man was sitting in his fat padded recliner in his living room, staring blankly out the window. At me. "Fucken senile old shet," I mumbled, giving the old man a stink-eye. The old man slowly leaned forward, got out of his chair, and shuffled off to another room.

I walked to Val's room. I knocked softly at the closed door. I turned the doorknob and pushed the door open a little. I looked into her room.

The midmorning sun was shining through the yellow curtains on the windows facing the front yard. Val's stuffed animals on the shelf above the head of her bed were all leaning back or lying down, taking in some of that sun. Rhinos, dogs, cats, elephants, and even turtles. A monkey hung from the end of the shelf, practicing for a starring role in some upcoming Tarzan movie. In the middle of that row of upholstered beasts sat the chubby snow-white bear with the red nose that I had won for Val at the Hongwanji carnival long time ago, small-kid time.

twelve years ago
Val in second grade
me in sixth grade

I was in the sixth grade, she was in second. I remember I had to stay with her at the Hongwanji carnival 'cause Mommy and Daddy said so. I walked with her, holding her hand, as we played all the games the carnival had.

"We get some more scrip, Vince?"

"Of course. We get plenty. What you like play?"

We played all the games. We rode most of the rides too. Except for the Round-up, 'cause we saw this guy get off the ride and puke his guts out. How sick. We saw my friend Duki who snickered at us.

I said, "What!"

He said, "Look the tilly holding hands with the baby girl."

Duki was razzing, but Val was my sister. I gave him a "how bizarre!" look and I led Val away to the Giant Ring Toss game.

"Play that one for me again, Vince!"

"Why you no like play?"

" 'Cause I not tall enough for throw the ring over the animals, that's why."

255

"Oh. Okay." I elbowed our way through the crowd, to the front of the booth, and nodded to the fat middle-aged Japanese lady with the mochi-dango face who was tending the booth. "Eh, lady. Excuse me, I like three rings, please."

"Nandeska?" She smiled a mochi smile.

I had to fumble into my pidgin Japanese. "Ah, boku, mitsu that kind man-marui rings suki des. Chodai. Onegai. I think."

"Ah! Guru boi, ne! Anta no Nihongo wa tot'temo joozu des, ne! Guru boi! Guru boi!" She wiped her hands on her white cotton apron. She patted my arm.

I forced a smile and mumbled under my breath, "Ye, ye. Howz about the rings, obasan?"

"Hai, hai." She heard! "Mitsu wa jyuu-go mai scrip narimas yo!" She held out three rings.

"Ha?" I gave Val a side-eye and whispered to her, "What she said?" Val shrugged.

I looked back at the lady. "What? I mean, nani?"

She smiled mochi. "Ara, ara. An'nani joozu ja nai, ne! Hai, 'Mitsu' wa 'three' des. You like three ringuz, ne? Boy-san?" Ye, ye. I know what "mitsu" means. "To, 'jyuu-go mai' wa 'fifteen scrip' des. You give me, ne?"

Oh I knew that all along. This was such a jiu-fut game anyway. So cheapskate, five scrip got you only one ring. More worse, three scrip could get you one ride on the Ferris Wheel. But this manju booth had all the good prizes—the giant stuffed animals that were thick and fluffy, with none of them having any eyes missing. I gave the lady fifteen scrip and she smiled, handing me three almost basketball-size wooden hoops.

"Here, Val. Go try one." I gave her a hoop.

"Well. Okay. But you gotta go first."

She took a hoop and stood to one side to let the pro do his thing. I leaned forward carefully and softly tossed the hoop towards a monstrous fluorescent orange walrus. The hoop floated down and snagged an upholstered walrus tusk. No good—shet.

"Almost though." Val was trying to be encouraging. I leaned forward again, this time putting my weight on the knee-high wooden beam around the edge of the booth. I aimed for the fat Filipino pig—it was purple—next to the walrus. Again I softly tossed the hoop. Again I missed. I caught the pig's curlicue tail.

"Oh, shet. Your turn, Val."

256

"Okay."

She didn't even aim. She didn't even take her time. She tossed the hoop overhand even. She was aiming for a chubby snow-white bear with a red nose. It was *all* the way on the other side of the booth. She just threw the hoop at it. No wonder she missed. The hoop didn't even go above the bear. Instead, it hit the bear on its pon-pon.

"Aw." Val was disappointed. But that's the way it goes.

"Hai, hai." The smiling Japanese lady again. "Too bad, ne, kawa-i gyoru! Here, I give mo-shtotsu chance!" The lady was smiling dango as she held out one more hoop in her mochi hand for Val.

Val looked at me and I nodded at her to go take it. She took it from the lady and mumbled, "Thank you."

"Nihongo de? Nani yuu ka?"

"Ah, arigatoo." Very good, Val. I knew you knew that one.

"Here, Vince. You throw for me. Aim for that bear I was going for." She handed me the hoop. The fat lady managed to frown while she was smiling. Apparently, I wasn't kawa-i enough for her.

I was figuring what a junk game anyway. Juice, in other words. Disgruntled, I just threw the hoop away in the direction of the bear.

"You got 'em! You got 'em!" Val was so happy. I was so surprised.

"Talent," I told Val.

The fat lady got off her dango ass and took the white bear off the square base around which the hoop I had just thrown nestled snug. She handed the big stuffed animal to Val, not to me, all the while smiling mochi at Val and frowning koge-gohan at me.

So I told her, "Thanks, eh, Babasan!"

When we walked away, Val hugged me and the chubby snow-white bear with the red nose. I grinned and said, "Only talent."

She said. "No act. You just lucky," and she took my hand and we went looking for our parents.

seven years later, back to five years ago
Val in ninth grade
me at UH

That same chubby snow-white bear with the red nose was still on the shelf in Val's room seven years later. She had been taking care of it—its smooth white fur wasn't even dusty.

Val was wrapped up in her blanket, the thin quilted futon that Obaachan had sewn for her long time ago. She was lying on her side, curled up, facing towards me at her door.

"Hui! Val! Val!" I just wanted to bother her.

She groaned and moved under her blanket. She lifted up an edge of the blanket and squinted out at me. Her eyes were red and puffy. She had been crying. She dropped the edge of the blanket back down and turned over to face the wall.

I looked behind me to make sure Mommy and Daddy weren't around. I walked into her room, closing the door behind me. Stepping over her summer school books, I sat on the edge of her bed and touched her shoulder.

"Eh, Val. You okay or what?"

"Leave me alone."

"Val-baby. Something the matter?"

"Leave me alone, Vince."

"You sure?"

"Vince. Come on." She wasn't mad. She just wanted to be left alone for now.

So I tucked the blanket in around her and left her in her room, closing the door again. I went into the kitchen and looked out the window at Taro. Mommy walked in from their bedroom.

She said, "You look like you looking for something to do."

"Not really." I wasn't looking forward to doing *chores*.

"How about cleaning out the garage?"

"Mommy!"

"I think that's a good idea. Most of the junk is yours anyway." She walked away.

I walked out the kitchen door and scratched the matted fur on Taro's back on my way to the garage. There were some car parts in the back of the garage. Greasy. I looked over the sheets of plywood leaning on a side-wall of the garage. Ah, righteous! My old paipo board! The one I used to use when I was in intermediate school. Heavy duty! This was a beauty. I had carved this out of three-quarter inch marine plywood. Most everybody else's paipo boards were just flat pieces of plywood with rounded edges. Mine was *contoured*, with no flats anywhere. It was carved, planed, and sanded smooth. It was a bust-ass job. But it turned out beautiful. It looked like this: maybe three feet tall and a little less than two feet wide. It was still beautiful. I hadn't used it since intermediate school time. The seven coats of marine varnish still gleamed with the dark brown wood grain showing through. Dings had been filled with linseed oil putty and revarnished.

I got this brilliant inspiration to paint a design on the top. I went into the storeroom and got some sheets of number one-fifty and four-hundred sandpaper. With the one-fifty I roughed an area of the top's varnish in the center of the board. I smoothed the sandpaper scratches out with the four-hundred paper. I got a small can of appliance-white paint and medium pointed brush. I imagined the design: a Hawaiian petroglyph of a guy throwing net. I pried open the can of paint with a screwdriver and I started painting. I figured—if look ugly, look ugly.

It looked ugly. Besides, Daddy once tole me that the ancient Hawaiians didn't know how to throw net in the old times of petroglyphs. The art was introduced by some crazy Japanese fisherman immigrant who had decided to bring his throw net along with him to Hawai'i, to the sugar plantations. Think— what good would a throw net be when you had to katchi-ken and hole-hole all day long.

I pounded the lid back on the paint can, rinsed the brush in some old paint thinner, and put everything away. I leaned the board against the back of the garage to let the ugly design dry. It looked stupid.

"Vince."

"What!" I was thrown off. It was Val. "Oh, You scared me, baby-girl. Good morning, Val." She had just gotten up. She was still in her sleep clothes—her red play shorts and the oversize 1973 'Iolani Carnival t-shirt I had given her last year. Her hair was a mess. She was looking down at the ground. She had on Daddy's bust-up leather zoris. Something was heavy on her mind.

She just stood there next to me, looking down at her toes sticking out of the zori straps. The quiet red nail polish she had brushed on her toes about two weeks before was showing its age—dulling and chipping. She rubbed at the nail polish on one big toe with the front of the zori on her other foot. The

259

hard nail polish became scratched—thin flat-white lines on the fading red gloss. She bent down, licked her thumb, and glided spit on the scratched nail polish on that big toe. The wet glistened over the shallow scratches, over the dulling red. The wet gloss of spit temporarily rejuvenated the old nail polish, making it look freshly brushed on. Like an illusion of nice and new all over again. I sat down next to her and put a hand softly on her shoulder.

"Hey, Val. How's everything?"

She was quiet, still intent on inspection of her big toe's nail polish.

"Val."

"Ah . . ." She looked at me. Her eyes were still red and puffy. "Everything's cool. Pretty much."

"Well, that's nice." I wasn't going to press the issue.

"Vince." She hesitated, and continued. "Except, you see . . ." She was looking at her big toe. One tear splashed on it.

"Vince." She was whispering. "I scared."

"How come?"

" 'Cause I think maybe I might be hapai." She was talking so soft I could barely hear her.

But I heard her. I stifled this "What!" that I felt forced to say. 'Cause I heard her. I managed a weak "Oh." She was still bent down on her ankles, looking at her toes. They were wet with her tears. I stood up and pulled her up too.

"Come, Val. We go take one walk, to the park maybe. We no can let Mommy and Daddy see you all sad like this."

"But look the way I . . ."

"Ye, ye. 'Look the way I dressed!' I knew you was going say that. Big duduz. Let's go take a walk, Val."

We walked down the driveway. I had my arm around her shoulders.

Mommy called to us from in the house, "Eh! Where you two kids going?"

I shouted back without turning around, "Ah, we just going to the park, look around little while. We come back."

"Everything okay?"

"Ye, ye. No worry."

We turned onto Pauoa Road and walked towards the park. Val wasn't crying or anything anymore.

She told me softly, "Was your friend, ye, but wasn't his fault, see, we got drunk at one graduation party at this hotel,

260

and, we was feeling good, you know, and, you know, we went into the bedroom, and . . ."

"Ye, I know. You no need tell me about it."

"I missed my period, two weeks already. You mad?"

"No. Why should I be mad? No can help, so no use come huhu. You went go see one doctor?"

"No."

"Well, you gotta go see one doctor. He can give you one pregnancy test."

"But I missed my period."

"Ye, but this way we can make sure. You know, if yes or no, stay for reals."

"Okay. Vince, no tell Mommy and Daddy."

I looked at her. She was pleading with me. "No worry, Val."

We walked to the park.

"Tell you what, Val. Duki's Uncle Sei, he one doctor. And he's cool. I know him. He not going tell nobody."

"Not even Mommy and Daddy?"

"Course not."

"Not even Duki?"

"*Course* not!"

"Okay."

We sat underneath a monkeypod tree.

"Vince, what if I for real hapai? Pregnant."

"You no can have one baby, no way."

"Ye, I know."

"Uncle Sei can fix that up. Abortion."

"Abortion? Scary, eh?"

"Ne, safe. Easy. He do 'em, and you stay in his office overnight, and then pau."

"Ye? How you know all this?"

"Duki's cousin Lei . . ."

"Lei? Ne! Lei?"

"Ye. She had. Duki told me."

"How Duki went find out if Uncle Sei so cool and quiet?"

" 'Cause Lei told Duki. They close, that's why."

"Oh."

We sat under the tree for little while and then we walked back home. Val was okay. I was surprised—I didn't know my baby sister was this strong.

I called up Uncle Sei that afternoon. He said to bring Val in to his office Sunday morning so he could take urine and

261

blood samples for the hapai test. He was real cool about it.

When I left to go to Al's house to help him fix car, Val was washing clothes. I came back home after the sunset. Mommy said that Val had gone out. She went out with that guy, the one who... I didn't understand. I was tired and all greasy from working on the car. I took a bath, ate dinner, and sacked out.

I woke up when I heard Val and the guy come home little before midnight. They came inside the house and Val turned the TV on soft. I didn't want to eavesdrop but I could hear them talking.

The guy was all sad about something. I think he was starting to sniffle. What a tilly. I heard him ask Val, "You sure you don't want to see me anymore?"

Val's voice was soft. "Yes."

"Why?"

"I just think would be better for you and me." Val wasn't going to comfort the nakimiso. Good.

"Oh." The tilly was sniffling. Shi, what a crybaby. More worse, he's only one year younger than me. I should slap his head for what he did to Val. Tell the muff off, Val!

The tilly squeaked, "Val. I was wondering. I don't want to worry you, but, you know, from that time, I was wondering if you could be pregnant or what?" The tilly kept on sniffling.

Goddam it. This was becoming unbearable, especially to a samurai like me. Chiksho! Aksame yo! Ukininam! What a sensitive performance. Give the silly-willy a Tony award. What a crybaby and a half! I wanted to run into the living room and scream the tilly. Just for scare the shets out of him.

I wanted to scream out with all my might:

Fuck, no cry. What crying going accomplish? What a dumb-shet panty! You supposed to flip out. You supposed to go pupule-kitchigai-mento. You supposed to get this blank look in your face as you think, think hard!

Hapai? pregnant? hara ga futoku nat'ta? remember something about that from Health class? one late period? period—menustration, menstruation. ovals, ovaltine, ovulation and uterine linings. blood, not blood, that's the menstrual FLOW. rags, tampax, kotex, modess—every month or so like the full MOON. rag-out 'cause of puberty. rag-in, rag-out, ovaries and fallopian TUBES. uterus and cervix and vagina. you cunt and clit. water retention and uncomfortability. that bloated feeling, hymens and hairy lips. if I was back in Health class, I'd stand up and scream the teacher, "WHATS IT ALL ABOUT, BRA!"

But this is not Health class. and the big deal is not about where the shi shi puka stay. no, not the scrotum bags and the testes balls—nuts and vas deferens. no, not kohes and bilots and botos and uleules. no, not the bone. no, not the anatomy of the genitalia, no, not the horrors of VD. this no stay one wet DREAM when you wake up sticky tomorrow morning. when you wake up, the girl still stay hapai. it's too late to "rap" about the problems of contraception and responsible parenthood with one of the good fun counselors. it's way too late for anything, kids.

Fuck, this not Health class anymore. no ways. nobody's giggling-snickering-cracking futs and dirty jokes in the back row with friends. no, everything's pretty serious now. pretty fucken serious.

Nobody paid any attention in Health class. everybody figured they knew all about all that shet. they all heard about it before. you know—balling, fucking, blowing, finger banging and K-Y jelly and rubbers and foams that taste gross. you know, the dick-cock, the two nuts-balls, the cunt, the clit. fucken ding-ding and ching-ching. big fucken shet. all the dirty pictures, all the positions all the moves.

Fuck that! You crybaby! Fuck that!

But I stayed in bed, lying very still. Screaming never helps the situation. I listened. Val let the crybaby sniffle a little bit more. I could tell she wasn't even patting his shoulder. She was probably sitting at the other end of the sofa. That's the way it ends, pal. The sofa springs squeaked as she stood up.

She told him, "It's time for you to go now. And no worry about me. I not pregnant." She's not? Since when? Ha?

She clicked the TV off and pulled him up from the sofa. She opened the front door for him. He put on his shoes. He got no goodbye-goodnight kiss. He stopped sniffling as he walked to his car.

Val locked the front door shut. On her way to her room, she stopped at my bedroom door. She pushed the door open and whispered to me in the dark, "What time tomorrow morning?"

"Nine."

"I thought you was sleeping, big ears." She shut the door.

She was teasing me again.

Next morning I drove Val to Uncle Sei's office. He took urine and blood samples from her with no lectures. He knew me, so he figured he knew her. Val and me, we ate lunch at Rainbows'. We drove to Diamond Head Road and watched the surfers from the cliffs. I called Uncle Sei up before we left for home. The tests were negative. Val wasn't hapai. That Christmas, I gave her the Winnie-the-Pooh bear.

five years later, back to just the other night
Val's a junior at UH
me four years older than her and cruising

The kitchen door opened and Val skipped back out of the house.

"Eh, dreamer! What you doing?" she called out to me.

"Ha?" I was leaning against the fender of my car. I hadn't gone back to fixing the distributor. I was doing nothing, just daydreaming. She slipped on her cork-and-leather sandals and walked up to me.

"I found 'em in the guitar case. I took two. Thanks."

"Nihongo de?"

"Arigatoo!"

"Who you going out with tonight?"

"Carol."

"Movies?"

"Ye."

Carol's car drove up into our driveway. Taro barked lethargically—he was old and hungry. Carol beeped her horn at us. I nodded at her. Val turned to go.

"Eh, Val. Try come."

"What?" She walked to my side and I kissed her on her cheek. She said, "Oh, yo! What was that for?"

"Nothing much."

"Gee, I hope you never mess up my make-up."

"What?"

"Ne! Just kidding."

"Go already. Carol stay waiting."

"Bye then, Vince." And she kissed me on my cheek and walked to Carol's car.

"Bye, Val."

In the car, Carol asked Val, "What was that all about?"

264

"I don't know. He was fixing his distributor. He's always a little bit stony. Maybe too much mosquito punk when he work on his car outside at night."

"For real." Carol drove off with Val.

I left the car as is and washed up. I fed Taro some dry dog food. I went into the house and, in passing her room, I saw the chubby snow-white bear with the red nose on the shelf and the Winnie-the-Pooh bear on her bed. I washed the dishes that night.

Wini Terada

Born of the Pacific _____

"My mother had a saying—'Grow up into a good Japanese and become a good American.' That was the whole genre of the Japanese school and community. It's okay as a child, you understand. But when you grow older, you see a contradiction. I had to acknowledge whether I was a Japanese or American."
—Toshi

The following is an excerpt, or more correctly, the remnant of the work which Toshiaki Fumio Suematsu began as a young writer in Waimea. Part of this work was published in the late 30s in a Honolulu Star-Bulletin column entitled, "I Am An American."

While he tried to accurately portray the plight of the Japanese in Honolulu surrounding the war years, Toshi was acutely aware of the sensitivity with which many of his people received what was written about them and how they felt it would affect their image—and future—in these islands. Having felt the pressure from friends, and after struggling to depict the situation among the local Japanese, Toshi gave up his writing. "You can't trust words," he would say often.

He turned, instead, to numbers. Building his mathematical towers which could "out-compute any computer" and endlessly scribbling figures; in notebook after notebook—he sought to bring to light lost knowledge which he believes would benefit the young and bring hope for the future.

Book I
A Letter to Hisae

Although conceived in Hawaii, she was born in Japan.

The cause of it was her grandfather's illness, which recalled her immigrant mother to Japan shortly before she, Hisae, was born. She was brought to Hawaii soon after her birth, but by then it was too late where American citizenship was concerned. As an oriental, naturalization, by law, was closed to her.

Thus, Hisae was doomed to the life of an alien in America.

That was a dark secret in her life. She guarded it as though it was something shameful to admit. As a result, only a handful of people outside of the family knew about her Japanese citizenship. Hisae herself was not aware of it until she started going to school. But still being too young then to let the accident of her birth in Japan bother her in any way, a few more carefree years passed before the import of not being an American citizen struck her.

When it did, she suffered a stunning blow she found difficult to overcome. Like a sensitive child who learns belatedly about his adoption, she deviated from what might have been her natural tendencies. Overnight it seemed, and like the sudden darkening of a summer day, her gay laughter succumbed to a gravity induced by a premature emergence from the age of adolescence.

Her friends could not understand why she, who used to chatter along with them like mynah birds of the evening, suddenly became quiet, reserved, and after a time, withdrew altogether from their circle. Her parents knew the cause of the change that came about in their daughter, but they were at a loss to understand why her being born in Japan and not in America should afflict her so. Besides, as they saw it, there was an easy way out: Hisae could remove herself from the scene that was somehow making her unhappy; Hisae could return to Japan. And this, they urged her to do.

Hisae, while brooding over her misfortune, was almost persuaded. Not unconsidered was the desire of her parents to bring up at least one of their offspring in the authentic atmosphere of their beloved homeland, and thereby convert that child into a bona-fide Japanese, inculcated with what they considered incomparably admirable Japanese virtues, as well

267

as refinement of culture. Hisae knew that her Japanese citizenship made her particularly fit for that role and how much her willingness to be educated in Japan meant to her parents. Cheerfully fulfilling that desire of theirs, without having to grapple with an awakened consciousness of her being, was something she honestly wished she could do.

Now if only she happened to be another Japanese American . . .

But no, she wasn't. She was a Japanese, period.

The finality of it was hard to accept, and hopeless as she felt it was, she fought against it. And because she felt that to leave America was to run away from the reality of the life she must face irrespective of where she lived, she decided against returning to Japan . . . trusting that she would have a better chance of finding herself, if not happiness, in America, American citizen or not.

She was to oftentimes wonder about that. However, as in the years that followed, she tried to reconcile herself with, first, her new status, and second, this now alien land. And as though her life—the form and texture of which depended so much upon amicable relationships between America and Japan—weren't complicated enough already, the Manchurian Incident had to break out . . .

That they were years of transition from being a Japanese to an American she was not to realize until a year afterwards. But the irony of trying to regain America only after losing her did not escape the poor girl.

For until she was overwhelmed by the circumstance of her life, it had never occurred to her to give serious thought to herself as an American. Well, yes, America was a wonderful country and it was good to be an American. That simply had been something she was taught in school, a lesson to be learned. Questioning where belief, with its personal touch called conviction, entered had never crossed her mind. She at first even doubted that she had been taking America for granted. Yet she must have been, she had to admit. For when all things commonly called American were wrested from her, she realized how closely she had been all along associating herself as a part thereof. And they became at once heartbreakingly precious and desirable. And there was remorse that she could have been so callous about American birthrights as to matter-of-factly assume that they were there merely to be enjoyed. And with deepening perception of American values her sense of loss deepened in proportion. And this, she wasn't sure, but probably it was out of a desperation to hang on to something tangible, she could act upon. She became obsessed with a passion to pattern her life as closely as possible to her concept of an ideal American.

And so it was.

The change came about slowly but surely. And people, noticing only its physical manifestations, were critical of her.

There was the way she carried herself—her back straight, her head held high, proud-like. ("I am proud to be an American, even if only in make-believe.")

There was the way she dressed—colorfully and distinctively; the way she fixed her hair in a unique combination of braids and bangs that formed a crown of a head. ("Well, why not? This is a free country!")

There was the way she spoke, grammatically correct and each word accorded its proper pronunciation and precise enunciation. (The Japanese-Americans were being criticized for their poor spoken English. "Think what they will of me, I am not going to speak like them.")

Then there was about her an air of aloofness, as of a person who holds an inordinately high opinion of herself. (This last was not intended, but the inevitable by-product of a guarded behavior.)

Add them all together and what do you get? Certainly not naturalness.

Hisae, in the idiom of the Japanese Americans, was "haolefied."

One night, I stayed up until dawn, writing a letter.

The Year: 1939—about a year and a half after Japan provoked the China Incident (1937) and invaded China.

The Place: Waimea, Hawaii—a small farm and cattle-ranch village, located some fifty miles from Hilo.

The Scene: A shabby room of a farmhouse, standing isolated at the edge of a field planted with corn and an assortment of vegetables, mainly head cabbage.

"Hisae-san," the letter began . . .

I am writing by the light of a kerosene lamp.

It is in a room, furnished only with a table, a chair and a bed. The floor is covered with Japanese straw matting; the wall, with store wrapping paper. Overhead, there is no ceiling to hide the rafters and the roofing of corrugated iron, turned brown with rust. There is no closet either, and clothes hang loosely from nails on the wall. A battered suitcase together with several cardboard boxes, filled with personal items that are normally kept in bureau drawers, are shoved underneath the bed.

The table where I sit writing is pushed flush against a corner of the room, facing the room's one window. Two layers of shelves, lined with books, protrude over the left edge of the table forming a part of what is my desk. The books look worn, both with age and usage. Among them are high school text-books and classics of English Literature—Charles Dickens' *David Copperfield,* to mention one; George Eliot's *Silas Marner,* to mention another. Also, there are books by American writers: Washington Irving, Cooper, Hawthorne, Emerson, Dreiser, Sinclair Lewis, Hemingway and others.

Many of the books are inscribed with the name of my older brother, Masao. Also inscribed are the schools he attended together with dates, 1913 through 1927.

Masao, rare for his day, was permitted to leave home and go to live in Kohala, a plantation town about 28 miles away in order to work his way through high school.

Apart from the books mentioned, there are several other books bearing Masao's name. Printed in Japanese and dating back to 1914, there are Japanese school textbooks Masao used while attending the Waimea Japanese Language School.

I have found these textbooks a great deal more formidable than the books published and distributed ten to fifteen years later by the Hawaii Japanese Educational Board, which is the governing body of the Japanese educational system in Hawaii. I remember trying more than once, to read Masao's sixth-year reader but failing. It contained too many kanji—Chinese characters—that were not included in my own reader of the equivalent year.

Evidently, the Hawaii Japanese Educational Board recognizes the fact that the later children of the Japanese encounter greater difficulty than the earlier ones in learning to read and write and even to speak Japanese. Accordingly, it has revised the textbooks in keeping with the trend of the times. The curriculum, too, has been somewhat revised. For one thing, traditional Japanese brush writing has given way to pen-writing in the penmanship class.

Clearly, this is a significant sign of the cultural evolution taking place in the lives of the Japanese Americans.

But that this cultural evolution has run its entire course, or that, culturally, the Japanese Americans are already alienated from their Japanese parents, as our leaders are claiming, I cannot agree.

For it is only presently, in the thirties, that the Japanese Americans are tentatively emerging from their Japanese background and becoming aware of themselves. And not necessarily as Americans.

(Of course, this is an opinion I can share with Hisae alone.)

"Hisae-san," the letter began . . .

I first knew her as a fellow student.

Her home was in Hilo; mine as already noted, in Waimea. The fact that the Waimea School ended at the 7th grade determined my going away to a school in Hilo. First of all, though, I had to gain permission from father, who preferred to see me go to work for the Parker Ranch. He could have used my help on the farm, but this he never considered, farming being so poor in those days. Parker Ranch offered the best outlet for the young men of Waimea—boys, really—who were forced by the necessity of helping out with the family finances by going to work as soon as they finished grade school, or even sooner, in many cases.

"Hisae-san," the letter began . . .

The ancient alarm clock, with its dome of a bell, says it is seventeen minutes after nine. Having lived for three years in Honolulu, I know that 9:17 for a city is still early. But the hour is already late for Waimea, where the farmers and the ranch hands go to bed as soon as possible after nightfall. Apart from having to get up early in the morning, there is hardly anything doing in the village to keep them up. Indeed, life outside the hastily closed front door is practically nonexistent once the sun disappears behind the distant mountain (Hualalai) and the chilly night wind sweeps down from the Kohala mountains, at the foothills where Waimea nestles. The best place is in bed, under heavy covers.

The house, a crudely put together collection of rough 1 x 12 boards, with gaps between them covered with lathings from the outside and stuffed with rags from the inside, serves as poor protection from the penetrating cold. The cold intensifies as the night deepens and the morning finds the grass almost white with frost-like dew.

In Waimea's cold climate must be compounded the beneficial elements that are so invigorating to all things that grow here, including rosy cheeked children. But for inducing out of its fertile soil the green of the vegetables and the golden yellow of the ripened corn on a commercial scale required settlement by the Japanese who fled from the sugar plantations.

Not many farms are discernible from the eucalyptus bordered roadside, nor can the grandeur of the vast reaches of the Parker Ranch be appreciated from the wire fence picketed highway. But climb any one of the grassy hills overlooking the village and you will be able to see, in panoramic view, the picturesque squares—green, yellow, brown—that are the farmlands, interlaced with windbreaks of trees. And beyond this, the cattleland, the amber-green expansiveness which stretches away for miles and finally gives way to the imposing height that is Mauna Kea, which at times looms near; at times, hazy blue and purple in the distance, depending upon your own mood or the atmospheric condition of the day.

Standing there, atop the grassy hill, my hair and clothes tugged at by the incessant wind that blows there, my eyes measuring the width and the length of the valley below, I have oftentimes wondered how Waimea managed to escape coverage by sugar cane.

I am glad that it has though. Glad too, that my parents left behind them the sugar-mill camp, where I was born. Not that I can recall experiencing life there, but I have heard too many stories told by the Japanese about that life on the sugar plantation.

"Hisae-san," the letter began . . .

"Haolefied."

No other single word could have described her so aptly.

Not a compliment. For a "haolefied" Japanese American to another was one who was ludicrously out of character; bluntly speaking, a Japanese American who appeared to be aping the haoles. Behind it was the jeering opinion that such a person ignored the fact that the Japanese shape of eyes and color of skin will never be denied.

Moreover, "haolefiedness" connoted "high-tonedness," superficiality, and other unfavorable characteristics that were said to be inherent in haoles; and these characteristics were considered to be all the more reprehensible when manifested in a Japanese American.

But for my part, Hisae's "haolefiedness" was not an intermediary object of the Japanese American's antipathy toward the haoles.

Partly this was because I grew up in Waimea, where its handful of haoles were personalities we villagers hardly ever encountered. Consequently, my mind was relatively free of disparaging thought association with haoles. But perhaps more pertinent was my familiarity with the characters in the books by Charles Dickens, Robert Louis Stevenson, Victor Hugo, plus a host of other writers.

A bookworm, I had started reading at an early age and had, by the time I finished grade school, read many of the required readings of high school.

Now I am not saying that I understood all that I read. But whatever I got out of all that reading must have given me a broader outlook on life than I would have had otherwise.

Anyway, haoles or no (as a matter of fact, raciality never entered the mind) the characters in the books I loved to read were people with whom I vicariously shared love, honor, duty, with the attendant sorrow and joy, despair and hope, defeat and triumph . . .

After reading, say, the life of David Copperfield, how could I not reflect that he, David Copperfield, was more human than I, or believe that he would not try to understand me any less than I tried to understand him.

Ah, yes! There I was loitering in the corridor of a world created by art . . . drenched, as it were, with an idealism that must, sooner or later, leave me high and dry on the ebbtide shore of reality.

In no other frame of mind, however, could there have developed such friendship as developed between Hisae and myself. Normal reaction to her "haolefiedness" would have repelled me from her.

As it happened, her peculiarness—her singular individualness, rather—raised her in my eyes above the rest of of Japanese Americans. And meeting her was like meeting a character out of a book. This impression was enhanced by the impression she gave of one cast in a tragic role.

For there she was, attractive (this in more ways than one) and with a studied indifference about her, as though nothing on earth could ruffle her composure. Yet, watching her, I detected signs that betrayed her; signs of inner despondency, as though carrying out her role was at times too much of a burden. Her shoulders would sag, and I could almost hear her letting out a sigh or two during some quiet interval in the classroom, when everyone was ostensibly occupied with his or her problem of a lesson. At such moments, with her defenses down, she looked almost pitiful, and I for one suspected that the face she was putting to the world was only a brave front after all. And I wondered about the nature of the tragedy that must have jarred her young life and which had not only left its mark on her but was affecting her still.

What neither I, nor anyone else in the classroom knew was that she was not an American citizen.

I do not know what difference it would have made to any of us even if we had.

"Hisae-san," the letter began . . .

I am the only one awake in the house.

A little while back, mother came, sleepy-eyed and muttering something about not staying up too late. Force of habit, I suppose. For she needn't have bothered, tomorrow being Sunday. I do not have to get up at 4:39 in the morning to work at the Parker Ranch store.

Force of habit on mother's part, I say, because from the time I was a little boy, a light burning in my room has made her get up once or twice in the night to check on me, whether I had passed on to sleep while reading. Looking back, it is a wonder that the house never caught on fire, reading as I used to do while lying in bed, laid out on the floor, with the kerosene lamp with its open flame close to my head. Of course, mother was watchful. Still, I remember waking up some mornings to find the lamp still burning or having flamed out of its own accord from lack of fuel, the chimney all blackened with soot.

With everyone else asleep, the house is quiet of human noise. All the windows are shut tight, but there is a current of air circulating through the house, what with its many cracks and openings. Now and then, gusts of wind rush at and slip into the house and set the flame of the lamp to flickering— which brings to eerie life the shadows of the objects in the room the lamplight casts.

Sleeping in the house are father and mother as well as a younger brother and sister. There are two other members of the family. Masao, I have already mentioned. An older sister lives in Hilo and it was at her home that I stayed while attending school in Hilo. Both are married, and each has a growing family. I had another sister immediately below me, but she died in infancy and lies buried in the cemetery, which is located in the backyard of the Japanese language school.

So the original couple, who are my parents, have now increased to seven—no, twelve, when grandchildren are counted.

With Japan's extraterritorial ambition creating tension in the Far East, we are headed toward some kind of a crisis. I am nevertheless glad that my parents immigrated to Hawaii.

But what about them . . . parents?

Our birthrights as Americans mean little or nothing to them.

They came to Hawaii, expecting to stay here for not more than three years. Yet here they are, more than a quarter of a century afterwards, still looking forward to that day when they can return to Japan. True, as they saw their children take root in this, to them a foreign soil, the motive behind their returning to Japan has changed. Now it is only for a pilgrimage home, to see their homeland at least once more before they died.

They came to Hawaii believing that money here was lying on the ground, and all they had to do was pick it up in order to gain riches. So what bitter disappointment theirs must have been to find out that all the wonderful stories they had been told about Hawaii were nothing more than part of a scheme to lure cheap Japanese labor to work in the sugar cane fields.

Looking back, it is a wonder how they endured their disappointment.

But endure it, they had.

Paradoxically, what helped them most was an added burden upon their hardpressed lives—children.

Yes, it was in the birth of us children that they reassembled what meaning to working and suffering and striving that was for a time, shattered within them; even as the waves which bore them across the Pacific curled against themselves and crashed and broke upon these then dispassionate, foreign shores. It was also in us children that they transplanted what hopes and dreams they had once had as man and wife, but which they now despaired of realizing on their own account.

And so it was for the sake of us children that they had set their hearts to establishing some semblance of home . . . trusting, in the meantime, that with proper inculcation of Japanese virtues, we would eventually do right by them, as duty-conscious children, within whose veins course Japanese blood, and whose hearts and minds were instilled with the spirit of Yamato.

"Hisae-san," the letter began . . .

Thus, Hisae . . . a strange girl, was different from any Japanese girl I knew up to the time I met her, and for a long time afterwards as well. A decade or so later, Japanese girls with suggestions of her likeness were to be a common sight. Back there in the early thirties, however, while the Japanese Americans were still strictly disciplined by the proud, unremitting "Japaneseness" of their immigrant parents, her sophisticated manner of carriage, dress and speech, was radically ahead of the times.

And on first impression, she was the last person from whom I expected the kind of friendship she extended me. Yet, apart from all others, it was she who seemed to sense the loneliness and the misplaced feeling I was experiencing as a new student in a large school, away from home. For upon learning that I was from Waimea, she seemed to go out of her way to show kindness toward me. And when I began contributing stories to the school literary magazine and newspaper, she began showing an uncommon interest not so much in me, but in my hometown. She would ask searching questions, thereby eliciting from me stories about the people and life in Waimea, many of which I hadn't thought I remembered.

In effect, she made me relive my boyhood in the village.

As to what purpose it all was, I did not, in the beginning, question. It was enough to talk to her; to have something to talk about in which she evinced keen interest.

"Hisae-san," the letter began . . .

Why Hisae's interest in me and my life in Waimea?

She had a definite purpose in mind. But it was only afterwards, after I left school and Hilo, returned to Waimea and began working on the farm, that it occurred to me that she had subtly tried to make me see myself for what I was: a Japanese boy raised in a closely knit Japanese village. In short, a hyphenated American who had grown up more a Japanese than an American.

"Hisae-san," the letter began . . .

Hisae-san, I wrote, what can I say in reply to your last letter? You sounded so troubled and unhappy. As a matter of fact, in all your letters of late, you sound both troubled and unhappy.

I know—it is this trouble in China, dissonant with undertones of war. It has reopened that old wound you suffered back in 1931, when Japan first incurred the enmity of America by invading Manchuria.

Why did the China Incident have to break out, just when you were emerging at last from the darkness of America Lost to the dawn-light of America Regained? Fate, would you say? The self-same fate that made you be born in Japan?

As I recall, you did not use the word fate. You blamed "chance and circumstance." "When I think how chance and circumstance can, and does alter one's life, I cannot begin to express my fear of them," was what you said, prefacing that to your telling me that you were not an American citizen.

But to tell you the truth, I was not able to understand what difference that should make to you. After all, Japanese or Japanese American, weren't we both being regarded as one and the same? And even after you told me how affected you were when you realized the full import of not being an American citizen, I was not able to fully understand why that should be so.

I sympathized, yes. I said it was a shame. I said it was sad and tragic and all that sort of thing. Moreover, I made you think that I understood how it must have been to grow up thinking that you were a part of all that you learned about America, and then to find out that you were not a part of it. That perhaps you could never be, because the diplomatic differences between America and Japan seemed so great you did not think they would be able to amicably resolve their differences.

I have been pondering over it these past weeks—this night, especially—as I sought for words that might be of some encouragement and comfort to you. I have been looking into the past of my life, weighing the part you have played in it against what my life might have been if I hadn't known you. I have done all this as objectively as possible, and the conclusion I have reached is this: I was not able to understand why you should be affected as you were because I had yet to know and feel what it meant to be an American, of what it should mean.

This is not to infer that I do now. If I did, I certainly would know what to tell you to relieve you of the anxiety you must be feeling this night.

How I wish I could tell you that the current war in China does not mean a thing. That it too, like that other war in Manchuria, will soon pass and that one of these days we will wake up to find that the fears we feared were utterly baseless.

Can I though, when I myself am affected by it? What grave concern America is manifesting over the situation in China! You want to close your ears to it, but you cannot help hearing disquieting whispers that before this crisis in the Far East is over, there will be war in the Pacific. Of course, war between America and Japan is still difficult to imagine. But it is not so far-fetched as it was at one time. For now that the prediction—"After Manchuria, China"—is a reality, the motive behind Japan's troop movements coinciding with tell-tale military activities within the security-bound border of Germany is becoming clearer. All in all, it is doubtful that America, this time, will stand idly by and watch China meet the same fate as Manchuria.

One thing is certain where we of Japanese blood are concerned: feelings against us will run at a higher and higher pitch, in relation to the rising criticalness of the times.

Already the newspapers are creating an atmosphere suggestive of war. Day after day, news dispatches from the warfront in China are featured on the front page, topped with banner headlines. Inexorably the Far East, which at one time seemed remote, is being drawn nearer and nearer. The general effect is that, while there may be some doubts to China fighting America's battle, there is little doubt that Japan is America's enemy.

. . . Japan is America's enemy, and what are you, Japanese in Hawaii, going to do about it? What are you thinking? What are you planning? What will you do, if and when America and Japan fight?

Gratingly, the oft-asked questions resound in our ears.

Now I ask you, is this a time for us to be looking ahead to the day when we expect to be accepted as bonafide Americans?

It appears not.

Faced as we are, with a future that is dark in its uncertainty, this appears to be a time when we ought to be satisfied—grateful even—just to be allowed to retain our status quo.

What do you say, Hisae-san?

Do you agree?

No, I do not think that you will.

At the moment you are troubled and unhappy, despondent. The pendulum swung, lethargically, to the other extreme. But given time, you will find your way out. You are bound to, just as you did that other time.

This I have to believe. At the moment, when it seems much easier not to care, I have to believe in you . . .

There was a time when I thought that I would be less perturbed by the attacks made against us if I were, in truth, a Japanese—say, like yourself. For then I would neither have the right nor the privilege of defending my rights and privileges as an American. And not having said rights and privileges and, also, not entertaining any ideas about the so-called Promise of America, I would not be giving up anything—sacrificing, that is, any of the ideals and principles of America—even if I were to let myself be beaten down to utter submission.

For it is because we know that we, as Americans, are entitled to the rights and privileges guaranteed us by the Constitution that when they are abridged and portions of them denied us and there seems nothing we can do about them, that we become frustrated, angry, bitter and perhaps in the end, turn our thoughts against America.

That is what I thought.

But then, I came to know you, and as I learned more and more about you, I realized how wrong I was. I realized that I was only trying to justify my shortcomings, not to mention my poverty of understanding.

For I found out that you are, in fact, a Japanese. And yet I did not know of any Japanese American who was more concerned about the dilemma of their problem. Still, I could not say that you were bitter. And though you held on to no hope of becoming an American citizen, you were always trying to think and live as though you were. And on the rare occasions you showed traces of anger, your anger was directed to your own self, rather than to anybody else. You were impatient with yourself for letting yourself be angered by something somebody said or something that happened on the racial front.

Now, I must confess that that was something I could not very well understand. But that your general attitude was related to something you once told me about ideals and principles, I was quite certain. You told me that American ideals and principles cannot represent the people. That it is people alone who can represent them. That some people may not live up to them, but the ideals, as ideals, and the principles, as principles, remain the same. That they do not change. You then went on to tell me that it was important that the Japanese Americans recognize whatever outrageous things said or acts committed against them for what they actually are, and not confuse them with anything else that might tend to make them think the less of America.

There I felt, you expressed the basis of your belief in America. And as I kept thinking about it, in time I let myself think that you succeeded in imparting that belief in me. But this was in the relatively peaceful year we enjoyed prior to the outbreak of the China Incident.

Well, what now? Now that an actual test of that belief is here?

Alas, I find myself falling flat on my face.

So there, now you know.

And I'm telling you that I am feeling tenfold worse than if I had never stopped to consider myself in relation to America in any way.

Who was responsible for it?

It was you, Hisae-san.

Now, don't misunderstand me. I am not blaming you in any way. I am simply stating a fact. For it is true, is it not, that if it hadn't been for you, I would today be like most Japanese Americans, irritated to be sure by the sharp words of those who choose to antagonize us, but not too much. Not at least, to the point of being waspish about it, as I sometimes suspect I am. And since there seems little or nothing that can be done, perhaps it is better not to be all fired up with ideas, not be overly sensitive to the situation at hand. One is less liable to get hurt, under the circumstances. So the apparent listlessness and indifference for which the Japanese Americans are being criticized, may be good for them for all we know. I don't know . . .

All I know is that I am not the fellow I might have been, if I hadn't known you. For which I am glad, though you may not think so considering the preceding paragraph. But I am! For, is not this problem you have made me face a problem all Japanese Americans must face if America is to mean anything to them?

What I am leading up to is this: that you, having brought me this far, cannot now give in to the apparent blank-wallness of the times. If you were to give in now, it would be the same as telling me to forget all that you have told me of what you believe.

I think your beliefs are sound, although God knows I am in no position to qualify them. They have helped you out of your first crisis. If they seem to crumble before the current crisis, is it your beliefs that are crumbling, or should it not be your belief in your beliefs?

There must be a better way of putting it. Anyway, what I am trying to tell you is that, if you find yourself doubting America, you are only reflecting your doubt in yourself.

Does that sound familiar? It should. I am only repeating what you have told me often enough. Yes, I am giving the thought back to you. I don't see what use I can make of it, if you can't.

Am I being ironic? Believe me, I do not mean to be. I am merely trying to impress upon you the fact that you have been in the past, and are today, the medium through which I judge America.

Judge, I say. That is a wrong word, judge. What qualifications have I to judge America? What qualification does anyone have to judge America?

Here might lie the root of the whole trouble with us: that we dare to judge. And judging, we are in turn, judged. And although irresponsible and insensitive to the consequence of the verdict we pass on to others, we on our part, react most illhumoredly to the verdict handed down to us.

That also, has a familiar ring to us.

Why, of course! Is not that the sum of what you have been

trying to tell me all along? Quoting scriptures from the Bible, even . . .

Strange how in the quiet of this night, they are all coming back to me, the many things you have told me, the views and opinions you have expressed on a thousand and one things. Stranger still, how I find myself receptive to them as though they originated in my own mind. Could this mean that I am finally thinking in the light of your understanding, and thus, observing myself all the more clearly for that?

Something is happening here . . .

Time seems to be standing still, and I am held in the sensation of being detached and elevated about the immediacy of my being, the immediacy of my surroundings. And though I have always thought of the past as the irretrievable past, I sense an intermingled intimacy of the past and the present. The past it seems, is coming back and relating itself to the present. Nay, the past, it seems, has never been the past, but an inseparable part of the present, and the way I have always thought of the past as the past, was only in the sense of it.

Am I making sense? I doubt it, but to me it is all very clear.

There is this kerosene lamp, giving off its yellow, flickering light. It could very well be the same lamp by which I, as a boy in grade school, used to read, late into the night. It is a wonder that the house never caught on fire, reading as I used to do: in bed, laid out on the floor, the lamp, with its open flame, close to my head. Of course mother was watchful. Still, I remember waking up some mornings to find the lamp still burning or flamed out of its own accord for lack of fuel and the chimney all blackened with soot. How I used to hate the chore of taking care of the lamps—refilling the fuel bowl with kerosene and washing the chimney I blackened . . .

Am I talking of the past? What I have said in connection with this lamp by which I am writing is more real to me now than it ever was.

There is this lamp, as I began . . . and the strawmatted floor, the store wrapping paper covered walls, the ceilinglessness overhead, showing the rafters and the roof of corrugated iron turned brown with rust . . . and there is the wind outside, rustling dryly through the plantings of corn and the scraping of the branches of the peach tree against the wall of the house . . . and there is the occasional stamping sound of the hoof of the horse tethered in the yard . . . and there is the distant moaning of cattle being driven by cowboys from pasture to seaport . . . and there is mother whom I expect any moment now to come sleepy-eyed and muttering something about not staying up too late . . .

These and many other familiar associations which would require pages to list, are the same as when I was a child. And I guess they will always remain the same, in fancy, if not in fact, for the rest of my life.

Where then, is the past? Where the present? Where the future?—except, in the sense of them?

So, again, I am standing atop one of the grassy hills overlooking this peaceful village. Here, where the outside world nudges itself in only through the newspapers. Here, where in most instances, momentous happenings of the world are no longer so by the time they enter because the newspapers arrive two to three days after publication. Yes, again, I am standing atop that grassy hill, my hair and clothes tugged at by the incessant wind, and I can see in panoramic view the picturesque squares—green, yellow, brown—that are the farmlands, interlaced with windbreaks of trees. And beyond that, the cattle land, the amber-green expansiveness of which stretches away for miles until it finally gives way to an imposing height that is Mauna Kea—at times, looming near; at times, hazy blue and purple, in the distance, depending upon your own mood, or the atmospheric mood of the day. And standing there, my eyes measuring the width and breadth of the vast valley below, I am wondering again how this place ever escaped coverage by sugar cane, but am concomitantly glad that it had. Glad, too, that my parents settled here, away from the sugarmill camp where I was born. Not that they improved their lot by settling here and setting themselves up as independent farmers. In fact, they were having a worse time of it, being so poor. And yet, here was a measure of independence. What did these Japanese people here, living together, in a closely-knit community, feel and think and aspire? And what about their children, for whom they were trying to create an atmosphere reminiscent of the home country? What did they, in turn, feel and think and aspire? Parents and offspring though they were, there was conflict between them. And what about their common conflict with the larger American community? When reflected in the light of these questions, was life in the village below as peaceful as it looked from here? No, no! Even as ocean tides flood and ebb, beneath the conventions of what outwardly appears to be an easy-going, leisurely country life, floods and ebbs a deep-set human tide . . .

I do not quite realize it yet, but I am thinking of the people and life in the village as you, Hisae-san, might. I am trying to visualize how I grew up here, as you yourself might. Then as I begin to see the picture you meant to evoke in mind, I know at last why you showed such uncommon interest in the stories you made me tell you about the people and life in my home town.

That was the way it was, many years ago, when I returned from school and Hilo, disappointed and maybe bitter too, for having had to start out in life long before I felt prepared for it. And it was to shut out the shame of the baseness of my thoughts, that I had gone off by myself to the grassy hilltop as though climbing to higher ground would cleanse my mind. And that is the way it is at this moment, when I sense no past, no present, no future, but only a great awareness of the now and its intimacy with that experience on the hilltop.

So the arc, you might say, has come full circle. I am back again to that beginning when you made me see myself for what I actually was—a Japanese boy, born of Japanese parents, raised in a Japanese community.

That first time, I was not able to accept this basic truth about myself. I don't see how I could be blamed for it, though. (Not that you have.) For the simple truth is that I was then not yet ready. There were so many other things you had to first awaken in my mind.

So I may have found myself, you might say. And I am going to be all right. Already, an idea of a story is developing in my mind. I am sure you can guess the nature of it without my having to tell you.

When, earlier this night—how ages ago it seems now—I sat down to write this letter, I did not know how to begin, did not know where I was headed. After I began, I did not know how and where I was going to end. Such was the muddled state of my mind. However, struggling along with this letter has clarified many things in my mind and I feel encouraged and exhilarated in a way I have not felt in a long, long time.

Now, let me check . . . Yes, the idea of the story is still there, and growing, and I am getting excited. I may still get to write that great American novel!

The flame of the lamp is fluctuating—becoming long then short, and black smoke swirls upward from its tongue, blackening the chimney. Symptom of the bowl running dry of fuel. Seems that I just made it. Something symbolic here . . . for though this flame is about ready to pass on, so too is the night, and I sense the quickening pulse of the dawn.

One last thought before I leave: I began this letter with the idea of comforting you and I end up by finding myself comforted.

Hisae-san, what will I ever do without you?

Fumio

Toshi

Go to Home

My mother enjoys telling my young daughters scary stories about the plantation days. The girls always ask to hear about the Coffin Lady. Mama sits down by the kitchen table, her face busy thinking. Her childhood and Obaban, her own mother, are ready to be called back. Mama pours us our sodas, passing out mochi-crunch or candy. Then she wipes her glasses, she has cataracts now, and clears her throat.

A long time ago, when Obaban was still new in the camp, she used to be the midwife for Union Mill Camp, outside of Kapa'au town. Obaban was young and pretty, yeah? But she had to do too much backache labor, because she was stuck with the housemaid work for Greenwoods and for the whole Sam Wells place, too. Also early in the morning she had to cook for all the single men down at Camp. Plus she had two or three kids, but I wasn't born yet.

She knew all the people living around there at the time, must have been 1890s, 1900. Those days Kohala was important like a small Hilo town. Union Mill was so dry and brown, though. Not like now. Not like when you folks went. In fact no more Union Mill now, right?

One family over there was not too lucky no matter how you look at it. When everyone was real poor, they were so poor people felt hurt even to look at them. Not just ricebag clothes like Obaban them, this family's came boro-boro falling apart and too junk for rags. They were shame, too. What was the name? Kaneyama, Tanegawa, Kurokawa? The lady was always sick, even from the day she got to Hawaii. Ten years later on, when she already had four children, the haole doctor found out she had tuberculosis. Her husband was working that time as a stevedore at the docks in Honolulu, because Kohala-side had no cash money.

When she found out she was going to die, because those days there was no hope if you were poor and had t.b., she cried and cried. All the four children cried, too. All the camp ladies who heard about it cried and cried with her. Pitiful, you know. But they were careful not to touch her or her clothes or her kids. The others would move far away if she even coughed.

Quickly somebody wrote a letter to her husband for her, because the poor thing could not write at all, not English, not

Japanese. And no telephone, right? The letter was in Japanese writing, but the neighbor's son tried out the English school lettering he was learning. So the outside of the envelope had on it, "Go to Home" in big, neat pencil letters. Obaban took it to the plantation office. She always remembered those English words from looking so long at that message while she took care of sending it to Honolulu. She use to practice when we were small; wrote it in the dirt or the air, "Go to Home," "Go to Home," while she told all us about the lady dying.

The mother. So young to know that she would be gone soon. And she looked at the little faces, the children so young to lose the mother's love. They hugged each other tight and cried until they would have drowned in each other's tears. But Obaban said to the missus, "You have to hold on, yeah? You have to be strong for the children until your man comes back." So Obaban cried some more with them until she had to leave their shack. Later on she told us she would never forget how the lady looked: j'like a little girl herself, j'like somebody who got hit with a stick for no reason by nobody you could see. She was surprised and sorrowful, but she didn't want to let go of those children. No, they sat together holding onto hands, legs, arms, necks, so skinny—those days they had only can evaporated milk, you know. Nobody had vitamins, only rice, rice, rice—all one heap of sad, bony children and the small lady blowing her nose on one rag.

So they waited. But in those days the boat between the islands never did run on time, and anyway only two times a month, maybe. So it could be the mister missed a boat or never had the money right away or didn't get the letter in time or what? Nobody found out. He got back in time for her funeral.

The camp was taking it hard; yet plantation days people pulled together when the time came for whatever it was they needed to do. All the folks took care of the ceremony. The church people made the service just the right way, and the neighbors took care the kids, because no more outside family, right? They were all walking to the graveyard with the casket, just a plain wooden box, slowly moving under the hot sun. Nothing around but burned out, chopped down canefields, miles and miles of nothing. Was pretty near the old Kohala town temple, yeah, but they were so sad, all those people, be cause it was so unfortunate, that they had to take their time, step by step, remembering all the sorrow.

Well, the husband comes running up the steps of the temple and far away he sees the line of all those friends; everybody was there, and the coffin that they were dragging with ropes, and he faints. Right there. After all, he had to rush from the harbor at Kawaihae, jump in a jitney all the way to Union Mill and then down his house place. And when he saw nobody anywhere, empty, empty, all gone, he knew right away she was make-die-dead. All pau. He knew where to find the people. He knew where she would be.

He got up hard on wobbly legs. He rushed to the road towards the hateful box.

"Wait, wait, wait," he waved, yelled and screamed at uncle them til they all spotted him running from far down the dirt road, kicking up dust.

A big man. Strong, after all, he could do stevedore work, you know. Throwing huge boxes around. He could match the Kanaka boys, not like the other short Japanese fieldworkers. Though they were steady, hard workers. But that's how lots of those old men use to be those days. Try look at all the old photos Mrs. Hamada's house. The big box. Some were sumo wrestlers, giants. How they could find enough to eat, I don't know. Some other ones liked to do cowboy work, heavy labor and low, low pay. Paid in beef. You would never know how strong and big they use to be with muscles all over, when you see them old and hunching down. J'like the grandpas sitting around at Ala Moana Center nowadays. But those are just the sons. The first old ones were tough guys, hard-headed though. Pakiki. They had to be.

They saw him. His children came running back when they heard the commotion. But they didn't touch him. No, it was out of respect and fear. They stayed back, hanging around and watching up at his face. They were so sad to see him too late.

He gripped the box crying, choking up with sadness. And then he went force them to pry up the thing. He was one hard one, a mean big man, aching so bad that nobody would argue. They must have thought he was pupule already, anyway.

He was looking down at his wife's dead body. Now he cried. Tears were rolling off in two wet paths. And everyone who saw him felt pitiful and cried at the uselessness of the waste. Poho.

He talked to his woman. He kept saying, "I'm sorry. Forgive me. I didn't know. Couldn't get home. I'm too late." Over and over.

And then he reached for her cold body, so they had to try to pull him back while he pushed them off with the other arm.

288

She was dressed so nice and neat. Pretty looking at the end.

"Give me a sign that you hear me, let me know you understand," he was shouting into her face, into her ear as if she could hear him. Her body was almost pulled out, because he had to struggle against all the neighbors holding on to him, begging him to stop

That's when it happened. She gushed out blood. Her jaw fell slack open, and it spread out all over her face and the front of the man. Soft red-black. Everyone backed off. But he was satisfied. She heard him. Stopped the tears. He put her down carefully and said a prayer kneeling on the ground with his head against the coffin: trembling, moaning, coughing, but not angry, not bitter now.

Our Obaban said everybody left that family alone for a long time after the burial. The oldest girl was in charge until they all grew up. They hanaied the baby brother with one Hawaiian family up in Waimea. Died already, but used to live in Makiki, long-time carpenter. That's the man who use to come see Obaban when she was sick. He said he wanted her to guide him after she died, the way his mother would always come home to visit his father in dreams.

"Baba, are you going to watch us, too?" My girls exchange looks and delighted shivers. They each look away as if lost in a long-forgotten landscape, but they always remember to ask the question.

"Sure, I'm going to do that for you folks later on." My mother looks around at our faces, notices that we are all paying attention properly.

"I will always watch everything that you do. So that you will do the right thing. And I can show you how to come home when you get lost." She looks so tired now.

"What if we don't listen?" says the little one. She giggles.

"Then I will choke you." My mother doesn't smile.

There is a long silence for us all. I change the subject. But I watch her gentle face knowing she'll keep her promise.

We are very lucky.

Mary Wakayama

The Prayer Lady

In late summer, when the spirits of the dead returned to eat with the living and to walk under the sky again, the villagers in the Japanese plantation camp put food out for the hungry ghosts and celebrated their coming with dance. On the last night of the festival, as time drew near for the lantern procession to light the spirits down to the sea, the old head priest woke from a dream of falling water and called his wife to dress him in his white silk laying-out kimono. It was nearly time for Kitaro to come for him, he said. Okusan stood in the doorway of her husband's study, trying to catch the drips from the wooden spoon she'd been using to stir the red bean soup, and stifled the impulse to point out that Kitaro wasn't likely to come back now that he'd finally gone to the only peace that anybody was ever likely to know. Instead, she said, "Papa, are you all right?" The old man sat in the musty darkness among shadowy stacks of dog-eared journals and sheets of rice paper covered with Chinese characters. "I would be a lot better if other people did not stand around asking foolish questions," he snapped. "Hurry, old woman! Kitaro will not wait."

Okusan walked over to her husband and looked closely at his face for signs of the falling down sickness. She wasn't sure exactly what she was looking for; three different doctors couldn't name the first attack which had come on suddenly during an argument with the new head priest at the annual huli huli chicken sale a few months before. Sensei had violently opposed his successor's latest revenue-making scheme of bringing in a popular singer from Japan to appear at the festival. "I built this temple with my own hands before you were even a smile in your Papa's sleep!" Sensei had shouted just before the ocean roared up inside him and the blackness came. The "fit," as Okusan called it, had passed as quickly as it had come, leaving him paralyzed in both legs. The villagers said that the old priest had finally been defeated by progress. For Okusan, who did not put much store either in progress or in medical science, her husband's "fit" had been an almost magical event—like all of the events that made up time; it worried her that she did not yet know the proper rite of propitiation. The old man was not making matters any easier.

"Ugh," he said, as Okusan bent over him. "You smell of chives." Each week, his wife smelled of a different miracle cure for arthritis that she'd heard about on the People Speak radio show. There had been lemon balm, mint, aloe, clove. He remembered favorite smells. The aloe had been worse than the chives. "I must make ready for Kitaro," he replied.

"Hush, old man," his wife chided. "Why are you in such a hurry to go away from me? The doctors didn't do any good . . . but they never do . . . we can still . . . let's . . . let's. . . ." She did not know how to go on. She did not know how to stop losing him. "I know you don't really approve. . . . But it won't hurt to try. Let's ask the Prayer Lady to come. I know she will." Taking her husband's silence as a sign of encouragement, she pressed forward. "Didn't Nobu Kobayashi, the fish vendor, go to the Prayer Lady for that heart condition that the doctors swore would kill him inside a year, and here he is, here he is, fifteen years later, even better than new? And what about Mr. Ah Sing, the vegetable man? On a rainy day, he couldn't get out of bed to make his deliveries, his gout was that bad. And remember, oh remember, the Koyama store lady?"

Sensei remembered. It was said that the Prayer Lady could heal people just by touching them with her hands; that the woman had acquired her special powers in a moment of revelation on a rainy summer afternoon when she was emptying the trash. As the story went, a sudden gust of wind had blown the torn page from a sutra book across a neighbor's yard into her hand, and as she held the page, the full meaning of the text had flooded her mind with an infusion of light. From that moment on, it was believed that she had a special connection with the kami, the spirits of the ancestors, who gave her the power to heal with her touch. For years, Sensei had regarded her as a less than creditable rival for the loyalty of his congregation. Who knows, he thought. If it hadn't been for that woman carrying on her services down the road, church attendance might have been higher. Maybe he would have been able to stop. . . . The image of the barely pubescent rock star with the duck-tail hairdo flooded into his consciousness.

"Humph," Sensei grunted.

Okusan pushed on, "I've heard such good things, such encouraging things, really. Mrs. Koyama and I were just talking about the Prayer Lady the other day. . . ."

"Oh, foolishness!" the old man cried. "That old crank! That garbage can Buddha! You will kill me with your foolish ideas before Kitaro even gets here!" His wizened face had drawn taut; his eyes were bright. The air between them shim-

291

mered like spun glass, then darkened again.

Outside, the last tour bus rattled in from Kaanapali. The doors hissed open, spilling out a metallic stream of tourist voices that flowed into the hum of the crowd across the temple yard. "That should be Tanji's vegetable wagon bringing the musicians from upcountry," Sensei said. He stared directly at his wife. His voice was suddenly very quiet. Tanji had been a friend of Kitaro. The sea had taken them both in the same fishing accident.

Okusan sighed. Old man. Old man, you will scare everyone away with this craziness and that will be worse than being dead. She did not say the words.

"Hot noodles! Hot dogs! Genuine good luck charms!" the hawkers cried, raising their voices above the sound of the crowd. Okusan wrapped her husband in funeral silk the color of old photographs. The old man closed his eyes. The silk flowed like falling water over him. The scent of camphor rose from its deep folds, like memory.

The dream seemed painted on his closed lids. Always the same dream. The sea. The boy. Strong brown limbs flashing against the white sand, hands reaching up to free the luminous white shape into the bright sky, like a prayer, "Oh look!" And up the kite soared—a dancing shape in that dream of blue. The boy had been the last. He had always belonged to the sea. The others were buried in the temple yard.

The priest had built the temple with his own hands—hauling stone, mixing mortar, sawing wood until his hands bled and it seemed he would never stand straight again. As he raised walls and roof, the temple shaped what he became. His body grew brown and taut. He hammered the roofbeams down, singing to the sky. He married in the temple and buried his stillborn sons in the graveyard, one by one, knowing that it was not the end of things. Each year, time was renewed for that brief while in summer when the spirits of the dead wakened and the dusty glow of the festival lanterns burned into the early morning.

In the dream, time held him like an embrace, continuous and whole. It seemed he could not tell the boy who sang from the roofbeams from that other boy who ran upon the sand, reaching eager hands toward the sky.

The old woman finished dressing him. "There," she said, settling him on the living room couch with a book of sutras on

292

his lap and his legs stretched out before him. "How handsome you look." The reflection from the reading lamp behind him glinted off his smooth, bald scalp like little stars.

From across the temple yard, the bamboo flute sang out, calling the dancers to the dance. The drums began to beat and the singers to chant. Okusan went to the window and peeked out through the blinds. "Is he coming?" the old man called. "What do you see?" Within the ring of lights formed by the festival lanterns, the dancers in summer kimonos circled the musicians' tower, their sleeves fluttering like white birds in the wind.

"Only dancers dancing, Papa," the old woman said. She sensed, rather than heard, the stirring of the sea that seemed to come from everywhere, like the quickening of touch.

The sound of footsteps crossed the porch and someone knocked at the screen door. "Konban wa!" a bright voice called. The door pulled open. The Prayer Lady stood on the stoop, with the light from the festival lanterns burning in the night behind her. She wore a Mama-san dress with tiny star-shaped flowers, and her white hair was pulled back neatly into a bun. She carried a bag of strawberry guavas and a bunch of golden chrysanthemums in her hands. "Hello, Okusan," she said, giving the flowers and the fruit to her. The Prayer Lady looked at Sensei installed in his funeral clothes upon the couch; she looked him up and down. Her voice was grave. "I heard you weren't feeling well and decided to pay my respects, but if I'd known it was this serious, I would have come sooner."

"You. . . ." Sensei glared at his wife.

"I'll go and get some tea and things," Okusan said, hastily leaving the room. "I won't be long. . . ."

The Prayer Lady turned back to the old priest. "To look at you," she said, "one could never tell . . . ."

"Um," Sensei grunted.

"I see it depresses you to talk about it, though I must say you are taking the whole thing very bravely." She went from window to window, pulling up the blinds. "Ah, but it's a splendid night, isn't it?" The night filled the room. The music swelled.

Sensei's lips were an angry white slit. "I heard you were in a retirement home," he hissed.

"No . . . the things people say! You wouldn't believe what they are saying down in the village—that you've lost your grip . . . oh, all kinds of things. No one has faith anymore, you know? Miracles aren't impossible, after all, though they're a bit out of style. But of course, I've considered it. Going into a retirement home, I mean." She glanced about the room at the kegs of rice and saké, the plates of sweets, and the fruits that well-wishers had brought. "How fine it must be to lie about on a night like this. . . ."

The old priest looked furious. "Oi!" he called for his wife. ". . . with well-wishers streaming in the door . . . and nice things to eat. . . ."

"Omae!" he yelled louder. Where was that old woman?

". . . everyone making a fuss over you. . . ." The woman was relentless. "You wouldn't have to lift a finger. . . ."

"Get out!" Sensei shouted. He was shaking with rage. "Get out, get out!"

The Prayer Lady walked to the door. "Oh, Sensei," she said. "Don't you know?" Her smooth pink face suddenly looked old. "Neither of us could have held back what is happening." She quietly turned and left.

"What is all the fuss?" Okusan asked, carrying a wooden tray of tea and cakes into the room.

The old man did not answer. He sat very still. Then, he laboriously got to his feet, hobbled past the old woman—waving aside her offer of help—and walked out the door. The night was alive with stars and the sound and smell of ocean. Okusan watched from the porch steps as he made his way across the temple yard and followed the procession of lights down to the bay. "Arya sa, koryaa," the singers chanted. "It has been so. It shall always be." The lanterns glowed on the dark water. The singers said the words, like the chant of memory through time.

Sylvia A. Watanabe

Nā Keiki O Nā-ʻIwi

"Father, why can't we go down to play with the children in Kalalau?" Ku-a-pōhaku asked. He was a small boy, with the same bushy hair and eyebrows of his father. He, his father Na-ʻiwi, and his sister Hiki-mauna-lei were sitting deep inside the cave that was their home. Across the cave's entrance, Nā-ʻiwi had placed a mat of woven banana leaves to keep out the sun's rays. The noise of children came faintly to their ears, brought to their cave above Kalalau by the winds flowing up the valley.

Nā-ʻiwi sat silently, his fingers continuing to mash pink-fleshed bananas into a poi for their supper.

"Why, father?" prodded Hiki-mauna-lei. She knew Nā-ʻiwi was a silent man and needed to be prodded to talk.

Nā-ʻiwi sighed. "I say you may not," he murmured without anger.

"But why?" Ku-a-pōhaku leaned forward to plant his elbow on his father's knee and stared boldly into his father's face. "We never play with the other children. We sleep during the day. They sleep during the night."

"We are the Mū people," Nā-ʻiwi said. "The people down there think of us as wild animals. They will hurt you."

Ku-a said, "Sometimes when my sister and I go down to trade banana for fish in the early evening, we meet some of the children who are still awake. They have not hurt us."

"We speak differently than they do," Nā-ʻiwi said. "Our speech sounds harsh and strange to them. They will laugh at you."

"They have not laughed," Ku-a said, "although we do not talk much. There was no time. We had our work to do, and they had to sleep."

Na-ʻiwi sighed again. He placed the bowl of mashed banana between them and carefully removed bananas that had been roasting in the hot ashes of the fire. He gestured to his children to eat, but sat turned away from them, staring at the light shining through the mat at the cave's entrance.

What would life hold for them, he wondered. They were Mū, the little forest people, the silent ones. They lived in the wet upland forests, for only here could the banana be grown all year long. The banana gave food, shelter, and clothing. But now the Mū were almost all gone from the island. Most had left with the Menehune, but a few like Nā-'iwi lived out their lives hidden in the upland forests unable to leave precious places or memories.

Nā-'iwi turned to gaze into the faces of his children. They looked so much like their mother, he thought. Within him sadness settled like a heavy weight. He reached out and drew his daughter onto his knees.

"You do not remember your mother, do you?" he asked sadly. He stroked Hiki-mauna-lei's hair where it fell down her back like the cascade of Nā-molokama.

The children shook their heads. They could not remember.

"I look into your faces," he said, "and I see her again. I wish she were here to help you. Until now, you have been content to do as you were told. But now your thoughts fly to those children who play in Kalalau in the sunlight. But we Mū are an ancient people, born of Lua-mu'u in the time of pō, the deep night. Like our cousins, the Menehune, we cannot go into the sunshine. We must never allow a ray of sunshine to touch us. If it does, we will be turned to stone."

"Then that is why we cannot play with the children," Ku-a said.

"It is why you cannot go into the sun," Nā-'iwi corrected. "It has nothing to do with the children."

"So we would be turned to stone if we are touched by the sun," murmured Hiki. "Is that what happened to our mother?"

Nā-'iwi replied softly, "Your mother heard the women below beating out their tapa and talking and laughing together. 'I am tired of being alone,' she told me. 'I long to be friends with these women I can hear.' Nothing I could say helped her to forget this desire of hers." He stopped for, as he remembered, grief sat on his tongue and weighed it down so it could barely move.

"Then what happened?" demanded Hiki.

"One day," Nā-'iwi continued, "she could bear it no longer, 'I do not believe it,' she cried. 'Nobody turns to stone. People die and their bones are left. Bones, not stone! I am going down to Kalalau!' She walked out of the cave, out of the forest, into a meadow of grass and fern. There the sunlight fell upon her. She turned to stone before my eyes."

For a time, there was no sound in the cave. Then a breeze rattled the mat across the cave opening and the faint sound of someone calling to another down on the floor of Kalalau echoed along the cliffs.

"We will not go into the sunshine," Ku-a promised. "Will we, Hiki-mauna-lei?" His sister shook her head. "We shall sleep in the day and play only at night," she said and yawned. "I am sleepy now."

"Come, sleep then," said Nā-ʻiwi. The children stretched out on their fragrant beds of fern and their father covered them with a thin, soft cover of woven banana leaves. They fell asleep, but Nā-ʻiwi remained beside the fire, remembering.

When the last ray of sunshine lifted from the ridges, Nā-ʻiwi woke his children. "I must tend to the bananas," he said. "Take as many bananas as you can carry down to the village and trade them for other food." In this way they had often bartered for food from the sea. The shore was not safe at night. The long swells could not be seen until too late.

Nā-ʻiwi set out in the darkness, but his large eyes were used to the starlight and he could see like an owl. There was much to do, for there were no seasons here in the uplands, and banana could be planted and harvested throughout the year. So each night, Nā-ʻiwi would find a place and dig a deep, wide hole. Then he would go to a banana tree and select a huli growing under a hanging bunch of fruit. This sucker would grow to bear fruit, for it had seen what it must do. Then Nā-ʻiwi sat down and ate until his stomach was full before he planted the huli, for if a farmer planted when his stomach was empty and thin, the bananas would become thin and sour, too. Next Nā-ʻiwi put the huli on his back and, bent over and staggering as though he was carrying a tremendous weight, went to plant the huli in the hole he had dug. Then he cultivated all his trees. When a bunch was ready, he would cut it down and place it in a large calabash where the fruit would ripen. Throughout his nights, Nā-ʻiwi was sad, for everything reminded him of his losses: the sad song of the ʻi-ʻiwi for whom he had been named, the heaviness of the huli which was like the heaviness of his sorrow, the banana plants themselves whose fruit hung like golden frozen tears.

Meanwhile, Ku-a and Hiki bundled up hands of bananas and carefully climbed down the ridge until they reached the village. The village women were glad to see them, for these wild, bush-haired children always brought the pink-fleshed bananas that were not forbidden to women. Men might eat any

297

banana, but women were allowed only to eat the iholena, the pōpoʻulu and the kaualau. So the children had no trouble trading their fruit for some red seaweed and mū, a fish the women saved especially for them since it carried the same name as the wild people. Ku-a and Hiki left the village as silently as they had stayed in it, but once they were beyond the light of the fire, turned to look at the houses.

"The children are sleeping in there," Hiki whispered to her brother. "I wish I could play with them."

"They only sleep at night," Ku-a whispered back. "They play during the day when we must sleep. Come, we must go back." She shook off his hand. "I want to at least see them," she said. "Let me at least watch them while they sleep."

The two children of Nā-ʻiwi crept up to a doorway and peered in where many children slept. Hiki stared for a long time. Tears filled her eyes as she turned away from the doorway. Silently the brother and sister began the long, steep climb to their home.

On their way, they picked the ʻākala berries, the wild raspberries that grew everywhere and gave its name to the valley. As they stopped to rest, Hiki said, "Couldn't we make some kind of cover that would keep the sunlight from touching us as we played with those children?"

"What could we make that would keep all the rays of sun from us?" Ku-a demanded. "No hat could have a brim large enough to shade us. But even if we could make such hats, who would play with us? We would look funny."

"I suppose so," admitted Hiki. She burst into tears. "But it is easy for you. You do not want to play with the children as much as I do."

"I do so," Ku-a said indignantly. "There are boys of my age living in Kalalau. They have bows and arrows to shoot at rats. I have made a bow, too, but I cannot use it at night. I cannot watch the flight of my arrow." For a moment his blood surged strongly through his body. He could beat anyone at hunting rats with bow and arrow. He knew he could. Then Ku-a remembered. In a flat, hopeless voice, he went on. "But since we can never play with the Kalalau children, we must try to forget them."

They could not forget, however. As they lay on their beds, the sound of children's laughter reached them. On the dark nights when they traded their bananas for fish, they would creep to the doorway and stare at the sleeping children. There was nothing they could do, nothing they could make that would help them.

But one night, the moon shone brilliantly in the sky, lighting all the leaves of the forest and all the pebbles in the path. "It will be easy to climb the trail tonight," Ku-a said happily. The children gathered up some hands of bananas and swiftly sped down the path into Kalalau.

They neared the village. They heard a burst of laughter coming from the grassy clearing just ahead. Startled, the children of Na-'iwi stood at the clearing's edge and stared with wonder. The Kalalau children were playing in the moonlight. Their shouts of laughter awakened the birds nesting on the cliffs. With greedy eyes, Ku-a and Hiki watched the games until their arms grew weary from holding the bundles of bananas.

Putting down the burden, Hiki reached out to touch her brother. "Ku-a," she whispered, "the children are playing in the moonlight!" Even in her wildest schemes Hiki had never thought of this and happiness filled her with such lightness that her feet began to dance.

"Ku-a!" she called, "this is moonlight! We can play with them!"

She danced out of the trees' shadow and into the clearing, pulling Ku-a with her. They came close to the playing youngsters and then stopped, shy and embarrassed.

With noisy welcoming shouts, the Kalalau children surrounded Ku-a and Hiki. Then all were off in a swift game of tag. All the longings of Ku-a and Hiki were forgotten in this breathless swift game. The moon sailed along her charted course as the hours sped by.

Hiki at last played pahipahi. Her hands slapped the palms of another girl in intricate rhythms and designs of seven, as the other girls, circling them, chanted an accompaniment.

Ku-a played pana'iole with the boys. While some scooped out a steep-sided hole, others caught rats. With arrows of cane tassels, the boys shot at the rats as they scurried and dodged in the trap. Ku-a was too excited to be finally playing to keep a steady hand. But that did not matter!

In the night winds, the children flew kites, the round

kites, the winged kites, and the crescent kites, honoring the moon that lit their play. The hours fled past, unmarked and unnoticed.

Hiki fell to the ground, breathless with laughter. She was facing the steep cliffs. Her eyes widened in surprise. She leapt to her feet, the laughter gone. "Ku-a!" she called. "Look! The east is red! The sun is coming!"

Swiftly the children of Naʻiwi ran up the trail toward their cave home so far above them. Fear bit at their legs like angry dogs. They climbed desperately, using any hold that their hands and feet could find.

"Ku-a, wait!" cried Hiki. "I am out of breath!"

"Hurry, hurry!" Ku-a urged. "We must get home before the sun comes!"

On and on they struggled. Ku-a turned to reach out for his sister's hand. In that moment, the sun rose from his resting place and stretched mightily. A finger of sunlight flew out to touch the children.

"Ku-a!" Hiki cried out and was still.

"My sister!" Ku-a cried out and was still.

Naʻiwi was waiting for his children to return home. When the sun had risen and they had not come, Naʻiwi was filled with dread. He tried to reassure himself that they had found shelter from the day, but he did not really believe it. He left the cave and searched the shadowy woods, calling their names. They did not answer.

He came to the edge of the forest and looked down the steep path to Kalalau. There on the steepest part of the razor-backed ridge, he saw two large stones that had not been there before. Tears filled his eyes.

"Now I am alone," he wept. "Oh, my children!"

He stayed at the edge of the forest through the long day, and when night finally came he walked down to the stones that are the children of Naʻiwi. He sat beside them in silent sorrow through most of the night.

At last he rose. He gently touched the stone that had been Ku-a-pōhaku. He stroked the stone that had been Hiki-mauna-lei. Then without looking back he walked swiftly up the path, past his cave, past his banana trees until he came to an open meadow. There, near the center, was a large stone. The sun was rising and the iʻiwi birds darted among the lehua blossoms to suck the nectar.

Na'iwi stood facing the rock as the first rays of sun fell into the clearing. "Our children are gone," he said. "Oh, my wife, I am lonely."

Na-'iwi wept and the heavy weight of his grief melted away. With a light step, he walked out to stand beside his wife in the bright sunshine.

Frederick Wichman

Waiting for the Big Fish: Recent Research in the Asian American Literature of Hawaii

Ignored and even denied to exist by all except its creators until the 1970s, the Asian American literature of Hawaii is now gaining long overdue recognition in its birthplace. This report on that literature—three generations of it—stems from research to which many contributed, we hope so that there will be no further claims that there is no such thing as an Asian American literature of Hawaii.

In 1959, Hawaii gained U.S. statehood, having been a territory since annexation in 1898. Not by mere coincidence, in 1959 two books important to Hawaii's literature were published. Although one far surpassed the other in popular appeal, both internationally marked historical and contemporary Hawaii's place in literature. But if today we are not particularly aware of Hawaii's literary distinction, if we hardly acclaim Hawaii as a truly literary setting, seriously, of any stature, it is no surprise. For the two landmark books published in conjunction with the granting of Hawaii's statehood are of dubious benefit to Hawaii's literature. One is James A. Michener's novel, *Hawaii.* The other, much less known, even obscure, outside of Hawaii, is an anthology edited by A. Grove Day and Carl Stroven, with an introduction by Michener, entitled *A Hawaiian Reader.*[1] The former has enjoyed worldwide fame. It fleshes out an attractive and popular dream of Hawaii as the setting for both paradisal indolence and, in sensational contrast to the indolence, the heroic adventures of men and women building an island civilization. It is magnificently the sort of stuff that readers would not want to take entirely seriously. Meanwhile, the anthology edited by Day and Stroven, meant to be taken seriously indeed, is crippled by glaring deficiencies which I shall shortly point out. These two works, it could well be said, were ostensibly summations of nearly two centuries of written literature and many more than that of the native Hawaiian oral tradition. And yet they made it seem somehow that nothing of real literary consequence was ever created in Hawaii by Hawaii's people.

Michener's *Hawaii* and Day and Stroven's *A Hawaiian*

Reader, however, have a far deeper significance to the development of Hawaii's literature than the former's label of being mainly "popular" in appeal and the latter's weaknesses and relative obscurity may suggest. The two statehood works helped to tighten the hatch that held down an indigenous Hawaii literary development in this century. Michener's came to be known as *the* novel of Hawaii. Whatever one may have thought about the novel's literary merits and demerits, the general feeling was that it, after all, was even by its sheer mass the most and the best those small tropical islands could muster. Why should anyone try to surpass it? Or why should anyone look for older works that have told Hawaii's story with any more authenticity or imaginative flair? Hawaii's criticism of the novel—unfavorable criticism which was quite abundant—lashed Michener for factual inaccuracies or, when he told the truth, for casting our ancestors in the lurid light of scandals involving family characters closeted generations ago. Michener and scholar A. Grove Day counter these charges with the obvious disclaimer that the novel is, after all, fiction.[2] But there has also been another dissatisfaction with the novel among certain people in Hawaii: that the novel considered to be *the* novel of Hawaii has been written by an outsider. Why did no one born and raised in Hawaii, someone steeped in the ways and the knowledge of Hawaii's cultures and history, write the novel? Why did no one among each of the major ethnic groups of whom Michener writes tell his or her people's story from the inside out? The dissatisfaction was also that somehow we in Hawaii had been robbed, and now it was too late to overtake the thief. And it was our own fault—somehow.[3]

But Michener of course is not to *blame* for his novel's popular success, so great that it would appear to have drowned out all other voices anyway. The real damage comes in his confirmation of a subsidiary and insidious popular notion: in this supposed paradise, hard-working Asians did not write, did not cultivate verbal expression while they cultivated Hawaii's soil, much less indulge in verbal creativity. There were utterly no Asian voices to drown.

The novelist's assertion of this belief is explicit. In his introduction to Day and Stroven's *A Hawaiian Reader,* Michener praises the editors' selection of works which "give recognition to the fact that Hawaii's population today is about fifty percent Oriental in ancestry."[4] These selections include, for exam-

303

ple, May Sarton's autobiographical tourist sketch, "Sukiyaki on the Kona Coast," a reminiscence of an evening the author spent dining in a Japanese American family's farmhouse.[5] The central image in the sketch is a lizard scurrying about the dining room walls. That lizard is imaginatively linked, whether deliberately or not, with the visitors' host, who comes and goes, waiting on the guests and seeing after their comfort. Such comparisons, needless to say, are not exactly relished by Hawaii readers of Sarton's sketch, though Michener, Day, and Stroven are apparently insensitive to the belittling inference that the Japanese American, Hawaiian host is like the lizard: charming and elusive, yet somehow alien to normal life. Still, one anthology selection in particular does nevertheless draw Michener's criticism in this regard. The selection, the only one in the anthology that employs an Asian as its central character, Jack London's "Chun Ah Chun," prompts Michener to point out that through such stories London "denigrated an entire body of people largely on racist grounds." Yet he goes on to praise the story's "sly warmth" and "much wit."[6] Why are such stories the anthology's only recognition of the very existence of Asian Americans in Hawaii? Why are there no selections authored by Asian Americans? Michener explains: "Having arrived in the islands as laboring peasants, these Orientals did not produce a literature of their own. . . ."[7] For nearly twenty years after it was published, Michener's statement was believed, or at least not seriously challenged, if anyone paid special attention to it at all, as far as I know.

I am very fortunate. Having gained a bit of knowledge on the matter, I can see now what a falsehood Michener perpetuated. I do not mean to imply that Michener was solely responsible for the idea that up until and beyond 1959, there was no Asian American literature of Hawaii. He was by no means alone in making the claim. In his company were those who presumably researched Hawaii's literature thoroughly: Pacific literature experts A. Grove Day and Carl Stroven, for example. And it is as if the rest of us were sitting dumbly in their class. Even in the next decade, in 1967, another Hawaii anthology editor, Gerrit P. Judd, found it necessary to fly pretty far afield to find some writings by an Asian which have something to do with "the Hawaiian experience." Judd's sole Asian "author" is Mitsuo Fuchida, with a true-to-life testimony excerpted from U.S. Naval Institute Proceedings, bluntly titled, "I Led the Air

Attack on Pearl Harbor."[8] Are we to understand that this galling selection represents, up to 1967, Asians' most significant contribution to Hawaii's literature and history?

I have presented this lengthly introduction to my paper in order to establish a context—both intellectual and emotional—in which Arnold Hiura and I conducted research in the Asian American literature of Hawaii, funded by a grant from the U.S. Office of Education's Ethnic Heritage Studies Program, 1978-79. The results of our research were the limited publication of *Asian American Literature of Hawaii: An Annotated Bibliography,* and an American Studies graduate course making use of our findings, offered primarily to thirty teachers who have gone on to introduce Hawaii's Asian American and other ethnic literature to their own classes in an impressive variety of ways.[9] This is literature that has not only been neglected, but whose existence, as we have seen, has been denied. As we were to find, it is a literature that goes back at least three generations, in some instances more, with hardly a break in the activity of writing imaginative works since the immigrants' arrivals in Hawaii from Asia through the later 19th and early 20th centuries.

Our published bibliography was limited to include only the publicly available works written in English by people of Chinese, Japanese, Filipino, and Korean descent in Hawaii. When we began the project, we frankly did not know whether we would find even ten pages worth of bibliographical entries. But the amount of material we found stunned us. Our bibliography, with some twenty pages of introduction, a subject index, and other apparatus, ended up being 210 pages long. We found nearly 750 works ranging from novels through two-act dramas to individual lyric poems and poetry collections. All of these, again, are imaginative works written by Hawaii's Asian Americans in English; and all are available either in published or in typescript form in public libraries in Hawaii, notably the University of Hawaii's Hawaii-Pacific Collection.

The account of three main generations of Hawaii's Asian American literature, however, reaches behind those written in English by the Hawaii-born. It was on the Big Island of Hawaii, in particular, that we saw how vital the history of Hawaii's literature in Asian languages has been and continues to be today. We were introduced to two still-active *haiku* clubs

305

and a *tanka* club begun by immigrant Japanese who devoted spare moments to writing and perfecting poetry following traditional Japanese conventions, using the Japanese language, yet in many instances adapting the poetry to its new setting. On another occasion, welcomed into the home of a Filipino immigrant couple long active in Hilo's polyethnic community, we were shown a treasure: an epic composed in Ilocano and cramped into the lines and margins of a thick, homemade booklet of now yellowing paper, an epic created in Hawaii by an inspired Filipino American immigrant, but as yet unread by anyone else, its present keeper being a Tagalog rather than Ilocano speaker. We could see what further work and reading we could look forward to, when the time and opportunity should arise to help make such Asian language works available to readers today.

Furthermore, we learned some rather startling facts about the history of Hawaii's Japanese immigrant poetry, which is especially vigorous even today. In a conference we devoted to the literature of the Big Island, in the summer of 1979, it was reported by members of the Hilo Shōu Kai (the Literary Society) that their haiku club, founded in 1903, is the oldest active one in the world. We were astonished to hear this. We asked the speaker to repeat himself. He did: this haiku club is the world's oldest, still active. He might as well have been discussing the island's volcanoes, we were so impressed.[10] In its eighty years, the Shōu Kai and its individual members have published a number of anthologies, collections of individual artists' poems, literary studies of their poetry, and individual poems in newspapers and haiku magazines, mainly in Japan. In a related development, four different *tanka* (31-syllable Japanese verse) clubs in Hilo joined together in 1923 to form the also still-active Gin-u Shi Sha, the Silver Rain Society, whose name is finely descriptive of Hilo's prevailing climate. Even the mere fact of the aptness of the name raises another: a Japanese poem by convention is required to contain mention or a suggestion of the season for which it is composed. How, the question was asked, have Hawaii's haiku and tanka poets been accommodating their works to Hawaii's far-from-Japanese seasons? The oldtimers on the panel were not at all surprised by the question. One replied that Hawaii's Japanese poets have developed a unique vocabulary of "season words" conventionally employed in their haiku and tanka. These words are based on growth cycles of tropical fruits, flowers, and crops, such as sugar cane; or on the seasonal appearances of certain fish or other wildlife; or on the apparition of snow on the distant peak of Mauna Kea. Indeed, it was reported, in the 1930s a Japanese literary scholar published, in Japanese and in Japan, a study of the season words and symbolism unique to Hawaii's Japanese poetry. The question arises, then, is this "Japanese poetry" at all?

Thus we find haiku such as the following: "Dawn's moon,/ Remnant snow on Mauna Kea/Still slumbering."[11] Another plays with the seeming paradox still fresh to the speaker, when she is struck by the sight of wintertime tropical greenery: "Amid winter verdance/Mynah birds feast on/Garden delicacies."[12] Some haiku go further than the use of place names, plants, animals, and seasonal imagery distinctive to the locale. As in the following, they evoke the mythology of the islands' original settlers: "Rising in darkness/Pele's red flame of ardor/Consumes the night rain," Pele being the Hawaiian goddess of eternal fire and thus of the island's volcanoes, her home.[13] The fire and the rain meet spectacularly in the haiku just quoted.

Yet somehow the most deeply moving fact we were to learn from the issei poets of Hilo came not from the high nor the middle reaches of literary art, but from folk arts. As in Japanese and Japanese American communities elsewhere, during the summer in Hawaii a festival is observed, the O-bon celebration honoring family ancestors and paying gratitude for the year's harvest. Over the century, plantation communities scattered throughout Hawaii have created their own lyrics for some O-bon folk songs to which the people dance. Members of the Hilo Bon Dance Club reported at the Talk Story Big Island Conference that since the town's resumption of observing the Japanese festival sometime following World War II, the old folks first introduced a song, and have expanded it year after year. This song, the Hilo version of Yamaguchi, Japan's "Iwakuni Ondo," tells the story of the famed 442nd Regimental Combat Team on which Hawaii's nisei served, fought, and many died.[14] Unable to understand the stylized Japanese language of the song, even those in the audience who had grown up dancing to the song once a year were warmed for the first time by its meaning. The lyrics' significance struck deeply home: here is a growing folk epic, in a sense, of the Japanese

307

American people. As the sansei, or third generation, members of the Hilo Bon Dance Club read a translation of a small excerpt from the song, then sang a few verses, young and old alike in the ethnically diverse audience wept quietly. Three generations were bound by the experience, a momentarily shared understanding of a major event in the recent history of Hawaii's people.

Asian immigrant literary activity continues to thrive today in each of the major Asian ethnic communities of Hawaii. The Chinese in Hawaii have literary societies with rather long histories and impressive successes. They have, for instance, presented elaborate classical Chinese dramas adapted to being performed in Hawaii. Meanwhile the Japanese, as we have seen, have cultivated the poetry of their homeland through their literary clubs. Poets among them have published extensively in Japan. Some have won Imperial poetry awards and recognition for their work, though they have long remained virtually unrecognized in their permanently adopted country. A notably active Asian immigrant literary association is GUMIL-Hawaii, whose purpose is to perpetuate the Ilocano poetry of the members' Philippine Island origin. In the 1970s alone, GUMIL-Hawaii published four anthologies of poetry, drama, and essays written by its members. The organization annually holds a drama writing contest, and the winning play is performed at a community cultural extravaganza little-known outside the recently immigrated Filipino community. Gradually the organization is turning to the composition of poems and dramas using Hawaii and other American settings and themes, and using the English language. These immigrant writers are in Hawaii to stay; the development of their writing reflects this fact. New immigrants from Korea, meanwhile, which is providing another major and growing Asian ethnic group in Hawaii, find some outlet for literary expression and creativity in the Korean language newsletters of the Korean community's Christian churches.

Like the writers among their parents' generation, the Hawaii-born Asian American writers first emerged in our research as members of literary and social organizations. But now, one of the common bonds holding the organizations together was not only ethnic heritage, but also education. In the 1920s and early '30s, the second generation writers were student writers, some still in high schools sparsely scattered through the islands, but most of them among those fortunate enough to be attending the University of Hawaii. With very rare exceptions, it appears, these students subsequently entered business and professional careers without later publishing more mature literary works of their own. But this does not mean that they made no contribution to Hawaii's literature. While they did write, they wrote prolifically—and sometimes very well.

Beginning with the 1919-20 volume of the *Chinese Students' Alliance Annual,* we were excited to find a yearly harvest of stories, poems, a drama or two, and essays prominently showcased in the yearbook's "Literary" section. Though we as yet have found no earlier literary works in English by Hawaii's Asian Americans, the student writers of the early '20s apparently saw themselves as heirs to an established literary tradition. What earlier tradition might the *Annual* editor of 1923 have in mind, when he exhorted the Alliance members to redouble their literary efforts, to emulate "the artists, the poets, the dreamers, literary geniuses of yesterday"?[15] Whoever the geniuses of yesterday, the passionate editor goes on to point out the direction the literature must now take:

> Who but we are more equipped to interpret the romance and tragedy of our own people—their passions, sentiments, desires? Is it not imposed upon us to overthrow such misconceptions as others sometimes so stupidly bring on our heritage? Yes, we Chinese students are the ones who must truly interpret the East to the West, formulate our views and opinions of the many complex problems confronting Hawaii, China, and the world at large, and share in bringing about a mutual goodwill throughout the world.[16]

As the editor implies in his exhortation, these early second generation writers looked to both the East and the West for literary material. But the matter is not really so simple as it may sound. Two stories by one especially talented member of the Alliance demonstrate the East-West duality and the complexities it entails.

One story by James Chun is a melodramatic romance entitled "Fate?" and set in China—a timeless China existing apart from the currents of world history, a China typical of works by this early generation of Hawaii-born Chinese American students. The story's elaborate plot seems so improbable that one is tempted to read the story as a fable.[17] Here is how we summarize Chun's tale in our annotated bibliography:

> Ah Kwong is adopted by Mr. Su, wealthiest man of Silk Grove. The young man falls in love with Bau Lin, daughter of Ah Kwong's teacher, Professor Lum of Green Plain. A marriage, however, is forbidden by the fathers because the neighboring home-villages of the Su and Lum families are hostile to each other. It turns out, however, that Bau Lin is actually Mr. Su's daughter who had been kidnapped as a child and taken to Green Plain. Professor Lum, knowing this, had forbidden marriage between brother (as he thought Ah Kwong to be) and sister. When it's found that Ah Kwong and Bau Lin are not brother and sister by blood, the two are wed—uniting the families and the feuding villages.[18]

Yet despite the timeless and exotic China setting of the story, the plot should not appear entirely implausible to an audience familiar with Western literature. Think of what a Shakespeare would do with this germ of a comedy.

James Chun's other story, "In the Camp," is set in contemporary Hawaii.[19] Like the earlier story, this one pivots on a twist of fate—but this time, twisting with a tragic irony. Here is our annotation:

> The first-person narrator of this strongly naturalistic story recounts the tragic life of Wong Mun Sing, a plantation laborer who fails to return to China to be reunited with his wife and his mother. At age 25, Wong was the camp's best worker, "strong, good-looking, . . . sprightlier than any of his companion workers." Having worked in a rainstorm, Wong falls ill and resorts to taking opium to relieve his pains. He explains to the young narrator, the son of a plantation storekeeper, that he's been unable to save enough money to return to China. Upon recovering from his illness, moreover, Wong remains addicted to opium. Twelve years pass. The narrator has established a career as a physician. He once more sees Wong, now a wasted gambler and opium addict. Wong wins a considerable sum by gambling but is informed by a letter from China that his wife has passed away. Wong at the end lies dying of an overdose of opium and liquor. . . .[20]

The author Chun, who perhaps figures in the story as the young physician who narrates it, charges the air with sunshine and with moldering gloom, as the season and the occasion demand:

> Outside the rain was pouring. It beat drearily upon the roof, dripped into the cracks and wet the walls within. It fell on the dirty porch, making it slippery and slimy. It flowed from the old

310

clothes that hung on the line. It formed puddles of brown water in the yard, filled up the empty cans scattered about, and ran into the pig pens where the animals wallowed in mud and mire. Inside the men were immersed in their game, unmindful of the storm outside. . . . Like the buildings that furnished them scanty shelter, their lives were moldering away.[21]

The Hawaii tragedy, unlike Chun's China romance, somehow seems both plausible and close to the author's own experiences and observations, as one would well expect of a young writer probably born and raised in Hawaii, and who perhaps has never been to his forebears' homeland.

But while the Hawaii writers of the 1920s, such as James Chun, wrote on the one hand about Asian or Asian American characters in Asian or Hawaiian settings, some of these same writers on the other hand questioned and sometimes rejected their identification with Asia.[22] James T. Hamada's novel, *Don't Give Up the Ship* (1933), poses some questions in this regard.[23] This novel is the earliest published of those we found, and it may very well be the first novel in English published by any Japanese American. And it cannot be faulted or slighted for being mainly autobiographical in nature, for this novel contains no Japanese American characters, despite its contemporary Hawaii setting. Hamada now and then decorates his narrative with details of Honolulu's Asian neighborhoods—a Shinto shrine, a Japanese grocery. But the hero is Bill Kane, "a white man," who, like Natty Bumppo, has his Chingachgook: in this case a couple of native Hawaiian pals. Hamada patterns his *Don't Give Up the Ship* after popular "epic" novels such as *Beau Geste,* Hamada's own being a tale of adventure climaxing on the high seas somewhere south of Hawaii. Lacking Japanese American characters of any consequence, Hamada's novel is virtually alone among all published novels subsequently authored by Japanese Americans. One wonders why he wrote it that way. It may be that Hamada wanted to forestall identification of his novel with somehow being "Japanese," or autobiographical. He perhaps wanted his novel to be seen as unquestionably "American," as Japanese Americans' "Americanness" was already being sorely questioned at that time. At any rate, one cannot help now but wish that Hamada had told a story of Hawaii's Japanese Americans as well, for he appears to have been a careful, a talented, and a dedicated enough writer to do the job.

311

The problem of dual Asian vs. American identification of Japanese Americans in particular had severe ramifications when the Japanese raided Pearl Harbor. The confusion persists through the decades since then, as when Gerrit Judd includes in his Hawaiian anthology a piece by the Imperial Japanese leader of the Pearl Harbor air attack, as I noted earlier in this paper. The confusion of identities persists today, when the general American public and scholars alike tend to think of Asian American literature as literature written in Asian languages and conforming to Asian literary conventions.

Yet World War II washed away some of that confusion, enough, at any rate, so that authentically local, Hawaii literature began unmistakably to sound its voice in the postwar years. This development was fed in part by a University drama writing class, where the use of local settings, situations, and colloquial language was encouraged. Moreover, the writers seemed now to be confident in identifying their work not with their parents' Asian traditions, nor with the Mainland American settings, language, and culture that Hawaii's people read about in books and saw in films; but with their own experience, even though many of its distinguishing features, it was thought, had never before been etched in literature.

The hallmark of authenticity was (and in some respects continues to be) the skillful use of Hawaii's pidgin English and creole. As early as 1936, members of the University of Hawaii drama writing class employed pidgin for more than merely comic effect in their work.[24] After World War II, a few locally widespread publications began carrying stories containing pidgin dialogue. One of the earliest published examples is "The Forgotten Flea Powder," by a young writer who had only recently graduated from high school, Philip K. Ige.[25] In his sketch of two Japanese American brothers and an incident involving their fleabitten farmdog, Ige deftly illustrates setting, speech, mannerisms, and values that local audiences have delighted in recognizing in the printed word: for example, a distinctively "local" and particularly Japanese American relationship between the older brother and the younger; likewise, the command that the boys' father has over the older boy, who commands the younger, who seems sometimes to be on the verge of taking it all out on the hapless dog. The pecking order is inviolate. And it may very well be universal.

But most clearly "local" of all is Philip Ige's use of pidgin English dialogue in "The Forgotten Flea Powder." The sketch begins:

> Two blocks past Johnson's Five and Ten in the town of Kaimuki, Satoshi Ikehara, standing in the rear of a jam-packed Honolulu bus, woke up from his stupor with a start, looked outside, and nudged his little brother who stood beside him. "Hey, Yuki, we pass da store again."
>
> "Huh?"
>
> "We forget to get off by Johnson Store an' buy flea-powder—you know, for Blackie."
>
> "Oh, yeah. How many times we goin' forget anyway? Four times already, no-o?"
>
> "Yeah. We no can get off now—too late. We got to go home."
>
> "'At's okay. We can buy 'em tomorrow—Saturday."
>
> "I know; but Blackie cry, you know. He get so many fleas. He feel itchy an' he cry, you know."
>
> "Yeah, I know. Yesterday I saw him scratchin' up. He no can scratch da back part 'at's why he onny cry, so I been scratch his back for him. He *f-e-e-l* good. He no cry."[26]

Ige's handling of pidgin was to become quite typical: standard English narration frames the pidgin dialogue, often with an implicit, ironical interplay between the two languages and the different worlds they represent. In the case of Ige's story, the clash between standard English and pidgin English is all but explicit. Immediately after the two boys talk excitedly about getting the flea powder for their dog Blackie, we see that "An old Caucasian woman, sitting in a seat before them, looked up and smiled at them. The boys smiled shyly back and quickly turned their eyes away. They stopped talking."[27] Whatever the woman's apparently kind intentions in smiling—not even talking—at the boys, her looks silence them, for, I would infer, through no personal fault of her own she represents a whole Mainland of standard English zealots, especially schoolteacher types, who sit in righteous judgment against the abominable pidgin English and its speakers. And yet of course, Ige and his fellow Hawaii writers are indebted to those who guided their literary talent and taught them the English language of books.

The postwar era of Hawaii's second generation Asian American literature also saw publication of the first of several works of fiction that chronicle Hawaii's Asian immigration. One author, Kazuo Miyamoto, specifically acknowledges Ole

Rolvaag's *Giants in the Earth* as both a model and an inspiration for his, Miyamoto's, *Hawaii: End of the Rainbow.*[28] Miyamoto's more than two decades of meticulous note keeping and writing, outside of his professional work as a physician, resulted in the 1964 publication of his Hawaii Japanese American immigrant and second generation novel. In addition to providing a fictional narrative of immigration and settlement, a fictional narrative stubbornly rooted in fact, Miyamoto tells the fullest story we yet have in literature, whether fictional or non-fictional, of Hawaii's people incarcerated in American World War II concentration camps. Miyamoto was among them.

Kazuo Miyamoto's chronicle appeared after statehood was granted to Hawaii. But the first of these immigrant sagas was published in 1951, well before Michener's novelistic account of Asian immigration in Hawaii. Shelley Ayame Nishimura Ota's turbulent novel, *Upon Their Shoulders* (1951), begins with a tale of abject poverty, injustice, and bigotry in Meiji Japan.[29] The novel's hero, Taro Sumida (whose very name, like "John Smith," signifies the common man), is driven to seek a living in Hawaii. What faintly resembles the Japanese immigrant success story that has become a stereotype is punched and battered again and again by reported or depicted incidents of rape, violence, economic setbacks, and other tragedies suffered individually and communally among the novel's Japanese American characters. Near the novel's end Taro Sumida dies, by then an esteemed grandfather, financially comfortable, yet weary to the core. He hears of Japan's surrender, is momentarily elated by the thought of modern reforms now to occur in Japan, and dies at least recognizing that he and his wife have given their descendants a better future, in Hawaii.

Sharply contrasting Ota's and Miyamoto's renditions of the Asian immigrant story in Hawaii is Margaret Harada's indeed sunny novel, *The Sun Shines on the Immigrant* (1960).[30] Here is the usual success story not necessarily written anywhere else in novel length but which is still thought of as being typical of Japanese Americans. Harada's narrative concludes just prior to World War II—that is, prior to the bombing of Pearl Harbor. It is somewhat strange that Harada should end her story there, her first and second generation Hawaii Japanese American characters fairly beaming with self-satisfaction as they gaze off toward sunny horizons of the fu-

314

ture. I do not think that Harada wanted or intended the nonetheless inescapable irony, that Japanese warplanes led by Mitsuo Fuchida were speeding to Hawaii from just beyond those same horizons. I want to believe that Harada simply could not bear to tell about the impact of Pearl Harbor on Japanese Americans, whether in Hawaii or elsewhere.

But whatever their authors' views, none of the immigrant sagas I've named should have to bear the burden of presuming to speak for every Japanese American family's history. Nor should Michener's *Hawaii* be presumed to speak for all Hawaii. But unlike Michener, each of these Hawaii writers— Shelley Ota, Margaret Harada, and Kazuo Miyamoto—shouldered a heavy thought, a responsibility: that she or he was writing alone, without knowing what predecessors each may have had in Hawaii's literary history. The entire weight of family, community, and public criticism and praise fell squarely upon the *only* person, each of these writers must have thought, to write the saga through both the point of view and the personal experience of the Japanese American subjects of the novel. Thus the title of Ota's novel, *Upon Their Shoulders,* applies not only to the Japanese immigrant pioneers and the load they carried for posterity's sake, but certainly applies to Ota's own act of writing her pioneering novel as well.

And so it is that a third generation of Asian American writers is now active in Hawaii. Thankfully, we have our predecessors' shoulders now to stand on; for now the predecessors are known, the burden shared. Broadly speaking, this generation has deep cultural roots in Hawaii, taking as its Asian heritage an eclectic mix of customs, traditions, foods, and values that their Asian immigrant grandparents adapted to the new climate. Much of Hawaii's literary activity today is polyethnic, with writers making deliberate use of elements of other heritages in Hawaii than one's own. There is an especially great admiration and even reverence for native Hawaiian culture, as it is undergoing a "renaissance" headed by new and revived legends, chants, and lyrics, the original literature of Hawaii. If a Hawaii writer today were called upon to choose a label for him- or herself identifying his or her cultural source, the writer would sooner answer "local," before thinking of "Asian American" or, say, "Japanese American." Of course, some would refuse any such labels altogether, for a

315

complex of reasons usually having something abstractly to do with "universality." But the active creative energy at present, anyway, seems to be with those who do acknowledge a local, Hawaii identity—an identity which automatically implies one's recognition of one's own ethnicity and a respect for others. Current activity also cuts clear across generational barriers that perhaps separated the Shelley Otas from the writers among the immigrants, whose works, we found, were rarely read by their own children. Second generation Asian American writers such as Kazuo Miyamoto, the much younger Milton Murayama, Philip Ige, Maxine Hong Kingston, and others are gradually becoming "elders" in the literary culture of Hawaii, both role and the culture itself in many ways lacking and unfilled when the second generation began writing, passionately, in earnest, but ignorant of their predecessors.

Yet current activity among Asian American and the rainbow host of other writers of Hawaii has followed the lead of the two preceding generations in at least one more important respect: their activities have been organized within associations aiming to serve both the arts and the communities from which they spring. Thus, in 1978, a then-new organization called Talk Story, Inc., held a conference that drew nationwide participation yet served to bring the young and the old generation of Hawaii's writers together for the first time.[32] The gathering has led in turn to some important continuing work, such as the publication of a journal, *Bamboo Ridge: The Hawaii Writers' Quarterly*, edited by poet Eric Chock and fiction and drama writer Darrell Lum. The 1978 Talk Story Conference itself has been succeeded by others: the Talk Story Big Island Writers' Conference of 1979, the Hawaii Literary Arts Council's Hawaii Writers' Conference of 1980, and, just to make sure we don't take ourselves too seriously, a zany, innovative, and very welcomed 1981 Talk Story Conference on local humor in literature, arts, and stand-up comedy, entitled "Crack Me Up."

In speaking of three generations of Hawaii's Asian American literature I have had to mention more writers by name than I could possibly discuss in any detail; and I have had to leave many, many names and titles unmentioned. After all, my partner Arnold Hiura and I found over seven hundred titles, hundreds of authors, where surely a good many of the stories must have been better than the account of "Sukiyaki on the Kona Coast" or "I Led the Air Attack on Pearl Harbor," to represent the existence of Asians in Hawaii and in Hawaii's literature, not only as characters, but also as authors.

But though I cannot supply here all the details on the works and authors I have mentioned, I would like to close with a general question relevant to all of them. And I wish to supply some speculative answers.

Why would Michener and Hawaii literary scholars A. Grove Day and Carl Stroven and others in word and effect deny the existence of this literature growing in their own yards for sixty, seventy, eighty years?

Lack of availability? No. These works are housed and are available precisely where the famous novelist and the anthology editors did much of their own research and reading: the University of Hawaii's Hawaii-Pacific Collection. Some of the Asian American works stand right alongside works by other writers whom the scholars do cite and anthologize.

Lack of a tradition in which to place and by which to understand and assess the works? This would be a problem, especially if one were expecting to find Asian, rather than American, literary works as examples of Asian American literature, whether in Hawaii or elsewhere. Among a few Hawaii Asian American writers in the '60s, it became fashionable to affect Asian literary forms—Japanese haiku, for instance. But aside from that transitory phenomenon and, as discussed earlier in this paper, the use of Asian settings in the '20s, the second and third generation Asian American literary works have been based in American literary traditions, with English as the authors' native tongues. Still, not much attention has been paid to the first generation writers, writing in Asian languages and traditions, by outsiders to these groups, anyway.

Lack of literary merit? Are the Asian American works in English somehow simply too poor in literary quality to be considered "literature"? I must say that for me, in our research, this was the most profoundly disturbing question of all. Told all my life that Hawaii's Asian Americans did not write—and were not verbally skillful enough even to understand— imaginative literature, I frankly was astounded by what we found. I realized how deeply I, too, had taken the claim for granted, or, worse, had always been afraid that it was true: that locals could never hope to write decent literature. Then I

317

found myself denying that the works we were finding and poring over had any "literary merit," in my vain attempt to preserve my lifelong misconception. But the denial was useless. There finally was no doubt that there indeed are such things as Asian American literary works written in Hawaii, about Hawaii, by and about Hawaii's own people. Once I capitulated to the force of evidence, my own career as an Asian American involved with literature is not quite so strange to me as it had been.

I do believe, though, that the works I have discussed did not go totally unnoticed by previous literary researchers. This raises my final speculation. Might there have been a lack of enough respect for these works and their authors to prevent one from "borrowing" stories and their elements without acknowledgment or recognition? Hawaii novelist O.A. Bushnell has charged on many public occasions that "outside" writers have shamelessly raided Hawaii for materials—and have mostly botched the job of writing them up. Indeed, some keepers of the community's culture in Hawaii are so sick of being pillaged that they refuse their knowledge to virtually every prospective or already proclaimed expert from the outside. One elderly man in Hilo calls visiting scholars and writers "steal baits," like the thievish little fish who nibble the bait off the hook, their mouths too small to be snagged—real pests. They leave nothing for the real catch. That man in Hilo is the local Japanese American community's self-appointed archivist and interim historian. His house is crammed with bait: news clippings, rare publications, photos, and memorabilia of the island's plantations and the families who made the sugar sweet with their sweat and labor. Grown reclusive through decades of continual vigilance, peering through the living room curtains to scrutinize the stranger approaching his porch, that man will not even open his door for any steal bait. And he waits still, today, for the Big Fish.[33]

20 November 1981

Stephen H. Sumida

Notes

[1]James A. Michener, *Hawaii* (New York: Random House, 1959); A. Grove Day and Carl Stroven, eds., *A Hawaiian Reader* (New York: Appleton-Century-Crofts, 1959).
For an account of Michener's writing his novel in order to meet the Hawaii statehood deadline, which Michener barely missed, see A. Grove Day, *James A. Michener* (Boston: Twayne Publishers, 1964), pp. 111-18.

[2]See, for instance, A. Grove Day, *Books about Hawaii: Fifty Basic Authors* (Honolulu: The Univ. Press of Hawaii, 1977), p. 31; and Day, *James A. Michener*, pp. 112-15.

[3]For an expression of this sentiment, see the reprint of a speech by Hawaii-born, historical novelist O.A. Bushnell, "Hawaii writers stifled at birth, one of them says," *The Sunday Star-Bulletin and Advertiser* [Honolulu], 25 June 1978, p. F-3. Bushnell laments the scarcity of "local" writers of any worth, castigates Hawaii for not nurturing creative literature, and looks forward with horror to further prospects of " 'Outsiders'. . . writing the novels [and] telling us what we are and what we think. They will turn out the stuff that the rest of the world will read. 'Outsiders' will be writing 'the great Hawaiian novels.' " Delivered as a keynote speech opening the 1978 Talk Story Conference on Asian American and Hawaii's ethnic American writers and their works, Bushnell's remarks aroused a nice stir.

[4]Michener, "Introduction," in *A Hawaiian Reader*, p. xiv.

[5]May Sarton, "Sukiyaki on the Kona Coast," in *A Hawaiian Reader*, pp. 299-307.

[6]Michener, "Introduction," *A Hawaiian Reader*, pp. xiv-xv.

[7]*Ibid.*, p. xiv.

[8]Mitsuo Fuchida, "I Led the Air Attack on Pearl Harbor," in *A Hawaiian Anthology*, ed. Gerrit P. Judd (New York: Macmillan, 1967), pp. 109-27.

[9]Arnold T. Hiura and Stephen H. Sumida, *Asian American Literature of Hawaii: An Annotated Bibliography* (Honolulu: Japanese American Research Center and Talk Story, Inc., 1979). Portions of the present paper are found in the "Introduction" to the bibliography.

[10]Information provided by Dr. Jiro Nakano, speaking on a panel entitled "Issei Poets of Hawaii" at the Talk Story Big Island Writers' Conference, 13 July 1979, University of Hawaii at Hilo. The information, to follow, on the Hilo Gin-u Shi Sha is supplied by Mr. Saburo Higa.
The Japanese American term *issei* refers to the "first" or immigrant generation. Used subsequently in this paper, the term *nisei* identifies the American (Hawaii-) born, or "second" generation of Japanese Americans.

[11]Haiku by Ryoseki Igawa. This and the following two haiku quoted in the text of my paper are translated from the Japanese originals by Dr. Kay Nakano and paraphrased into English haiku by Carol Reynolds. The haiku are from a collection entitled *Sei-u-kai Haiku* (Banana-Plant Rain Haiku Poetry Anthology), selections from which were sent to me by Dr. Jiro Nakano of the Hilo Shōu Kai. I am deeply indebted to Jiro and Kay Nakano, Carol Reynolds, and the other poets of the Shōu Kai for their making these poems available.

[12]Haiku by Tsurujyo Miyada.

[13]Haiku by Keijyo Shiba.

[14]Information provided by Ken Okimoto of the Hilo Bon Dance Club, speaking at the Talk Story Big Island Conference on the panel identified in n. 10, above.

[15]"Literary Lethargy," *Chinese Students' Alliance Annual*, 6 (May 1923), p. 5.

[16]*Ibid.*

[17]James Chun, "Fate?" *Chinese Students' Alliance Annual*, 3 (May 1920), pp. 43-48, 50.

[18]Hiura and Sumida, *Asian American Literature of Hawaii*, p. 69.

[19]James Chun, "In the Camp," *Chinese Students' Alliance Annual*, 6 (May 1923), pp. 27, 29-31.

[20]Hiura and Sumida, p. 70.

[21]Quoted in Hiura and Sumida, p. 7.

[22]Interesting early examples of this questioning are found in the works of Gladys Li, a member of the Chinese Students' Alliance and a writer, not for the Alliance, but for the Hawaii Quill, the University of Hawaii's first literary society, founded in 1928. See her "The Submission of Rose Moy," *The Hawaii Quill Magazine*, 1 (June 1928), pp. 7-19; "The Law of Wu Wei," *The Hawaii Quill Magazine*, 2 (January 1929), pp. 20-26; and "The White Serpent," *The Hawaii Quill Magazine*, 5 (May 1932), pp. 24-31. The first two of these dramas center on conflicts between presumably traditional Chinese marriage dictates and supposedly American freedom of marital choice. Though the Chinese-Hawaiian or Chinese-American heroine's sympathies are with the American way, she ends up subject to the Chinese laws of custom, in both these plays. The third play is set and styled entirely in China, in a Chinese manner, dramatizing a Chinese legend of an evil white serpent tormented by her love for a mortal.

Gladys Li appears to be one of the few Hawaii writers of her generation to pursue a career in writing. According to information on the dustjacket of *Life Is for a Long Time* (New York: Hastings House, 1972), a biography of a Chinese family in Hawaii, the author now-known as Li Ling Ai has been "playwright, performer, director, and moviemaker" in connection with producing film documentaries on China and serving as a director for Ripley's "Believe It or Not" Far Eastern Department. And according to Mr. Kum Pui Lai of the Hawaii Chinese History Center in Honolulu, this adventuresome and creative Li Ling Ai is the same one once known as Gladys Li at the University of Hawaii in the late '20s and early '30s.

[23]James T. Hamada, *Don't Give Up the Ship* (Boston: Meador Publishing Co., 1933).

[24]See Wai Chee Chun, "For You a Lei," *College Plays* (University of Hawaii Department of English, 1937), pp. 57-72, for the earliest example of this use of pidgin.

Typescripts and carbon copies of dramas written for classes and playwriting contests connected with the University of Hawaii are collected in bound, annual volumes in the University's Hawaii-Pacific Collection.

[25]Philip K. Ige, "The Forgotten Flea Powder," *Paradise of the Pacific*, 58 (November 1946), pp. 24-25; reprinted in *Bamboo Ridge: The Hawaii Writers' Quarterly*, no. 1 (December 1978), pp. 56-59.

[26]Ige, ". . . Flea Powder," *P of P*, 58 (November 1946), p. 24.

[27]*Ibid.*

[28]Kazuo Miyamoto, *Hawaii: End of the Rainbow* (Rutland, Vt.: Charles Tuttle Co., Inc., 1964), p. 7.

[29]Shelley Ayame Nishimura Ota, *Upon Their Shoulders* (New York: Exposition Press, Inc., 1951).

[30]Margaret N. Harada, *The Sun Shines on the Immigrant* (New York: Vantage Press, 1960).

[31]Milton Murayama is the author of a revolutionary little novel, *All I Asking for Is My Body* (San Francisco: Supa Press, 1975), the first novel employing pidgin dialogue, set in a Hawaiian sugar plantation camp, and authored by one raised in such a camp to gain a widespread readership in Hawaii. Murayama was in fact the first Asian American author to appear in a Hawaiian anthology edited by Day and Stroven, when in 1968 his story, "I'll Crack Your Head *Kotsun*," was reprinted in Day and Stroven's *The Spell of Hawaii* (New York: Meredith Press, 1968), pp. 323-35. Originally published in the *Arizona Quarterly* 15 (Summer 1959), pp. 137-49, and later as Part I of *All I Asking for Is My Body*, "I'll Crack Your Head *Kotsun*" inspired the anthologists to remark rather belatedly that here is evidence of Hawaii's young Orientals' "becoming aware of their background as a source of unique literary material" (p. 323). A drama by Murayama on the historical Japanese figure Yoshitsune is scheduled to be produced in Hawaii in May of 1982.

The author of "The Forgotten Flea Powder," discussed above, Philip K. Ige wrote the only scholarly commentary on selected writings in English by Hawaii's Asian Americans, prior to our bibliography. In 1968 Ige completed his massive dissertation, "Paradise and Melting Pot in the Fiction and Non-Fiction of Hawaii: A Study of Cross-Cultural Record," Diss. Columbia Univ. 1968, which he has been revising for publication. Without segregating Asian American writers and their works from others, Ige implicitly shows how these writers have contributed their visions of what Hawaii is or ought to be. In recent years Ige has been active among Hawaii's writers as a scholar, critic, and a creative writer himself.

[32]For the fullest single account and analysis yet published centering on the 1978 Talk Story Conference, see Katharine Newman, "Hawaiian-American Literature: the Cultivation of Mangoes," *MELUS*, 6 (Summer 1979), pp. 46-77. Newman was a busy participant in the conference. In rereading her article, I find that Professor Newman calls attention to a number of points that I have touched upon in this paper. I thank her for discussing our shared topic with me in our previous talks and meetings.

For a sampling of Hawaii's contemporary poetry, fiction, and drama, see Eric Chock *et al.*, eds., *Talk Story: An Anthology of Hawaii's Local Writers* (Honolulu: Petronium Press/Talk Story, Inc., 1978).

[33]First hand information supplied to me by Arnold T. Hiura, who in a recent year spent several unforgettable, fascinating hours learning from the gentleman to whom I allude.

321

Contributors' Notes

Eric Chock sold the celebrated '64 Valiant "Bamboo Ridge" (metallic blue on rust white) staff car. Let him take you for a ride in his new silver blue 1986 Honda Civic.

Janice Day Fehrman: Even though I'm now living at the bottom of "Big America" on the last bit of Delta, I think of Hawaii every day. I like it down here with the Creoles and Cajuns but there's something about Hawaii that never leaves you. Aloha to my friends in the Kauai Writers Group, a.k.a. Saimin's Last Stand.

Wanda Fujimoto works as a paralegal in a downtown law office. She a a member of Nahuluaho'oululahuihou under kumu hula Ho'oulu Cambra.

Caroline Garrett: Frost said " . . . that every poem solves something for me in life. I go so far as to say that every poem is a momentary stay against the confusion of the world." And as predicaments continue to arise throughout life, so do the poems.

Dana Naone Hall is the editor of *Mālama, Hawaiian Land and Water* (Bamboo Ridge, No. 29). "T'ang Fishermen" reflects her Hawaiian-Chinese background.

Violet Harada is a School Library Services Specialist with the Department of Education. She has taught a course in Asian American children's literature at the University of Hawaii and presently coordinates the "Children as Authors" project for the D.O.E.

Norman Hindley's collection of poems, *Winter Eel*, was published in 1984 by Petronium Press.

Dean Honma lives in California, working, writing, and regretting that he ever left home.

Clara Mitsuko Jelsma, country girl, vividly recalls the "good old days" in Glenwood and Mt. View, Hawaii and writes about them as she presents the Issei story in *Teapot Tales* and *Mauna Loa Rains.*

Diane Kahanu: Wini Terada is my hero. His pidgin English poetry is mystical; he's made a believer out of me. I know he looks like he works in a service station, but he's taught me. Mahalo, Wini!

Dennis Kawaharada, formerly the Managing Editor of Bamboo Ridge Press, currently lives in San Francisco.

Hiroshi Kawakami: When my essays were first selected for publication in *Bamboo Ridge*, I was just a retiree with more time than money. Thanks to Darrell Lum and the Bamboo Ridge, "Who Da Guy" has become a series publication for the *Hawaii Herald.*

Gary Kissick's "rain quietude" won first prize in the 1975 Honolulu Commission on Culture & the Arts Poetry Competition. He received a writing fellowship grant from the National Endowment for the Arts in 1982 and won the Pacific Poetry Series Competition for *Outer Islands* (University of Hawaii Press, 1983).

Jody Manabe Kobayashi lives on the island of Kauai with husband Joseph and daughter Julie Alisa. She teaches in the Poets-In-The-Schools program and weaves baskets for the Waioli Fishing Company in Hanalei.

Juliet S. Kono: I was born and raised in Hilo, Hawaii. I presently work for the Honolulu Police Department and am the office manager for the Hawaii Chapter of the Sierra Club. I am a graduate of Hilo High School and am currently attending the University of Hawaii.

Laurie Kuribayashi lives in Honolulu.

Tony Lee: I ran into Junior the other day at Holiday Mart. He no longer fishes at Bamboo Ridge, but he gave his gear to his grandson.

Darrell H.Y. Lum is the proud husband of *Mae A. Lum* who, on August 4, 1978, became the proud mother of *Lisa Terumi Kwai Oi (T.K.O.) Lum.* A knockout! (From "About the Contributors", *Bamboo Ridge #1,* December 1978.) Darrell is still very proud of wife and daughter. Lisa, like *Bamboo Ridge,* is eight years old.

Wing Tek Lum's first volume of poetry is scheduled to be published by Bamboo Ridge in 1987.

Michael McPherson still lives in Maui. His second book of poems, *The Alien Lounge,* is forthcoming from Petronium Press.

Rodney Morales is a lifelong resident of Oahu and has been living there all his redundant life.

Susan Nunes was born on the Big Island and now lives in Honolulu. Her short fiction has appeared in *Hawaii Review, Bamboo Ridge, Hapa,* and a high school anthology *Asian-Pacific Literature.* A collection of her Hilo stories, *A Small Obligation,* was published by Bamboo Ridge Press.

Ty Pak, on leave from the University of Hawaii, is in California writing a novel.

Kathy Phillips teaches English at the University of Hawaii.

Patsy S. Saiki: Bamboo Ridge Press is a real boon to Hawaii writers for the Press encourages hopefuls like us to continue putting our thoughts and experiences into words to share with others.

Cathy Song's first book, *Picture Bride,* won the Yale Series of Younger Poets Award in 1983 and was nominated for the National Book Critics Circle Award. Her new poems appear in *Seneca Review, Columbia, American Poetry Review,* and *Poetry.* She has been recently included in *The Morrow Anthology of Younger American Poets.*

William Stafford, well-known poet, teacher, critic, Poetry Consultant for the Library of Congress, conscientious objector in World War II, husband, father, biker, hiker, and photographer says, "Thanks for your kindness to my work!"

Joseph Stanton grew up in St. Louis, where he developed a fondness for Michelob beer and Cardinal baseball. He now lives in Aiea with his wife, his two children, and his kim-chee-loaded refrigerator. Since 1972 he has worked for the University of Hawaii as a researcher, writer, and editor of textbooks on literature and language. His latest text is *British & European Literatures.* His poems have appeared in most of Hawaii's literary magazines—*Bamboo Ridge, The Paper, Hawaii Review, Ramrod, Hapa, Seaweeds and Constructions*—as well as in many mainland publications.

Stephen H. Sumida is an assistant professor of the Departments of Comparative American Cultures (Asian/Pacific American Studies Program) and English at Washington State University, Pullman. His full-length study of Hawaii's literature is forthcoming from Bamboo Ridge Press and Topgallant Publishing.

Raynette Takizawa:
> my father fished bamboo ridge thirty years ago
> when fish were bigger than the stories told of them
> and hiss of whirring reels became poetry to men
> dad, i've followed you to cast my line here too—
> the first strike goes to you.

Wini Terada, keiki o ka 'aina, farms kalo Hawai'i at the Kānewai Cultural Garden in Mānoa and teaches at Farrington High School and at Pūnana leo o Honolulu Hawaiian language pre-school. E aloha ʻaina Kākou.

Debra Thomas, age 30, was born and raised in Honolulu. She is an assistant editor for *HONOLULU Magazine* and a teacher of the Transcendental Meditation Program.

Jean Yamasaki Toyama was born and bred in Hawaii. She teaches French at the University of Hawaii and is now learning Japanese. Aside from poetry and scholarly articles she also writes short stories.

Mary Wakayama: My purpose as a writer is to celebrate what it means to live in Hawaii with truth, justice and concern for the beauty here. The Talk Story motto still holds me: "Words bind; words set free." As one of many in the fragile network of local writers, I would like to thank Ozzie Bushnell and Stephen Sumida for their steady encouragement and solid scholarship . . . and Chock, Lum and Co. for keeping something intangible alive for all of us.

Sylvia Watanabe lives in Honolulu. She teaches English and is currently working on a collection of short stories.

Martha Webb and her daughter, Helen, are once again living in Volcano. She is now working on the translation of a biography of Robert Wilcox from Hawaiian into English.

Frederick B. Wichman is a haku moʻolele, telling the ancient tales of Kauai so that they will not be forgotten.

Rob Wilson's poems have appeared in American and South Korean journals. The 25th Anniversary issue of *Korea Journal,* a UNESCO publication, features fourteen of his poems on Korea. He is an avid basketball player for "Sakuma Productions."

Tamara Wong-Morrison is Hawaiian, Chinese, English, Irish and Scots, and the seventh child of Larry Ah Chin and Miriam Mundon Wong of Koloa, Kauai. She teaches poetry writing on the Big Island of Hawaii where she lives in Volcano Village with her husband, artist and designer Boone Morrison.